Second Language Writing Research

Perspectives on the Process of Knowledge Construction

Second Language Writing Research

Perspectives on the Process of Knowledge Construction

Edited by

Paul Kei Matsuda
University of New Hampshire

Tony Silva
Purdue University

LEA LAWRENCE ERLBAUM ASSOCIATES, PUBLISHERS
2005 Mahwah, New Jersey London

Lawrence Erlbaum Associates, Inc., Publishers
10 Industrial Avenue
Mahwah, New Jersey 07430
www.erlbaum.com

Cover design by Kathryn Houghtaling Lacey
Cover concept by Paul Kei Matsuda

Library of Congress Cataloging-in-Publication Data

Matsuda, Paul Kei.
Second language writing research : perspectives on the process of knowledge construction / edited by Paul Kei Matsuda, Tony Silva.
p. cm.
Includes bibliographical references and index.
ISBN 0-8058-5045-7 (cloth : alk. paper)
ISBN 0-8058-5046-5 (pbk. : alk. paper)
1. Language and languages—Study and teaching—Research. 2. Rhetoric—Study and teaching—Research. 3. Second language acquisition—Research. I. Silva, Tony. II. Title.

P53.27.M38 2005
418′.0071—dc22

2004053337
CIP

Books published by Lawrence Erlbaum Associates are printed on acid-free paper, and their bindings are chosen for strength and durability.

Printed in the United States of America
10 9 8 7 6 5 4 3 2 1

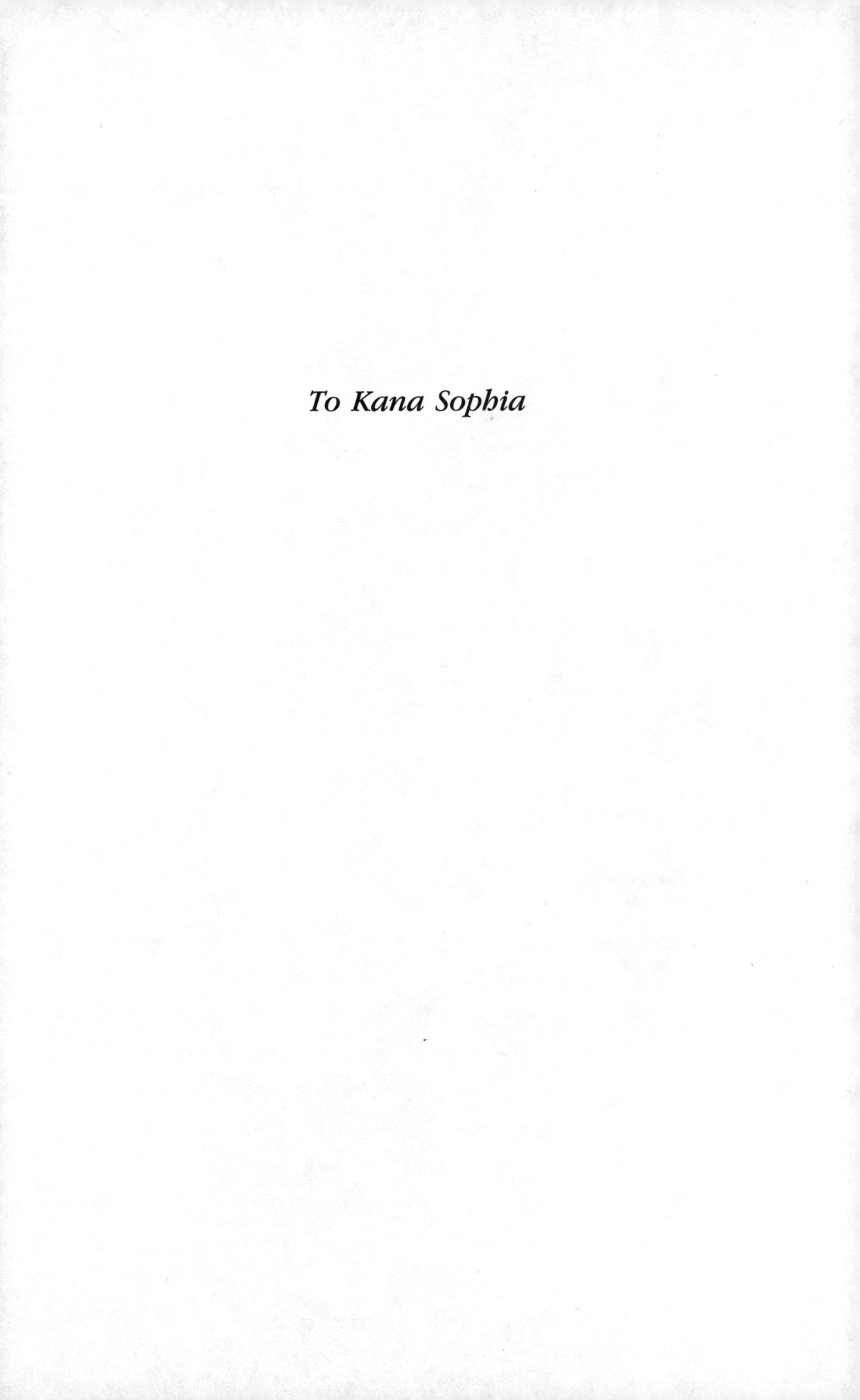

To Kana Sophia

Contents

Preface

The field of second language writing has grown exponentially over the last decade and a half. Once a neglected topic, second language writing today is arguably one of the most viable fields of inquiry in both second language studies and composition studies. With the growth of the field, second language writing research has become increasingly sophisticated, requiring researchers to negotiate various disciplinary, theoretical, and methodological perspectives as well as practical issues that arise in the process of research.

To develop methodological expertise, novice researchers have often relied on books that focus on research methods in second language studies or composition studies. In their effort to help novice researchers understand various methods, however, most books divide research methods into clearly delineated categories, inadvertently creating the false impression that research methods are discrete and transportable from one context to another. Those publications often do not account for the ways in which researchers combine various methodological tools in response to research issues or questions situated in their own context of inquiry, nor do they reflect the complexity of decision-making processes that researchers go through in conducting research. Furthermore, few of them discuss issues that are specific to second language writing research.

To explore the complexity of second language writing research and promote a situated understanding of actual research practices in the field, we organized the 2002 Symposium on Second Language Writing around the theme of knowledge construction in the field of second language writing. We sought to capture the complexity of second language writing research by asking 18 internationally known second language writing researchers—representing a wide range of disciplinary, philosophical, and methodological perspectives—to reflect on their own knowledge construction processes in the context of a specific research project. We then asked them to develop a written version of their presentations suitable for publication. All of them graciously agreed, and the result is the book you are holding in your hands.

Second Language Writing Research: Perspectives on the Process of Knowledge Construction is an edited collection of 16 original chapters on various methodological issues in second language writing research. This volume is an attempt to fill the gap between the neat and orderly worlds of introductory methodology publications, on the one hand, and published research reports, on the other hand. In other words, it provides a glimpse into the messy space of situated practices of inquiry in the field of second language writing. It brings together 18 second language writing researchers from different parts of the world who explore various issues in constructing and negotiating knowledge in the field. Although the contributors are experts on the methodologies they have used, they do not present their insights from the perspective of disinterested methodologists. Instead they share their insights in the form of reflections on their own experience as researchers.

Taking a broader conception of research as inquiry, this volume includes philosophical (Silva), narrative (Casanave), and historical (Matsuda) modes of inquiry that are often taken for granted in the discussion of research methods in second language studies. The discussion of empirical inquiry includes both quantitative (Haswell; Sasaki) and qualitative (Atkinson; Blanton; Brice; Hudelson; Li; Parks; Manchón, Murphy, & Roca de Larios) approaches as well as those that strategically combine them (Flowerdew; Hyland; Weissberg). This volume also includes a discussion of the "nuts and bolts" of developing research programs (Ferris).

This volume is not meant to be a comprehensive survey of research methods or an introductory "how-to" book—for those purposes, we refer the readers to existing publications on research methods. Rather this book is designed to highlight some of the key issues, assumptions, questions, and strategies in conducting second language writing research through contributors' reflections on a specific research project they have completed. Some of the key assumptions underlying many of the chapters include:

- Any approach to research is based on a set of assumptions about the nature of reality and knowledge as well as ways of arriving at that knowledge.
- Second language writing research draws on multiple modes of inquiry, including philosophical, historical, empirical, and narrative.

- Knowledge is not simply "found" or "revealed," but constructed and negotiated by researchers who interact with philosophical assumptions, established knowledge, and various forms of data.
- Research design is driven by the researcher's sense of purpose and cannot be disinterested.
- Research is a situated act of knowledge construction rather than a simple application of prefabricated methodological principles.
- Research methods are heuristics—sets of guidelines or rules of thumb—for knowledge construction; they are not rigid rules that guarantee the outcome.
- Research results can be interpreted and reinterpreted from multiple theoretical perspectives.

The primary audience for this book includes novice researchers who have some familiarity with various research methods and are entering the messy world of situated research practices. Master's students and beginning doctoral students who have only begun to read research articles in the field may also benefit from personal insights provided by authors of published research studies. Established researchers who are interested in expanding their methodological repertoire might also find this book useful.

Although particular examples discussed in this book come from English-as-a-second- or foreign-language contexts, many of the principles, issues, questions, and strategies highlighted in this book are also applicable to researchers who are working on second or foreign languages other than English. We also believe that this book has much to offer researchers in composition studies regardless of their interest in second language issues. For an increasing number of researchers in composition studies who are seeking ways to integrate a second language perspective into their research practices, this goes without saying.

OVERVIEW

This book is organized into four parts based on the primary focus of each of the chapters. Although the physical characteristics of an edited book impose a linear order, chapters in this book overlap with one another in multiple ways; some of the chapters could even fit comfortably in more than one section of the book. Yet we have decided not to superficially treat various research issues as if they are discrete. In fact we see the overlapping nature of the chapters to be one of the distinct features of this collection. This volume engages the readers with various issues recursively. Depending on their level of methodological expertise and interests, readers may wish to read the chapters out of sequence.

Part I, "Research as Situated Knowledge Construction," features three chapters that deal with the nature of knowledge and knowledge construction from a broader perspective. Chapter 1, "On the Philosophical Bases of Inquiry in Second Language Writing: Metaphysics, Inquiry Paradigms, and the Intellectual Zeitgeist" by Tony Silva, reflects on the fundamental philosophical issues underlying the nature of knowledge construction in the field of L2 writing. In chapter 2, "Uses of Narrative in L2 Writing Research," Christine Pearson Casanave uses her expertise in narrative inquiry to highlight how narratives inform and shape various aspects of L2 writing research. In chapter 3, "Historical Inquiry in Second Language Writing," Paul Kei Matsuda discusses an approach to metadisciplinary inquiry that provides a way of identifying, constructing, and critiquing existing narratives about the nature and status of the field—narratives that provide contexts for empirical research.

Part II, "Conceptualizing L2 Writing Research," presents six chapters that deal with various issues in conceptualizing L2 writing research programs. In chapter 4, "Situated Qualitative Research and Second Language Writing," Dwight Atkinson emphasizes the complex and situated nature of research in L2 writing, suggesting the importance of developing research methods for the particular context of study, rather than relying on readymade methods. In chapter 5, "A Multimethod Approach to Research Into Processes of Scholarly Writing for Publication," John Flowerdew discusses the use of a multimethod approach to research in investigating applied language issues in a series of studies. In chapter 6, "Hypothesis Generation and Hypothesis Testing: Two Complementary Studies of EFL Writing Processes," Miyuki Sasaki discusses how she generated and tested hypotheses in a series of related studies. In chapter 7, "Talking About Writing: Cross-Modality Research and Second Language Speaking/Writing Connections," Robert Weissberg explores one of the fundamental conceptual issues in the field of L2 writing—the relationship between speech and writing and its implications for L2 writing research. In chapter 8, "Researching Teacher Evaluation of Second Language Writing via Prototype Theory," Richard Haswell sheds light on the use of conceptual categories and how it affects the ways in which L2 writers are evaluated. In chapter 9, "Composing Culture in a Fragmented World: The Issue of Representation in Cross-Cultural Research," Xiaoming Li comes to terms with the issue of representing culture and L2 writers, which has been one of the most contested issues in the field of L2 writing.

Part III, "Collecting and Analyzing Data," includes five chapters that explore issues in collecting and analyzing data. In chapter 10, "Qualitative Research as Heuristic: Investigating Documentation Practices in a Medical

Setting," Susan Parks addresses key issues in qualitative research of academic and workplace literacy, focusing on (a) the design of the study, (b) the representativeness of data, and (c) researcher stance and the role of theory. Her broad perspective forecasts a number of key issues that are explored further in chapters that follow. In chapter 11, "Mucking Around in the Lives of Others: Reflections on Qualitative Research," Linda Lonon Blanton further explores the thorny issue of the researcher–participant relationship. Chapter 12, "Coding Data in Qualitative Research on L2 Writing: Issues and Implications" by Colleen Brice, takes up issues that arise in coding data, which are often taken for granted. In chapter 13, "Digging Up Texts and Transcripts: Confessions of a Discourse Analyst," Ken Hyland identifies and discusses various issues in working with textual data. Chapter 14, "Using Concurrent Protocols to Explore L2 Writing Processes: Methodological Issues in the Collection and Analysis of Data" by Rosa M. Manchón, Liz Murphy, and Julio Roca de Larios, discusses the authors' efforts in minimizing the problems of concurrent protocol data. Finally, in chapter 15, "Taking on English Writing in a Bilingual Program: Revisiting, Reexamining, Reconceptualizing the Data," Sarah Hudelson shows how the same set of data can be reanalyzed from multiple theoretical perspectives to produce a deeper understanding of the phenomenon.

Part IV provides a "Coda" to this volume by focusing on practical issues of conducting scholarship in the field of L2 writing. In chapter 16, Dana Ferris presents "Tricks of the Trade: The Nuts and Bolts of L2 Writing Research," which puts L2 writing research practices in perspective by discussing issues that researchers face in developing sustainable research programs.

Together the contributors to this collection provide not only a deeper understanding of some of their research projects, but also insights into various issues in the messy process of conceptualizing, conducting, and composing L2 writing research that are not readily apparent from published works that often give a false sense of neatness and coherence.

ACKNOWLEDGMENTS

We are grateful to Alister Cumming for his constructive and supportive comments that guided us in the editing process and to Ann Johns for believing in the usefulness of this book for researchers in mainstream composition studies. We would also like to thank Lawrence Erlbaum Associates and especially Naomi Silverman, our editor, for her support and expert guidance.

I

RESEARCH AS SITUATED KNOWLEDGE CONSTRUCTION

1

On the Philosophical Bases of Inquiry in Second Language Writing: Metaphysics, Inquiry Paradigms, and the Intellectual Zeitgeist

Tony Silva
Purdue University, USA

This book is largely about reflection—the reflections of L2 writing researchers on projects they have done. This involves self-disclosure—telling the story behind the study. My chapter is also a story about a project—the story of how I have come, over the past 25 years, to the opinion that it is important and necessary to look at the philosophical bases of inquiry in L2 writing. In a sense, this story is about me. However, I do not believe that it is idiosyncratic. In fact, I believe that, to a certain extent, it parallels the development of the field with regard to its view of the relationship among theory, research, and practice.

FROM PRACTICE TO THEORY

I began work in second language studies as a teacher concerned primarily with how to teach better, more effectively. I did not see a need for research, theory, or philosophy in my work. In fact I gave such matters little, if any, attention.

As a graduate student, I was exposed to empirical research and at first resisted it because it seemed largely irrelevant to my teaching. Also, it was hard to understand. It involved thinking in a different way. It involved acquiring the vocabulary of empirical research. It involved grasping abstractions like validity and reliability. It involved understanding alien concepts and terms like *means*, *standard deviation*, t *tests*, *ANOVAs*, *multiple re-*

gression, and, later, *thick description*, *grounded theory*, and *triangulation*. Not only was it scary, but it seemed like a whole lot of effort for very little gain.

However, I soon came to the belief that reading empirical research was a necessary evil and I probably would even have to do an empirical study at some point. If I wanted to make claims about teaching—what "worked" or "did not work"—I would need to base them on empirical evidence and not just on my interpretation of my personal experience in the classroom. After all there was no logical reason to assume that what worked for me in one context would work for someone else in another. In addition, as with any new convert, I began to renounce my former beliefs—I began to believe that other types of inquiry (i.e., nonempirical) produced mere speculation.

At first I saw empirical research as a rather cut-and-dried affair—you collected your data, analyzed it, reported on what you "found," and said what you thought it meant for the classroom. Again I was focused on how—how to do research "the right way" so as to support my views on teaching. It all seemed unproblematic—follow these rules (whatever they might be and wherever they might come from) and you will find success.

But after reading a substantial amount of empirical research, I began to have questions. Researchers disagreed. How could that be? I guessed that some did research "right" and others did not. What made a methodology right or wrong, good or bad? Where did these research methodologies come from anyway? How did one decide on which methodology to use in a given study?

Soon I came to the conclusion that a researcher's questions would determine the design—this now seems patently obvious to me, but it was an epiphany then. It was all a matter of what you wanted to be able to claim on the basis of your research findings. But where did these questions come from? Enter theory (and the notion that research supported theory and theory supported practice). Okay, but what theory should I follow? There were different ones out there. Where did they come from? How could you tell which was right and which was wrong? On what basis could you choose? Could I make up my own theory? If so, how?

Enter philosophy—particularly the philosophy of science—and inquiry paradigms, which were based on ideologies, which were made up of metaphysical notions like ontology, epistemology, and axiology, and which were supported by, well, personal beliefs, which were strongly affected by experience, politics, ideology, and so on. Isn't this where I started? Was the trip worth it? In a word, yes. Is this trip over? Unlikely. Given the (d)evolving nature of my thinking described above, I do not anticipate closure. Therefore, I offer the caveat that what I have written here may not be exactly what I believe by the time you read this.

I now move on to the central objective of this chapter: to lay out some of the conceptual and terminological apparatus necessary for talking and thinking about the inquiry process in the area of second language writing at the present time. Another caveat: In this chapter, I voice my particular views, some of which may not necessarily reflect those of the other authors whose chapters appear in this collection.

THE PHILOSOPHICAL TRADITION

I would like to ground this chapter in the classical western philosophical tradition—not because I see this as the only or best tradition, but because it is the only one I know well enough to talk somewhat intelligently about. Specifically, I would like to begin with a contrast of some of the work of two ancient Greek philosophers/rhetoricians: one extremely well known, Plato, and one fairly obscure, Gorgias. I do this because I think the clash of their views in many ways mirrors oppositions in today's intellectual climate.

I begin with Gorgias, also known by some as "the nihilist," who was actually from Sicily, but is best known for strutting his rhetorical stuff in Athens and throughout ancient Greece. He is said to have achieved fortune and fame by teaching his disciples the practical art of persuasion, which some (e.g., Plato) would define as the ability to make a convincing argument on a particular topic or issue without really knowing anything or much about that topic or issue—that is, as favoring style over substance, rhetoric over reality.

Gorgias's most well-known work is called *On nature* or *On the nonexistent* (Freeman, 1957). Here he makes three basic points in a straightforward manner: (a) nothing exists; (b) if anything did exist, it could not be known; and (c) if anything did exist and could be known, it could not be communicated. Now you see why they called him the nihilist.

He argues his points thus: (a) if anything exists, it must have had a beginning; also it must have arisen either from being or not being; if it arose from being, then there is no beginning, and arising from not being is impossible because something cannot arise from nothing; (b) because sense impressions differ in different people (and even in the same person at different times), the object as it is in itself (i.e., a physical reality) cannot be known; and (c) knowledge (seen as a product of physical sensation or sense perception) has meaning only for a particular sensor/perceiver, and thus cannot be communicated in any meaningful way to others (Freeman, 1957).

What are the ramifications of this view? Taken to its logical limits, paralysis, chaos, and, eventually, anarchy. Imagine that someone has burned your house down and this someone has Gorgias on retainer. In court,

Gorgias argues: "Your honor, this house never existed; if it existed we could not know it, and even if it did exist and could be known, we could not communicate it." Case closed.

Plato, a native Athenian, came from a well-to-do and well-connected aristocratic family. (Interestingly, however, I have never heard anyone refer to him as "the aristocrat.") Plato did believe in a reality, a permanent and unchanging reality, a reality of universal truths and idealized eternal forms and substances.

Although Plato did not completely reject the validity of sense experience and, thus, empiricism, he did see the knowledge arising from it as second best—that the objects of sense experience are changeable phenomena in the physical world, and thus not objects of proper knowledge. Proper knowledge (i.e., certain, infallible knowledge) could only be attained via reason developed by dialectic—the rational pursuit of truth through questions, answers, and more questions (in other words, via the Socratic method). For Plato, empiricism produces opinion; dialectic, properly used, produces truth.

In his work on politics, Plato was also an idealist. He claimed that the ideal society would have three kinds of citizens: merchants (to generate wealth), soldiers (to provide security), and philosopher kings (to provide leadership). The philosopher kings would be the most able—those who could grasp the truth and thus make the wisest decisions. (Guess which group Plato identified himself with?) Where Plato was going was toward a totalitarian state run by an aristocracy. Here is Plato in his own words from *Laws*:

> The greatest principle of all is that nobody, whether male or female, should be without a leader. Nor should the mind of anybody be habituated to letting him do anything at all on his own initiative; neither out of zeal, nor even playfully. But in war and in the midst of peace—to his leader he shall direct his eye and follow him faithfully. And even in the smallest matter he should stand under leadership. For example, he should get up, or move, or wash, or take his meals . . . only if he has been told to do so. In a word, he should teach his soul, by long habit, never to dream of acting independently, and to become utterly incapable of it. (Cited in Popper, 1962, p. 7)

One day I was grazing on Amazon.com's Web site and somehow wound up looking at reader reviews of Plato's work, *Republic* or *Laws*, I forget which. The first review described this work as "the insane ramblings of a proto-fascist." In light of the foregoing, that works for me.[1]

---

[1]I recognize that there are other, more sympathetic readings of these passages from Plato and Gorgias.

So will it be nihilism (leading to anarchy) or idealism (leading to totalitarianism)? Fortunately, these are not the only choices. To look into this, I would now like to move on to a tighter focus on matters of ideology.

IDEOLOGY[2]

I define *ideology* as being constituted by ontology, epistemology, axiology, and methodology, and I offer definitions for these terms. *Ontology* is the study of the nature of being and the structure of reality. *Epistemology* is the study of the origin, nature, and limits of knowledge. *Axiology* is the study of the nature of value—of what is good. *Methodology* refers to the means of inquiry into a given subject—the procedures for constructing knowledge.

From ideology are derived paradigms of inquiry—basic sets of beliefs that guide action and generate research. I address what I see as the three most influential contemporary paradigms, and I do not pretend that I do not have a favorite.

INQUIRY PARADIGMS[3]

Positivism, the dominant perspective in the philosophy of science during the first half of the 20th century, is now typically used as a term of ritual condemnation or derision. That is, labeling someone a positivist typically constitutes an act of vilification, of name calling. Positivism's ontology is realist; that is, reality or truth exists "out there" and is driven by unchanging natural laws and mechanisms. These laws and mechanisms are presented in the form of general statements and are seen as being unaffected by time or context. Some generalizations take on the form of laws of cause and effect. Positivism's epistemology is objectivist; that is, reality can be known objectively and completely. This connotes that it is both possible and necessary for the inquirer to adopt a distant, noninteractive posture. Personal values and other biasing or confounding factors are thus excluded from influencing the outcome. In terms of axiology, positivism values certain knowledge and absolute truth. Positivism's methodology is experimental and manipulative. Hypotheses, arrived at via induction, are

[2]See Table 1.1 for a tabular representation of ideological positions and inquiry paradigms.

[3]For the sake of clear presentation, I sharply distinguish these paradigms here. I recognize, however, that, in practice, these distinctions are not always so clear cut. For the basic work on the notion of inquiry paradigms, see Kuhn (1996); for an overview of particular paradigms (to which my formulation owes much), see Guba (1990).

TABLE 1.1
Inquiry Paradigms

Paradigm	*Ontology*	*Epistemology*	*Methodology*	*Axiology*	*Zeitgeist*
Positivism	Realist	Objectivist	Experimental	Truth	Modern
Relativism	Constructivist	Subjectivist	Hermeneutic	Consensus	Postmodern
HPR	Modified Realist	Interactionist	Multimodal	Knowledge	Eclectic

stated in propositional form and subjected to empirical tests under carefully controlled conditions. The aim of positivism goes beyond description and explanation to prediction and control.

Relativism typically has a constructivist ontology, whereby realities exist in the form of mental constructions that are socially and experientially based, local and specific, and dependent for their form and content on the persons who hold them. Relativism's epistemology is subjectivist—reality is solely a creation of the human mind. With regard to axiology, what relativism values most is consensus. Relativism's methodology is hermeneutic (i.e., interpretive, depicting individual constructions as accurately as possible). It is also dialectic (comparing and contrasting these constructs). Individual constructions are elicited and refined hermeneutically and compared and contrasted dialectically with the aim of generating one or a few constructions on which there is substantial tentative agreement. Relativism requires the replacement of positivism because it holds that reality exists only in the context of a mental framework or construct for thinking about it, that no unequivocal explanation is possible, and that although there may be many constructions, there is no foundational way to choose among them.

The third paradigm is typically referred to as *postpositivism* or *critical rationalism*. I am not comfortable with either of these terms. I find postpositivism rather uninformative and opaque, as is the case with other terms prefixed with *post*. The term *critical*, in my view, has been overused and underdefined to the point of meaninglessness. I also find its use condescending in that it often seems to me to imply that views not explicitly labeled as *critical* are necessarily uncritical and, by extension, naive and unworthy of serious consideration—that is, they are simply wrong. In my view, this usage reflects a positivistic orientation.

Therefore, I label this third paradigm as humble pragmatic rationalism (HPR). No, I am not kidding.[4] *Humble* reflecting the limits of one's knowl-

[4]I contrast this "kinder, gentler" rationalism with that practiced in, for example, the generativist tradition, wherein the views of those not behind the program are often harshly and summarily dismissed.

edge and *pragmatic* in the sense of a pluralistic and eclectic approach that accommodates different worldviews, assumptions, and methods in an attempt to address and solve specific problems in particular contexts. Given the complex nature of the phenomenon of L2 writing and the serious consequences that learning how to write in a second language often entail, I believe that humility and pragmatism are in order.

In any case, HPR's ontology is that of a modified realism; that is, reality exists, but can never be fully known. It is driven by natural laws that can only be incompletely or partially understood. HPR's epistemology is interactionist—a result of the interaction between subject (researcher) and object (physical reality), wherein a human being's perceptual, cognitive, and social filters preclude any totally objective or absolute knowledge. Regarding axiology, HPR values knowledge—knowledge that is tentative, contingent, and probabilistic. HPR's methodology is multimodal—involving the integration of empirical study (qualitative as well as quantitative) and hermeneutic inquiry (the refinement of ideas through interpretation and dialogue, through conjecture and refutation).[5]

In my view, a strong positivist orientation for second language writing research is not viable because of its inductive basis; its lack of recognition of perceptual, cognitive, and sociocultural screens through which reality is filtered; and its bias toward the so-called "hard" sciences (i.e., dealing with inert matter is a lot easier than dealing with people, who are more complex entities affected by a lot more slippery variables). A rigid relativist orientation is also unacceptable, in my view, because there really seems to me to be something out there—a physical reality that can be understood, if only partially, and because consensus alone will not make something so (e.g., a group of people can develop a consensus that human beings are immortal, but this will not keep them from dying). HPR is attractive to me not only because it accepts the notion of the existence of a physical reality, but also because it recognizes that this reality can be seen, albeit through a glass darkly. I see HPR as well balanced in the sense that it has not only what it takes to generate viable theories of complex phenomena, but it is also pragmatic enough to be useful in addressing real-world problems and concerns.

TYPES OF INQUIRY

I would like to move now to an examination of types of inquiry within HPR, the two basic types being hermeneutic and empirical. I use the term *hermeneutic* to refer to interpretation via reasoning, logic, and dialectic. It

[5]My formulation here owes much to the work of philosopher of science, Karl Popper, and to O'Shea's (1991) application of Popper's ideas to the area of composition studies.

is implicated, for example, in philosophical, historical, and narrative inquiry. It is the most common way research is done in the Humanities. It involves identifying a motivating concern, posing questions, developing answers via deductive and analogical reasoning, creating a new theory or hypothesis, and testing and refining that theory through argumentation. Because hermeneutic approaches to inquiry are addressed by other authors in this collection (Casanave looks at narrative inquiry, Matsuda at historical), my major focus in this chapter is on empirical research. I define *empirical research* as the construction of knowledge by means of systematic observation, analysis, and representation of behavior and/or its artifacts. All that said, I would like to note at this point that hermeneutic and empirical research are similar in that they both identify concerns, pose questions, investigate, interpret results of the investigation, and theorize on the basis of those results. These two types of inquiry also interact with one another—historical studies often use empirical evidence (artifacts); empirical research is also inevitably hermeneutic to some extent. They are probably better understood as differing emphases, especially within the framework of HPR

TYPES OF EMPIRICAL DESIGNS[6]

Research designs are typically categorized as descriptive or experimental. Descriptive designs examine variables without manipulating environments. Descriptive designs include case studies (studies of the behaviors of one or a small group of individuals), ethnographies (examinations of particular contexts), surveys (sampling of groups to extrapolate to larger populations), quantitative descriptive research (analyses of relationships between variables—e.g., correlational studies and factor analyses), and prediction or classification studies (analyses of individual characteristics to predict future behavior—e.g., regression analyses).

Experimental designs are said to identify cause-and-effect relationships. Experimenters manipulate contexts by forming experimental and control groups, applying different treatments to these groups, and measuring the results of these treatments. Experimental studies include true experiments (which use randomized samples), quasi-experiments (which work with nonrandomized, intact samples), and meta-analyses (analyses of the cumulative results of a number of experiments).

I think it is important to note at this point that many, if not most, empirical studies done on L2 writing use a mixed methodology—that is, they

[6]My account here owes much to Lauer and Asher (1988). See Fig. 1.1 for a pictorial representation of research designs.

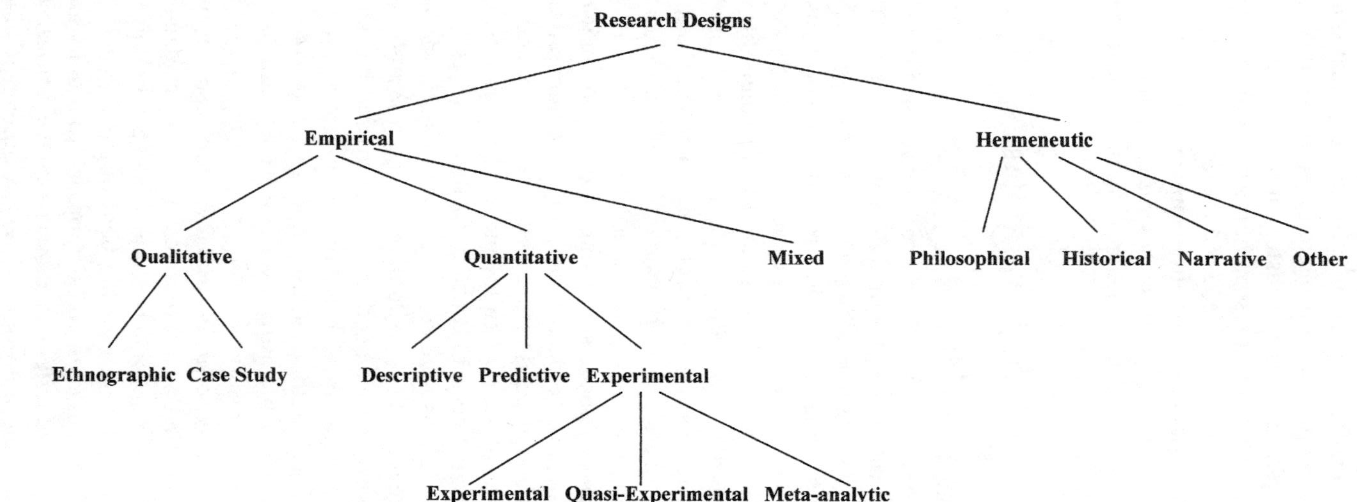

FIG. 1.1. Research designs.

combine both qualitative and quantitative designs, that quantitative designs need not be positivistic in orientation, and that qualitative designs can be positivistic. For me it is all a matter of researchers' epistemologies; that is, studies are positivistic if researchers assume implicitly or claim explicitly that their findings provide certain knowledge or absolute truth. Such a positivistic orientation is often implicit in the terminology researchers use—for example, patterns *emerging* from data or analyses *revealing* new insights (i.e., shifting agency from the subject to the object).

MULTIMODAL INQUIRY

I am working from an assumption that research questions should drive and determine the type of inquiry and design used in a particular study in second language writing. Simply put, different jobs require different tools. Therefore, I believe that second language writing researchers: (a) can and should study second language writing from the perspectives of the social sciences, humanities, and even the physical sciences; (b) can and should mix modes of inquiry where appropriate to overcome the limitations of any single mode and add breadth and depth to a study; and (c) can and should reject (what I see as profoundly unproductive) arguments about the superiority of quantitative or qualitative empirical research methods and feel free—and be encouraged—to use any type of existing design, to modify designs, to combine designs, and/or to develop new designs. I see quantitative and qualitative designs as complementary rather than oppositional, and I am encouraged that it is becoming more and more difficult to find studies which do not employ more than one type of design.

In light of these beliefs, I find troubling the attempts by some second language studies journals to micromanage the research designs of potential submitters—that is, to specify (and thus prescribe and/or proscribe) in great detail what researchers need to do: how to conduct studies, how to report studies, how to analyze data, how to report data, how to interpret results, what statistical methods to use or not use, and so on. I believe that attempts to exercise such control over researchers are based on the assumption (conscious or subconscious) that research design is a static rather than a dynamic enterprise—that there are absolute and unchangeable rules that govern empirical research. I see this as dangerously limiting, stifling, and counterproductive—an unnecessary and unacceptable orthodoxy for a vibrant and evolving field of study.

In short, I welcome an ecumenical approach to inquiry and methodology, wherein any type of systematic inquiry—be it empirical (qualitative or quantitative), historical, philosophical, or any other type of analysis—can inform the knowledge base of second language writing.

THE INTELLECTUAL ZEITGEIST

Postmodernism to the rescue? Well, maybe not. To work into this, I need to first address modernism, postmodernism's alter ego. Modernism is an intellectual current that is said to have grown out of the age of enlightenment, also known as the age of reason. Generally and reductively speaking, modernism sees truth as absolute, knowledge as certain, and language as an expression of thought. It values the notions of progress, optimism, rationality, depth, essence, universality, and totality. Postmodernism, in contrast, sees truth and knowledge as relative and contingent and language as deterministic of thought. It is identified with the notions of pessimism, irrationality, superficiality, difference, and fragmentation.

Although I believe it is important for second language writing professionals to engage with larger intellectual currents (like postmodernism), it is also important to consider whether such currents are truly current. Let me try to explain what I mean by quoting from theorist Mark Taylor's (2001) *The Moment of Complexity*. In this passage, Taylor talks about postmodernism in terms of the work of Foucault, Derrida, and Baudrillard:

> The theoretical resources informing social and cultural analyses for more than three decades have been exhausted, and alternative interpretive strategies have yet to be defined. Innovative perspectives once bristling with new insight by now have been repeated and routinized until they yield arguments that are utterly predictable and familiar. For more than thirty years, there has been a widespread consensus that the most pressing critical challenge is to find ways to resist systems and structures that totalize [function in a totalitarian manner] by repressing otherness and by reducing difference to sameness. So called hegemonic structures, it is argued, must be overturned by soliciting the return of repressed otherness and difference in a variety of guises. For many years, writers and critics who were preoccupied with the theoretical problem of alterity [otherness] were institutionally marginalized. . . . As critics who had built careers on the resistance to centralized authority assume positions of institutional responsibility, they frequently repeat precisely the kind of exclusionary gesture they once suffered. Accordingly, critics of the Western canon now canonize noncanonical modes of analysis, thereby relegating other approaches to the periphery. As the marginal becomes institutionally central, the theoretical concern with difference and otherness is gradually transformed into a preoccupation with the same. Though critics repeatedly claim to recover *difference*, their arguments always come down to the *same*: systems and structures inevitably totalize by excluding difference and repressing otherness. Since the point is always the same, difference in effect collapses into identity in such a way that this undeniably influential critical trajectory negates itself and turns into its own opposite. At this moment, theory, as it recently has been understood, reaches a dead end. (pp. 47–48; italics original)

Taylor adds that, therefore:

> Any adequate interpretive framework must make it possible to move beyond the struggle to undo what cannot be undone as well as the interminable mourning of what can never be changed (p. 71) . . . while criticism is important, it is not enough to convey to students a wisdom that is merely negative. Nor is it sufficient for critical practice to have as its primary aim the production of texts accessible to fewer and fewer people, which promote organizations and institutions whose obsolescence is undeniable. A politics that is merely academic is as sterile as theories that are not put into practice. (p. 269)

In essence, the message is "meet the new boss—same as the old boss" (Townsend, 1971). In effect, that which was cutting edge is now status quo. However, I would not be as harsh as Taylor, not wanting to throw out the postmodern baby with its bathwater. I think that, despite its excesses, postmodernism still has interesting and important things to say. This chapter, after all, is to a great extent postmodern in its orientation.

It seems obvious to me that these intellectual movements parallel in many ways the inquiry paradigms of positivism and relativism. As with the inquiry paradigms, I do not believe it is necessary to totally buy into modernism or postmodernism or to exclude one or the other from consideration. Why should artists limit the number of colors on their palettes?

I believe that modernism is not acceptable because of its requirement of certain knowledge; my basic problem with postmodernism is its implication that knowledge has no relation to physical reality. In my view, a researcher strictly following one or the other current here would either be saddled with the unrealistic goal of divining transcendental and absolute truth or be doomed to perpetually stumble around in the dark. So why not an amalgam of modernism's notions of progress, optimism, and rationality with postmodernism's view of truth as relative and contingent and its recognition of the importance and necessity of honoring difference?

CONCLUSION

I am not suggesting here that one should avoid advancing one's ideological agenda, but I believe it is necessary to keep an open mind, to avoid bandwagonism and exclusionary rhetoric, to be willing and even eager to listen to and honestly consider even drastically opposing views, and to adopt the attitude that honest people can disagree. In short, I believe that, in matters of inquiry, inclusivity is not a weakness and compromise is not capitulation.

REFERENCES

Freeman, K. (Ed.). (1957). *Ancilla to the pre-Socratic philosophers*. Cambridge, MA: Harvard University Press.

Guba, E. E. (1990). *The paradigm dialog*. Newbury Park, CA: Sage.

Kuhn, T. S. (1996). *The structure of scientific revolutions* (3rd ed.). Chicago, IL: University of Chicago Press.

Lauer, J., & Asher, J. W. (1988). *Composition research: Empirical designs*. New York: Oxford University Press.

O'Shea, C. S. (1991). *Post-positivism in rhetoric and composition: Kuhnian epistemology and a Popperian alternative*. Unpublished doctoral dissertation, Bowling Green State University, Bowling Green, Ohio.

Popper, K. R. (1962). *The open society and its enemies: Volume 1. The spell of Plato* (5th ed.). Princeton, NJ: Princeton University Press.

Taylor, M. C. (2001). *The moment of complexity: Emerging network culture*. Chicago, IL: University of Chicago Press.

Townsend, P. (1971). Won't be fooled again. *Who's next*. London, England: Polydor Records.

2

Uses of Narrative in L2 Writing Research

Christine Pearson Casanave
Teachers College, Columbia University, Tokyo, Japan

In this chapter, I explore the uses of narrative in L2 writing research—uses that overlap with how narrative is used in educational research more generally. In discussing this topic, I am interested in contributing to efforts by scholars in the L2 writing field to expand the ways we think about, investigate, and ultimately teach L2 writing. In particular, a narrative approach to the study of writing does not centrally concern textual analyses of narratives or how students learn to write narratives and stories, but how researchers, teachers, and students deal with conflicts and find meaning in the events and actions that make up the activities of studying, teaching, and engaging in writing. In the first part of the chapter, I provide a conceptual background to the study of narrative. I then examine uses of narrative in L2 writing research from five perspectives: metadisciplinary narratives (or how we construct the stories of our field), narrative inquiry as a research approach, research reports as narratives, narratives as data, and pedagogical narratives (our stories of teaching and learning). In my conclusion, I argue that as researchers we need to be more honest about our roles as the tellers of tales in our research, and that narrative approaches can help break down narrow stereotypes of who L2 writers are and what constitutes L2 writing.

THE ROLE OF NARRATIVE IN STRUCTURING AND INTERPRETING EXPERIENCE

Narrative is considered to be the primary means by which human beings create meaning from their life experiences, both individually and socially

(Bruner, 1986, 1990, 1991; Polkinghorne, 1988). Narrative configuration occurs as a process of emplotment (Polkinghorne, 1991; Ricoeur, 1984–1986) in which disconnected temporal actions and events are transformed through language into a "unified story with a point or theme" (Polkinghorne, 1991, p. 141).

Understanding the meanings created by the language of narrative requires us to use interpretive strategies rather than formal logic or concrete empirical evidence. This division has led scholars like Bruner (1986, 1990) to posit two basic modes of thinking: the logicoscientific (paradigmatic) mode and the narrative mode. The former typifies the kind of thinking in formal science where people make connections among natural phenomena, seeking causal and logical explanations. The narrative mode typifies how people make connections among and then interpret the meaning of the events and actions of human experience. In other words, a series of otherwise isolated events becomes a narrative when humans connect those events to form a story. Bruner (1991) points out that narrative versions of reality are deemed acceptable by convention rather than by empirical falsification, verification, or logic.

Echoing Bruner, Polkinghorne (1988) describes narrative as a form of "meaning making" (p. 36). Descriptions of actions are drawn together, usually as a sequence in time, and given meaning. It is this power of narrative to ascribe meaning to parts, and to configure them into wholes, that defines narrative as a meaning-making phenomenon.

An example of how narrative constructs this wholeness can be seen in the life stories of professional people in the life history research of Linde (1993). In her research, Linde found that people reinterpreted and reconstructed their life stories depending on the circumstances they found themselves in, such as needing to make sense of sudden changes in fortune. Giddens (1991) also discusses how people reconstruct their narrative biographies over a lifetime as a way to construct a sense of coherence from potentially fragmented life experiences. In educational settings, the work of Clandinin and Connelly (1991, 2000; Connelly & Clandinin, 1990) shows how teachers, administrators, and students "story" and "restory" the events in their lives (Clandinin & Connelly, 1991) as a way to make sense of their educational experiences. This process, they claim, leads to both individual and social growth. Similarly, the critical personal narratives of educators themselves, in the view of Burdell and Swadener (1999), are evolving into a new genre of "autoethnography."

In short, narrative connects and configures parts of human experiences into meaningful larger chunks, weaving them together in a storylike way such that episodes are seen as related to each other in time. This way of constructing meaning is considered basic to human existence and is an ability that develops from earliest childhood. Narrative constructions of reality pervade our lives from the levels of individual identity to broader cultural and historical perspectives. In educational settings, including ones where L2 writing lies at the core of research and teaching, narrative is a particularly powerful way for educators and students to make sense of their experiences over time (e.g., Belcher & Connor, 2001; Bell, 2002; Blanton & Kroll, 2002; Casanave & Schecter, 1997; Witherill & Noddings, 1991).

NARRATIVE IN L2 WRITING RESEARCH

Metadisciplinary Narratives (The Stories of the Field)

At the broadest level, narratives help structure how scholars think about their fields at different moments in history. Like all narratives, metadisciplinary narratives look on events in the past and discursively construct them into coherent stories of a field or subfield (see Matsuda, chap. 3, this volume). Many of the metadisciplinary narratives in L2 writing, such as the story of how process approaches developed, have their origins in those of L1 writing (for a more detailed history, see Matsuda, 2003). Particular tales become summarized and cited by later scholars who generally have little interest in or use for the historical complexities.

In L1 writing, for example, Young (1978) drew on Kuhn's (1970) notion of paradigm to suggest that, despite diversity, the field had been dominated for several decades by the current-traditional approach, with its focus on the written product, analysis of sentences, and classification of discourse into groups such as description, narration, and exposition. As one would do in any good narrative, he then describes a "crisis," in this case, a paradigm that failed to tell us anything about composing processes. The crisis, so goes the narrative, was followed by the response to the crisis—a need to attend to invention and composing processes, as did Flower and Hayes (1981). Hairston (1982) labeled the response a "Kuhnian paradigm shift," ensuring that Kuhn would become one of the protagonists in this tale of the L1 writing field. In L2 writing, Zamel (1976, 1982, 1983) built on the work in L1 and offered persuasive arguments for turning away from an obsession with final products, grammar, and errors and toward exploring instead how expert and novice L2 writers compose. The narrative continued with the expected backlash as scholars constructed a new crisis—namely, the inadequacy of an approach to writing thought to overemphasize personal writing in preparing students for the kinds of writing required in academic settings, such as essay exams (e.g., Horowitz, 1986). This crisis was followed by the happy pseudoending (until the next crisis) that it is desirable and feasible to attend to writing strategies and processes within an approach such as EAP that explicitly teaches students the genres they need in academic and workplace contexts (e.g., Cope & Kalantzis, 1993). Metadisciplinary narratives such as these get told and retold in ways that make the shifts seem progressive over time as well as causally connected, each shift solving problems arising from previous trends despite caveats about overlaps and continuities (Leki, 1992; Raimes, 1991; Silva, 1990).

Another example of metadisciplinary narrative concerns the stories that educational researchers tell about themselves and their research. For instance, Smith (1997) reports on the ongoing vigorous debate between the so-called *quantitative* and *qualitative* enthusiasts about what constitutes appropriate research in literacy education. On the one hand are the proponents of whole language education, and on the other hand are the proponents of a more traditional language arts education that can be studied in more controlled, "objective" ways. The stories told by the two camps bypass each other because the vocabularies they use to construct their stories, and hence their worldviews, differ so greatly. The vocabulary of whole language revolves around perspectives, narrative, context, and voice. That of traditional language arts features the concepts of distance, objectivity, neutrality, prediction, and control. The traditional story, notes Smith, is one of the separation of researchers from what is researched. In contrast, the new stories, such as the ones told by Edelsky (1990, 1997) about whole language, highlight themes of connection, messiness, inconclusiveness, and interpretation. In short, the vocabulary and stories that researchers tell with it announce "to both them and to others who they are as researchers, how they got to be that way, the goals they strive for in their research, how they are able to achieve those goals, and so on" (Smith, 1997, p. 7).

L2 writing scholars rely on metadisciplinary narratives to link past and present practices, to interpret these practices as meaningful or deficient, and to maintain the comforting sense that the L2 writing field is progressing in some way. However, closer historical examination of the events and practices in writing over time reveals that these broad metadisciplinary narratives construct vastly oversimplified stories of the field. Practices in both L1 and L2 writing have historically been far more diverse than is implied in these narratives (Faigley, 1992; Matsuda, 2003), and writing educators and researchers are wisely cautioned against assuming historical accuracy in the metadisciplinary narratives of their fields (Matsuda, chap. 3, this volume). Yet in their telling and retelling over time, the narratives, which impose structure, meaning, cause, and a sense of development on diverse practices, come to represent the field, providing frameworks for our writing and teaching. Metadisciplinary narratives can also be imbued with political import, as has happened with the narratives about L1 and L2 literacy education and about bilingual education. Each narrative has its heroes and villains (e.g., whole language and phonics advocates—choose your hero/villain), its descriptions of crises and conflicts, and its tales of what has and has not worked in the past to solve the problems.

In sum, metadisciplinary narratives tend to take the complexities of past practices and turn them into simplified tales. Researchers rely on such narratives to contextualize past and present beliefs and to plan future solutions. Recognizing that their views of a field and of themselves within a field are constructed as narratives, sometimes using vocabularies that do not translate from one narrative camp to another, can help L2 writing researchers fend off bandwagon fads and develop flexible, multifaceted perspectives on their work. This awareness needs to be situated within an understanding of the historical complexities of how knowledge and practice develop: Things are not always as straightforward as they seem to be from the tales we tell of our field (Matsuda, 2003).

Narrative Inquiry as a Research Approach

In the social sciences, narrative inquiry of various kinds has been attractive to L2 writing researchers who are interested more in the text-related experiences of teachers and writers than in the formal analysis of the texts that writers produce. Models include life histories (Linde, 1993), interpretive sociolinguistic studies (Eckert, 2000), analyses of published autobiographies of bilingual writers (Pavlenko, 2001), experiential narratives and autobiographies of people involved in language learning, teaching, and academic writing (Bell, 1997; Braine, 1999; Blanton & Kroll, 2002; Casanave & Schecter, 1997; Casanave & Vandrick, 2003; Clandinin & Connelly, 1995, 2000; Code, 1999; Connelly & Clandinin, 1999; Witherell & Noddings, 1991), and interview-based case studies of multicultural writers and learners (Casanave, 2002; Kanno, 2000, 2003).

Probably the most influential work on narrative inquiry as a research approach has been done by Clandinin and Connelly (1994, 2000), who have tried to articulate what is involved in their all-encompassing narrative approach to the study of teacher knowledge and experience. They view narrative inquiry as an empirical research approach (Connelly & Clandinin, 1990) that focuses on the stories of the lived experiences and personal practical knowledge of participants (including researchers themselves). The intention is to learn from the stories they tell about participants and themselves what teachers know and how they interpret their experiences. At least two levels of story are involved. At one level, participants tell and retell stories over time to researchers; at another level, researchers construct a story of the participants' stories for the final research text.

One of the problems that Clandinin and Connelly point out with narrative inquiry is that it is almost always impossible at the beginning of a project to clearly describe the research questions and phenomena to be investigated. The specific themes and stories often do not get articulated until the end of the project, when the many field texts and interim texts get written up as the final research text. Although Clandinin and Connelly do not explain the problem in this way, narrative itself is a coherent construction of events from the past rather than an interpretation of the present or a prediction of the future. This character of narrative makes it difficult for narrative inquirers to pose clear research questions and plans before they have experiences on which to reflect.

Like other kinds of qualitative research, narrative inquiry also depends on close observation of people and their settings, detailed description, and the writing and collecting of many kinds of fields texts such as notes, journals, letters, and transcripts of interviews. However, the intent is to listen to, record, and construct stories of lived experience within the narrative dimensions of time, place, and personal-social relationships. Describing how narrative inquirers go from field texts to research texts, Clandinin and Connelly (2000) note how the process of poring over field texts leads to narrative coding, which resembles categories that pertain to stories more than does coding in other kinds of qualitative research:

> Although the initial analysis deals with matters such as character, place, scene, plot, tension, end point, narrator, context, and tone, these matters become increasingly complex as an inquirer pursues this relentless rereading. . . . For example, names of the characters that appear in field texts, places where actions and events occurred, story lines that interweave and interconnect, gaps or silences that become apparent, tensions that emerge, and continuities and discontinuities that appear are all possible codes. (p. 131)

Then in the final narrative report, the researcher-writer needs to appear as an "I," given that narrative inquiries are always "strongly autobiographical." Research interests "come out of our own narratives of experience and shape our narrative inquiry plotlines" (Clandinin & Connelly, 2000, p. 121). A challenge to narrative inquirers, then, is to avoid accusations that have plagued Clandinin and Connelly's work—namely, that narrative research tends to be overly personal and "narcissistic." The "I" must connect to "they"—to an audience of readers who expect to find social significance in the narrative (Clandinin & Connelly, 2000). Narrative inquiry, in other words, does not result simply in a collection of stories that are personally meaningful only to the authors and participants. The narrative is a complex reconstruction of many tales designed to end with a message of significance for an audience.

These same principles apply in general to variations of narrative inquiry in writing research, such as literacy autobiographies in which authors construct stories of themselves as writers (e.g., Belcher & Connor, 2001; Casanave & Vandrick, 2003) or in inquiries about such narratives, as in Pavlenko's (2001) analysis of the published autobiographies of bilingual writers. The point is that as a research method, narrative inquiry revolves around the telling, retelling, and interpreting of stories told by people about themselves and others. In sharing stories during the research process, researchers and participants may find that they need to reconfigure plotlines, construct new perspectives, articulate tensions, and then shift and perhaps resolve those tensions. In L2 writing research, stories about how, why, and what people write and what they know and believe about their writing stand to fill in the many gaps that exist in our knowledge of writing and writers.

Reports of Research as Narrative

Many reports of research in the sciences and social sciences are structured as narratives even if they represent "logicoscientific thinking" (Bruner, 1986, 1990), in the sense that they identify a problem, describe the events and procedures used to investigate that problem (paths that are sometimes fraught with obstacles), and arrive at some kind of felicitous, if not definitive, conclusion (Mishler, 1990; Newkirk, 1992; Sheehan & Rode, 1999). Researchers, notes Brodkey (1987), are fundamentally storytellers because research reports rarely reflect what actually happens in the research process. Instead the messiness and contingencies in both experimental research and qualitative interpretive studies get smoothed out and constructed into a relatively seamless story that fits conventions of academic and professional writing and political realities within fields (Gilbert & Mulkay, 1984; Latour & Woolgar, 1979). The stories are evident not only in the structure of whole research reports, but also in separate sections that can be considered narratives within the broader narrative of the research experience. An introduction and literature review, for example, can be viewed as a story of what happened in the past, what is missing, and where a researcher's own work will fit (Berkenkotter & Huckin, 1995; Swales, 1990). Likewise the methods and results sections in a traditional research article are often presented as a series of events designed to solve a problem and lead to a conclusion. Qualitative research reports are even more obviously narrative in structure, again covering up the extraordinary complexity and messiness of actual research processes even when data are presented in abundance for readers to evaluate for themselves (Mishler, 1990).

Several examples demonstrate the narrative-like character of research texts. Pointing out the parallels between narrative and scientific discourse, Sheehan and Rode (1999) show how Newton and Einstein both constructed narrative accounts of their theories of light, Newton in first person and Einstein in third person. Similarly, Bazerman (1999) shows how Edison rhetorically constructed accounts of how his inventions came into being, placing himself as hero at the center of his stories. In the L2 writing field, two examples will show that even studies that feature quantitative analyses rely on narrative structures to make a meaningful and coherent story of some problem and solution in L2 writing.

In the study of teacher commentary and ESL student revision by Conrad and Goldstein (1999), the main structure of the article follows the standard research article format, which, as I suggested earlier, resembles features of narrative structure: introduction to a problem area, description of the study (including context, data, analysis), results, and implications for pedagogy and research. In other words, a problem is identified, the main characters and scenes are described, paths toward the solution are described and analyzed, and an ending is reached even though the main problem is not fully solved. In addition, the results section contains two very different displays and descriptions—one in the form of seven tables that display numbers and categories of different kinds of teacher comments and student revisions along with a description of the tables, and another in the form of actual stories (the authors' term) of the three individual writers whose revisions they studied (described further in the next section).

Another example comes from an article on writing and the critical thinking abilities of Japanese students (Stapleton, 2001). This article introduces a problem that L2 writing scholars are familiar with—that of the depiction of Japanese students as deficient in critical thinking skills. The article continues with a conventional research article format: methods, results, discussion, and conclusion. Here there are heroes and villains of a sort: Japanese students unfairly depicted as deficient in thinking skills can be seen as underdog heroes, supported by their champion, the author. Villains include other authors who have made exclusionary universal statements about different cultures and used labels that are reductive. Stapleton's review of the debates over cultural constructs in L2 studies itself shows how researchers in the field construct stories about how people in different cultures think, learn, and are educated. Typical of a good story, Stapleton's follows a path toward resolving the tensions created by the debates on critical thinking. He deconstructs the myth of deficient Japanese thinkers by demonstrating that topic familiarity, more than culture, may enable critical thinking in students' writing. The happy ending to his story is that, in his telling, his Japanese students indeed had individual voices, and they were able to think critically on topics familiar to them.

In constructing any research report, then, L2 writing scholars go through processes that can be called *narrative*. They identify problems, conflicts, and tensions having to do with people and their experiences. They search for and examine pieces of the puzzle on the path toward a solution. They fit the pieces together in a story and bring it to some kind of conclusion. It is difficult to imagine a way to approach L2 writing research that is not narrative in this sense.

Narratives as Data

Narratives in the form of actual stories often get inserted as data into larger research reports. In other words, one does not have to be committed to a narrative approach to inquiry to rely on narrative as part of a project that studies writing in other ways. Yet in some studies of L2 writers, stories by participants may constitute the main source of data. I briefly discuss narratives collected by researchers of other people (usually of student writers) and then writers' own narratives that they use as data to construct stories about themselves as writers.

The most common kind of narrative that gets inserted into studies of writers is stories of writers, as told to researchers in interviews and conversations and as observed by researchers and teacher researchers who spend time with student writers. As data, these narratives tend to appear as paraphrases and retellings by the researcher and as snippets of direct quotes and dialogues from transcripts. In the Conrad and Goldstein (1999) article mentioned earlier, these authors interviewed three students, wishing to learn in particular why some of the students' revisions were either unsuccessful or unattempted. As the authors state, "Analysis of the comments themselves fails to shed light on the . . . exceptions to the typical patterns of success in revision. To understand the variation, we must move beyond the characteristics of the feedback and consider the individual student writers" (Conrad & Goldstein, 1999, p. 161). The stories, in other words, provide the authors with the kind of deep understanding of students' knowledge, decision processes, and affective states that can only be hinted at from non-narrative data. In this study, the stories are (rather unusually) told in the present tense, adding a vivid narrative presence. For each of the three students, a sample of dialogue from interviews is also included, giving readers a hint of the participants' real voices. It is the stories, the authors claim, that help show how "the teacher's comments interact with individual factors that students bring to writing and revision" (p. 162). Without the stories, students' decisions about what and how to revise remain a mystery. In short, this article structures the research story as a whole in narrative form and then incorporates several actual narratives into the structure as explanatory data.

As in other kinds of research, L2 writing researchers have also used qualitative case study approaches to construct stories of people. The people are described; their problems, progress, and changes are framed in their own words through the use of extracts from interview data; and the extracts are then woven by the researcher into a narrative that has a specific trajectory and purpose. My own case study of several bilingual Japanese faculty members (Casanave, 1998) reflects this approach, which is built nearly entirely on the stories told to me over a year and a half by colleagues at my university in Japan. They were all writing in both English and Japanese at a professional level, but we used their texts as loci for discussion rather than as objects for textual analysis. As is typical for narrative research, the researcher–participant boundaries were fuzzy, and over time two of the participants became both trusted colleagues and friends.

In my reporting, I used paraphrases from interview tapes and transcripts, quoted words and phrases, and longer extracts in the words of participants. By the time I had to write the final research text from more data than could ever be reported, I had to find ways to select, pare down, extract, and then reconstruct these pieces into thematic retellings. These are the problems faced by any researcher of course, particularly those who conduct qualitative (interpretive) research, but in case studies of writers like this one, the main data consist of participants' stories of their activities, motivations, frustrations, and successes. I had to piece together my own story, from these stories told to me, of how bilingual writers manage to write for publication in two languages.

In addition to stories told to researchers by participants, L1 and L2 writers tell their own stories about their identities and activities as writers. Their data are stories from their lives told in conversations, journals, letters and e-mail, drafts, and finally in published form. We have seen increasing numbers of published narratives by L2 writing teachers and researchers in the form of literacy autobiographies and first-person narratives of writing and teaching experiences (Belcher & Connor, 2001; Blanton & Kroll, 2002; Braine, 1999; Casanave & Vandrick, 2003; Vandrick, 1999; Villanueva, 1993). Such first-person narratives are often overtly constructed in story form and perhaps in chronological or flashback-flashforward order, documenting a writer's experience over time in some aspect of writing that he or she found difficult or transforming. It is tempting to view such stories as made up of "raw" data—untransformed by the outside influence of a researcher but such is not the case. The stories that writers tell of themselves do not magically pour out of them as truths in brilliant and unedited form. I discovered this first hand in my negotiations with contributors to an edited volume of first-person narratives by language educators (Casanave, 2002; Casanave & Schecter, 1997) and in my reflections on how I struggle to construct an appropriate identity in my own published writing (Casanave, 2003). The stories of self as first or second language writer or writing teacher are as carefully crafted from fragments of evidence from our pasts as are our stories of other people. Pieces are left out, retold in new ways, and adjusted to fit the requirements of an editor or publisher. These data are not raw, but "cooked" many times over. They contribute to the story with the self as protagonist facing tensions and conflicts and seeking ways to resolve them.

Finally, narratives of the self in the form of published autobiographies and literacy autobiographies can become the data for analysis by others, as is the case for Pavlenko's (2001) study of the autobiographies of bilingual authors mentioned earlier. These data are doubly cooked, once by the original author in the process of constructing a published piece and then by Pavlenko the analyst, who was looking for some things and not others in the autobiographies. Thus, she carefully selected narrative extracts about language, culture, gender, identity, and ethnicity as a way to put across her own message about the complexities of bilingual-bicultural identity.

Pedagogical Narratives

In writing research, narrative is used not only to tell the stories of people and their experiences with writing. There are also narratives, implied or explicit, about how L2 writers of various kinds best learn to write and, by implication, how L2 writing should be taught. Carter (1993) refers to this kind of story as the "curriculum story line," or how teachers use story to "transform knowledge of content into a form that plays itself out in the time and space of classrooms" (p. 7). If we examine our textbooks and course syllabuses, for example, we may find evidence that our teaching activities are implicitly grounded in a narrative of learner development. I presume it is rare in L2 writing pedagogy to see randomly ordered writing activities in course syllabuses. Rather, they tend to be ordered according to our beliefs about where learners are beginning and where we hope they will end. For instance, in the pedagogical plotline, the predicament is that beginning L2 writers don't know or can't yet do what we think they need to do to become proficient writers. Teachers as protagonists therefore engage them in this or that kind of writing activity with the intention of helping them reach their (teachers') goals. Students struggle through obstacles, overcome difficulties, develop proficiency and independence as writers, and eventually take on agency and autonomy as protagonists in their own stories of development as writers.

Various pedagogical debates in the L2 writing field also fit into the pedagogical narratives of what the predicaments, obstacles, and paths to solutions are in L2 writing. For example, in her fluency first argument, Mac-

Gowan-Gilhooly (1991) claims that basic L1 and L2 writers benefit from a pedagogical sequence of literacy activities that begins with extensive fluency activities and culminates several courses later with attention to form and accuracy. Similarly, the error correction debates (Ferris, 1999, 2001; Truscott, 1996, 1999) identify the predicament of how to reduce errors in L2 student writing and suggest alternate routes to the goal. Truscott identifies those teachers who insist on correcting all the errors in their writing as villains who do no good to and may even harm L2 writers. Ferris, for her part, holds up the well-meaning teacher as hero, who has an ethical responsibility to provide what students want and who may even help them in the long run. In both cases, events that happen over time (i.e., writing activities and practice of various kinds) are presumed to help solve a problem that the characters in the story face (L2 writers who need to develop linguistic and rhetorical skills) and to lead to a happy conclusion (improvement in their writing).

Stated in such ways, the pedagogical narrative sounds unrealistically simple. However, the point is that such narratives are not intended to portray the truth of what happens in our writing classes. Rather they underlie our planning, strategizing, feedback, practice, and assessment activities as a kind of structural plotline that guides and frames how we conceptualize the purposes and activities of our teaching. At the end of a teaching-learning experience, pedagogical narratives likewise help us as teachers and researchers look back and interpret what happened, when such interpretations elude us at the moment we live our experiences.

CONCLUSION

In this chapter, I looked at uses of narrative in L2 writing research from several perspectives—from the level of metadisciplinary narratives that construct how L2 writing researchers and educators view the field of L2 writing and composition to ways that narrative is used in research and teaching. It is clear that the field of TESOL and L2 writing research, narrative is playing increasingly important roles (Bell, 2002; Pavlenko, 2002). To conclude, I point out several implications for us as L2 writing researchers of looking at scholarly work more narratively than we are accustomed to doing.

First, L2 writing research is inevitably about people who write, even if the main interest of writing researchers is in textual analysis. Narrative is fundamentally about how people construct meaning over time in their lives, including sociocultural and sociohistorical influences on their writing (Pavlenko, 2002). Learning more about people who write from the stories they tell of themselves and their experiences can only enhance what researchers know about L2 writers and the challenges and processes they experience when writing.

Second, L2 writing research of many kinds needs to do what good narratives do: confront a problem, identify the characters in the story, develop a plotline, follow a series of events over time and forge links between those events, and make a point that will connect with the consumers of research. But as is the case for other qualitative methods, narrative researchers in L2 writing also need to confront issues of how their work will be assessed: What will the criteria be for how scholars evaluate this work (Bell, 2002; Carter, 1993; Clandinin & Connelly, 2000; Lazaraton, 2003)?

Third, seeing our research in more narrative ways means that as L2 writing researchers we need to position ourselves clearly and honestly in our texts, as narrators and constructors of stories about writers. It is we who choose who to describe, how to portray the details of their characters and activities, what themes to highlight within our narrative plots, and how to interpret and ascribe significance to what we learn. This is so regardless of the kind of research we undertake. *We construct our tales*. They do not emerge like magic from our data. Therefore, I urge all scholars of L2 writing to avoid attributing our goals, interests, and methods to something besides ourselves.

Finally, more actual narrative inquiry in L2 writing research can potentially help L2 writing researchers dismantle stereotypes of cultural patterns in writing and of writers labeled simplistically as representatives of their respective cultures. Although narrative inquiry is not immune from oversimplifying and stereotyping, learning the stories of both L1 and L2 writers over time, and investigating our own stories as researchers and teachers of writing and as writers ourselves, will help us recognize the fascinating complexities of writing that surround and support what we usually focus on—the drafting and analysis of text (e.g., Prior, 2002). If we work at it, we may be able to construct and interpret patterns without invoking the stereotypes. Equally important, we can also learn to appreciate the idiosyncrasies that characterize human experience and weave those idiosyncrasies into our L2 writing research. Without them, our stories are incomplete.

REFERENCES

Bazerman, C. (1999). *The languages of Edison's light*. Cambridge, MA: The MIT Press.

Belcher, D., & Connor, U. (Eds.). (2001). *Reflections on multiliterate lives*. Clevedon: Multilingual Matters.

Bell, J. (1997). Shifting frames, shifting stories. In C. P. Casanave & S. R. Schecter (Eds.), *On becoming a language educator: Personal essays on professional development* (pp. 133–143). Mahwah, NJ: Lawrence Erlbaum Associates.

Bell, J. S. (2002). Narrative inquiry: More than just telling stories. *TESOL Quarterly, 36*(2), 207–213.

Berkenkotter, C., & Huckin, T. N. (1995). *Genre knowledge in disciplinary communities: Cognition/culture/power*. Hillsdale, NJ: Lawrence Erlbaum Associates.

Blanton, L. L., & Kroll, B. (with Cumming, A., Erickson, M., Johns, A. M., Leki, I., Reid, J., & Silva, T.). (2002). *ESL composition tales: Reflections on teaching*. Ann Arbor: University of Michigan Press.

Braine, G. (Ed.). (1999). *Non-native educators in English language teaching*. Mahwah, NJ: Lawrence Erlbaum Associates.

Brodkey, L. (1987). Writing ethnographic narratives. *Written Communication, 4*, 25–50.

Bruner, J. (1986). *Actual minds, possible worlds*. Cambridge, MA: Harvard University Press.

Bruner, J. (1990). *Acts of meaning*. Cambridge: Harvard University Press.

Bruner, J. (1991). The narrative construction of reality. *Critical Inquiry, 18*, 1–21.

Burdell, P., & Swadener, B. B. (1999). Critical personal narrative and autoethnography in education: Reflections on a genre. *Educational Researcher, 28*(6), 21–26.

Carter, K. (1993). The place of story in the study of teaching and teacher education. *Educational Researcher, 22*(1), 5–12.

Casanave, C. P. (1998). Transitions: The balancing act of bilingual academics. *Journal of Second Language Writing, 7*, 175–203.

Casanave, C. P. (2002). *Writing games: Multicultural case studies of academic literacy practices in higher education*. Mahwah, NJ: Lawrence Erlbaum Associates.

Casanave, C. P. (2003). Narrative braiding: Constructing a multistrand portrayal of self as writer. In C. P. Casanave & S. Vandrick (Eds.), *Writing for scholarly publication: Behind the scenes in language education* (pp. 131–145). Mahwah, NJ: Lawrence Erlbaum Associates.

Casanave, C. P., & Schecter, S. R. (Eds.). (1997). *On becoming a language educator: Personal essays on professional development*. Mahwah, NJ: Lawrence Erlbaum Associates.

Casanave, C. P., & Vandrick, S. (Eds.). (2003). *Writing for scholarly publication: Behind the scenes in language education*. Mahwah, NJ: Lawrence Erlbaum Associates.

Clandinin, D. J., & Connelly, F. M. (1991). Narrative and story in practice and research. In D. A. Schön (Ed.), *The reflective turn: Case studies in and on educational practice* (pp. 258–281). New York: Teachers College Press.

Clandinin, D. J., & Connelly, F. M. (1994). Personal experience methods. In N. K. Denzin & Y. S. Lincoln (Eds.), *Handbook of qualitative research* (pp. 413–427). Thousand Oaks, CA: Sage.

Clandinin, D. J., & Connelly, F. M. (1995). *Teachers' professional knowledge landscapes*. New York: Teachers College Press.

Clandinin, D. J., & Connelly, F. M. (2000). *Narrative inquiry: Experience and story in qualitative research*. San Francisco: Jossey-Bass.

Conle, C. (1999). Why narrative? Which narrative? Struggling with time and place in life and research. *Curriculum Inquiry, 29*(1), 7–31.

Connelly, F. M., & Clandinin, D. J. (1990). Stories of experience and narrative inquiry. *Educational Researcher, 19*(5), 2–14.

Connelly, F. M., & Clandinin, D. J. (Eds.). (1999). *Shaping a professional identity: Stories of educational practice*. New York: Teachers College Press.

Conrad, S. M., & Goldstein, L. M. (1999). ESL student revision after teacher-written comments: Text, contexts, and individuals. *Journal of Second Language Writing, 8*, 147–179.

Cope, B., & Kalantzis, M. (Eds.). (1993). *The powers of literacy: A genre approach to teaching writing*. London: Falmer.

Eckert, P. (2000). *Linguistic variation as social practice*. Malden, MA: Blackwell.

Edelsky, C. (1990). Whose agenda is this anyway? A response to McKenna, Robinson, and Miller. *Educational Researcher, 19*(8), 7–10.

Edelsky, C. (1997). Working on the margins. In C. P. Casanave & S. R. Schecter (Eds.), *On becoming a language educator: Personal essays on professional development* (pp. 3–17). Mahwah, NJ: Lawrence Erlbaum Associates.

Faigley, L. (1992). *Fragments of rationality: Postmodernism and the subject of composition*. Pittsburgh: University of Pittsburgh Press.

Ferris, D. (1999). The case for grammar correction in L2 writing classes: A response to Truscott (1996). *Journal of Second Language Writing, 8*, 1–11.

Ferris, D. (2001). *Treatment of error in second language student writing*. Ann Arbor, MI: University of Michigan Press.

Flower, L., & Hayes, J. (1981). A cognitive process theory of writing. *College Composition and Communication, 32*, 365–387.

Giddens, A. (1991). *Modernity and self-identity: Self and society in the late modern age*. Stanford, CA: Stanford University Press.

Gilbert, G. N., & Mulkay, M. (1984). *Opening Pandora's box: A sociological analysis of scientists' discourse*. Cambridge, England: Cambridge University Press.

Hairston, M. (1982). The winds of change: Thomas Kuhn and the revolution in the teaching of writing. *College Composition and Communication, 33*, 76–88.

Horowitz, D. (1986). Process not product: Less than meets the eye. *TESOL Quarterly, 20*, 141–144.

Kanno, Y. (2000). Kikokushijo as bicultural. *International Journal of Intercultural Relations, 24*, 361–382.

Kanno, Y. (2003). *Negotiating bilingual and bicultural identities: Japanese returnees betwixt two worlds*. Mahwah, NJ: Lawrence Erlbaum Associates.

Kuhn, T. S. (1970). *The structure of scientific revolutions* (2nd ed.). Chicago: University of Chicago Press.

Latour, B., & Woolgar, S. (1979). *Laboratory life: The social construction of scientific facts*. Princeton, NJ: Princeton University Press.

Lazaraton, A. (2003). Evaluative criteria for qualitative research in applied linguistics: Whose criteria and whose research? *Modern Language Journal, 87*, 1–12.

Leki, I. (1992). *Understanding ESL writers: A guide for teachers*. Portsmouth, NH: Boynton/Cook Heinemann.

Linde, C. (1993). *Life stories: The creation of coherence*. New York: Oxford University Press.

MacGowan-Gilhooly, A. (1991). Fluency first: Reversing the traditional ESL sequence. *Journal of Basic Writing, 10*, 73–87.

Matsuda, P. K. (2003). Process and post-process: A discursive history. *Journal of Second Language Writing, 12*, 65–83.

Mishler, E. G. (1990). Validation in inquiry-guided research: The role of exemplars in narrative studies. *Harvard Educational Review, 60*, 415–442.

Newkirk, T. (1992). The narrative roots of case study. In G. Kirsch & P. A. Sullivan (Eds.), *Methods and methodology in composition research* (pp. 130–152). Carbondale: Southern Illinois University Press.

Pavlenko, A. (2001). "In the world of the tradition, I was unimagined": Negotiation of identities in cross-cultural autobiographies. *International Journal of Bilingualism, 5*, 317–344.

Pavlenko, A. (2002). Narrative study: Whose story is it, anyway? *TESOL Quarterly, 36*, 213–218.

Polkinghorne, D. E. (1988). *Narrative knowing and the human sciences*. Albany, NY: State University of New York Press.

Polkinghorne, D. E. (1991). Narrative and self-concept. *Journal of Narrative and Life History, 12*(2 & 3), 135–153.

Prior, P. (2002, June). *Disciplinarity: From discourse communities to dispersed, laminated activity*. Plenary talk presented at the Knowledge and Discourse 2 Conference, University of Hong Kong, Hong Kong.

Raimes, A. (1991). Out of the woods: Emerging traditions in the teaching of writing. *TESOL Quarterly, 25*, 407–430.

Ricoeur, P. (1984–1986). *Time and narrative*, Vols. 1 and 2 (K. McLaughlin & D. Pellauer, Trans.). Chicago: University of Chicago Press.

Sheehan, R. J., & Rode, S. (1999). On scientific narrative: Stories of light by Newton and Einstein. *Journal of Business and Technical Communication, 13*, 336–358.

Silva, T. (1990). Second language composition instruction: Developments, issues, and directions in ESL. In B. Kroll (Ed.), *Second language writing: Research insights for the classroom* (pp. 11–23). Cambridge, England: Cambridge University Press.

Smith, J. K. (1997). The stories educational researchers tell about themselves. *Educational Researcher, 26*(5), 4–11.

Stapleton, P. (2001). Assessing critical thinking in the writing of Japanese university students. *Written Communication, 18*, 506–548.

Swales, J. M. (1990). *Genre analysis: English in academic and research settings*. New York: Cambridge University Press.

Truscott, J. (1996). The case against grammar correction in L2 writing classes. *Language Learning, 46*, 327–369.

Truscott, J. (1999). The case for "The case against grammar correction in L2 writing classes": A response to Ferris. *Journal of Second Language Writing, 8*, 111–122.

Vandrick, S. (1999). ESL and the colonial legacy: A teacher faces her "missionary kid" past. In B. Haroian-Guerin (Ed.), *The personal narrative: Writing ourselves as teachers and scholars* (pp. 63–74). Portland, ME: Calendar Island Publishers.

Villanueva, V. (1993). *Bootstraps: From an American of color*. Urbana, IL: National Council of Teachers of English.

Witherell, C. (1991). The self in narrative. In C. Witherell & N. Noddings (Eds.), *Stories lives tell: Narrative and dialogue in education* (pp. 83–95). New York: Teachers College Press.

Witherell, C., & Noddings, N. (Eds.). (1991). *Stories lives tell: Narrative and dialogue in education*. New York: Teachers College Press.

Young, R. (1978). Paradigms and problems: Needed research in rhetorical invention. In C. R. Cooper & L. Odell (Eds.), *Research on composing: Points of departure* (pp. 29–47). Urbana, IL: National Council of Teachers of English.

Zamel, V. (1976). Teaching composition in the ESL classroom: What we can learn from research in the teaching of English. *TESOL Quarterly, 10*, 67–76.

Zamel, V. (1982). Writing: The process of discovering meaning. *TESOL Quarterly, 16*, 195–209.

Zamel, V. (1983). The composing processes of advanced ESL students: Six case studies. *TESOL Quarterly, 17*, 165–187.

3

Historical Inquiry in Second Language Writing

Paul Kei Matsuda
University of New Hampshire, USA

Historical inquiry in the field of second language writing is a form of metadisciplinary inquiry—self-reflexive investigation into the nature and development of a field of study (Matsuda, Canagarajah, Harklau, Hyland, & Warschauer, 2003). As such it may not contribute directly to *raison d'être* of the field—that is, disciplinary inquiry into second language writers, writing, writing instruction, writing assessment, and writing program administration. Nevertheless, historical inquiry is important for the field because it provides a way of constructing, exposing, and examining metadisciplinary narratives (Casanave, chap. 2, this volume) that inevitably shape the ways in which we as members of the field conduct our work. In other words, historical inquiry can contribute insights into the socially shared and discursively constructed identity of the field and its members. It can also help identify what issues have been discussed, what questions have been posed, what solutions have been devised, and what consequences have come of those solutions—and why.

My goal in this chapter is to highlight the importance of historical inquiry in constructing and examining metadisciplinary narratives. I begin by considering the current status of historical inquiry in second language studies. I then discuss my own historical study (Matsuda, 1999) to show an example of a metadisciplinary historiography that is based on careful and critical processes of collection, corroboration, and interpretation of historical data. I conclude by discussing the importance of ongoing communal dialectic in constructing and assessing metadisciplinary narratives.

HISTORICAL INQUIRY IN SECOND LANGUAGE STUDIES

Historical inquiry was once an important part of second language studies in general.[1] During the formative years of second language studies and its constituent fields, a number of scholars made serious attempts to take stock of the past to understand the present and consider directions for the future (e.g., Allen, 1973; Darian, 1972; Diller, 1978; W. McKay, 1965). These studies not only described pedagogical practices in the past, but also provided a shared sense of tradition and identity to a growing number of people who were beginning to identify themselves as professionals in the field of second language teaching. By the 1980s, however, historical studies seemed to have fallen out of favor as social scientific research methods took hold as the dominant mode of knowledge making. As John Swales (2001) notes, book-length historical studies have been few and far between since the appearance in 1984 of A. P. R. Howatt's *A History of English Language Teaching*. Margaret Thomas (1998), historian of applied linguistics, has also problematized what she has called *ahistoricity* in the field of second language acquisition. She points out that "L2 theorists consistently ignore the past as discontinuous with the present," thus "render[ing] the past invisible" (p. 390).

This is not to say that historical inquiry into second language studies has ceased to exist completely. There are a few notable exceptions, such as Bernard Spolsky's (1995) *Measured Words* and Diane Musumeci's (1997) *Breaking Tradition*. Historical studies also continue to appear in specialized journals such as *Historiographica Linguistica* and at conferences such as the North American Association for the History of the Language Sciences, the Henry Sweet Society for the History of Linguistic Ideas, and the Society for Historical Studies of English Teaching in Japan. Yet these conversations seem to have been taking place outside the mainstream discourse of second language studies. In contemporary second language studies, which tends to privilege empirical knowledge making, historical perspectives have often been relegated to literature reviews or chronologies of events accompanied by established researchers' personal recollections.

I do not mean to deny the importance of stories told by people who have been in the field for a long time. In fact for historical studies that focus on relatively recent periods, written reflections and oral history of

---

[1]For the purpose of this chapter, I use the term *second language studies* as a catch-all shorthand for various and overlapping fields that provide primary sights for the study of second language learning and teaching, such as applied linguistics, bilingual education, education, foreign languages, linguistics, second language acquisition, and TESOL.

those who lived through the events are indispensable because they provide important information about people's perceptions of certain historical events. Yet they are no substitute for historical inquiry; rather, they provide the raw materials with which historians work. The task for the historian is to take insights from these narratives and corroborate them with other types of historical evidence—published documents, textbooks, oral history interviews, archival materials, and other available sources—to construct a plausible narrative that has significant implications for the field.

Today, doctoral education in second language studies, at least in North America, usually includes training in empirical research methods, which continues to be an important mode of inquiry, but not in historical or other modes of inquiry. Although most doctoral programs require coursework in research design, those courses are not likely to include readings or discussion of philosophical or historical modes of inquiry. It is even less likely that graduate programs in second language studies require coursework in the history of second language studies or in historiography. As a result, the same researchers who would approach empirical studies with a high degree of methodological rigor would treat historical knowledge uncritically, often making unsubstantiated or unverified claims about historical events or developments.

Indeed the conventional history of L2 writing, which not surprisingly echoes the dominant historical narrative of L2 studies in general, is based on many of those unsupported claims. It goes something like this: Before the 1960s, writing was neglected in L2 studies because of the dominance of the audiolingual approach, which focused exclusively on spoken language. During the 1960s, the fall of the audiolingual approach and the sudden influx of international students in U.S. universities made writing an important agenda in L2 studies—especially in TESOL, where ESL writing gained recognition as one of its subfields. Historical accounts of the field that began to appear in the early 1990s (with the exception of Silva, 1990) usually accepted this dominant narrative, taking the 1960s as the starting point of their historical narratives. Today many L2 writing researchers continue to reproduce this received view of history, often relying solely on secondary sources such as Silva (1990) and Raimes (1991).

Although the received view of history may seem plausible, many of the details are questionable. As I have documented elsewhere (Matsuda, 2001), the audiolingual approach could not have been the cause of the neglect of writing. The term *audiolingual approach* was not coined until 1960 (Brooks, 1960), and those who began to argue the importance of writing during the early 1960s were the proponents of the oral approach (Erazmus, 1960; Marckwardt, 1961), a precursor to the audiolingual approach. Furthermore, although the Sputnik crisis did prompt the U.S. government to provide funding for the education of ESL teachers through the

National Defense Education Act of 1964, no evidence has been presented to suggest that there was a sudden influx of international students in the 1960s or that the rise of writing issues was prompted by it. In fact the presence of international students in the writing classroom had already become an issue by the early 1950s, and those issues had been discussed at conferences such as the Conference on College Composition and Communication and the National Association for Foreign Student Affairs (Matsuda, 1999).

This conventional historical narrative also tends to focus on the classification of pedagogical approaches. Silva (1990) identified four major approaches—controlled composition, current-traditional rhetoric, the process approach, and English for academic purposes—and characterized the relationship among them as the "merry-go-round of approaches" that "generates more heat than light and does not encourage consensus on important issues, preservation of legitimate insights, synthesis of a body of knowledge, or principled evaluation of approaches" (p. 18). Similarly, Raimes (1991) characterized the history of L2 writing as the development of competing pedagogies with differing foci: focus on form, focus on the writer, focus on content, and focus on the reader. Although Silva suggested that L2 writing teachers and researchers move beyond the pedagogical conflicts and focus on developing a broader and more principled understanding of L2 writers and writing, his article is usually cited for his descriptions of pedagogical approaches.

Such classifications are useful in understanding the development of the dominant pedagogical emphases; they may even help teachers avoid reinventing the wheel or repeating the same mistakes. Yet the exclusive focus on pedagogical approaches is limited because it tends to take those approaches out of their historical contexts, ignoring larger institutional changes that have affected the field in important ways. To overcome this limitation, the field needs other kinds of history. To illustrate this point, I discuss my own attempt to construct a disciplinary history, "Composition Studies and ESL Writing: A Disciplinary Division of Labor," which has appeared in *College Composition and Communication* (Matsuda, 1999).

THE MAKING OF A DISCIPLINARY HISTORY

The issue I examined in my 1999 article was the development of the disciplinary division of labor as the dominant metaphor for the relationship between composition and ESL. This metaphor creates a dichotomy between L1 and L2 writing, placing L2 writing in the context of L2 studies, but not composition studies. Initially, this dichotomy encouraged the creation of separate ESL courses to meet the needs of ESL writers that were not being addressed in mainstream composition courses or basic writing courses (Braine, 1996; S. McKay, 1981). It also facilitated the development of L2 writing pedagogy and research apart from those developed in composition studies (Silva, 1993). In the long run, however, the disciplinary division created a different kind of problem.

During the 1990s, it was typical for composition teachers to consider themselves as L1 composition teachers by default. This tendency was being reinforced by some L2 writing specialists who characterized composition studies as *L1 composition* (e.g., Atkinson & Ramanathan, 1995; Santos, 1992). But the *L1 composition* was an inaccurate label for the field of composition studies because ESL writers—both international and resident students—were constantly finding their way into mainstream composition classrooms. Yet, too many composition teachers seemed to think that it was not their job to work with those ESL students in their own classrooms. Composition teachers' attitude toward ESL students became a source of frustration for a group of L2 writing specialists who were active at the Conference on College Composition and Communication (CCCC). Many L2 writing specialists attended CCCC conventions primarily to help composition teachers learn about L2 writers, but their sessions attracted the same group of people who already considered themselves L2 writing specialists (Johns, 1993). To make all writing courses more ESL friendly, I felt the need to argue that division of labor was not a productive metaphor—that composition studies was not L1 composition.

In the spring of 1996, I tried to address this issue by writing an article that described the problem of the division of labor metaphor and suggested alternative metaphors. In that article, which was later published in *Written Communication* (Matsuda, 1998), I traced the origin of the metaphor to the late 1940s, when the presence of international ESL students became a serious concern in U.S. higher education. I also identified a 1951 *College English* article by George Gibian, which documented the creation of a special section of the required composition course at Harvard in 1949. However, there were many more questions that I had not answered. How did the division of labor metaphor emerge and how did it evolve? Was Harvard the only place where a separate ESL course was created? Why did the division of labor become the dominant metaphor for the relationship between composition and ESL? How did it affect the status of ESL issues in composition studies? In other words, I had some understanding of what had happened, but not how or why. These questions seemed to call for a more detailed historical study.

In the fall of the same year, *College Composition and Communication* (CCC), the flagship journal in composition studies, issued a call for papers for its 50th anniversary issue with a focus on the history of composition studies. When I saw the announcement, I decided to write a historical article tracing the development of L2 writing as an area of specialization rather than a common concern for writing teachers and researchers. My goal, according to my ambitious proposal, was to "lay the foundation for further efforts to situate ESL writing research and practice in composition studies" by examining the history of marginalization.

As Robert J. Connors (1992) wrote in "Dreams and Play: Historical Method and Methodology," historians "start from theory, at least from a theory about building challenging, supportable hypotheses, and historians seldom work through serious archival search unless they have a hypothesis that they tacitly think is supportable" (pp. 22–23). My initial hypothesis, which came from my 1998 article, was that L2 writing did not suddenly become an issue in the 1960s; rather, it became an issue sometime after the late 1940s and gradually drifted away from composition studies. With that initial hypothesis in mind, I began to identify relevant sources in the process known to historians as external criticism. I decided to begin by examining the representation of ESL issues in the program books for the annual conventions of CCCC, and I counted the number of sessions that dealt with L2 issues. I was also able to identify the names of ESL specialists who were active at CCCC in the 1980s, including Barbara Kroll, Nancy Lay, Ann Raimes, Joy Reid, Alice Roy, and Tony Silva. I learned that ESL issues, although marginal, were represented at CCCC meetings throughout the 1980s and 1990s, but my collection of program books only went back as far as 1980.

Then I remembered reading a passage in Jim Berlin's (1987) *Rhetoric and Reality*, where he mentioned the practice of publishing workshop reports in *CCC*. To examine those reports, I went into Periodicals Stacks in Purdue's Humanities, Social Science and Education (HSSE) Library in the Stewart Center—the building in which L2 writing specialists now gather for the biennial Symposium on Second Language Writing. I sat in the dark and dusty stacks for hours and days, browsing through early issues of *CCC*. There I found the voices of such influential figures in TESOL as Harold Allen, Virginia French Allen, Kenneth Croft, Robert B. Kaplan, Robert Lado, Clifford Prator, Betty Wallace Robinette, and Paul R. Sullivan.

I also learned that, between 1955 and 1966, ESL discussion took place regularly at the annual meetings of CCCC (Table 3.1). More important, in the 1950s, those sessions attracted not only L2 specialists, but also administrators and teachers of what some of us now call "L1 composition." They were all trying to figure out what to do about the growing number of L2 writers in their classrooms. In 1956, Paul Sullivan even pointed out that all writing teachers are *de facto* ESL teachers (Studies in English as a Second Language, 1956). By the early 1960s, however, the site of ESL issues had begun to shift from composition courses to separate ESL courses. Evident in many of the workshop reports in the 1960s were arguments for the cre-

TABLE 3.1
ESL Sessions at CCCC: 1947–1966

1947	CCCC established	
1950	*CCC* inaugural issue	
1955	Workshop.	"The Foreign Student in the Freshman Course." (Ives; Lado; Sullivan)
1956	Workshop.	"The Foreign Student in the Freshman Course." (French Allen)
	Panel.	"Studies in English as a Second Language." (Sullivan; Lado)
1957	Workshop.	"Teaching the Foreign Student to Speak and Write—Materials and Methods." (Hunt)
1958	Workshop.	"Composition/Communication Programs for the Foreign Student."
1961	Panel.	"The Freshman Whose Native Language is Not English."
1962	Workshop.	"English for Foreigners in the U.S.A." (Croft)
1963	Workshop.	"English for Foreign Students." (Kaplan, co-chair)
1964	Workshop.	"Composition for Foreign Students." (Kaplan, chair)
1965	Workshop.	"ESL Programs: Composition and Literature." (Kaplan, chair; Robinette; Marquardt)
1966	Workshop.	"Teaching English as a Second Language." (Kaplan, chair)

ation of separate courses and the recognition of ESL as a respectable profession. I was also struck by frequent references to the teaching methods and materials being developed at Michigan's English Language Institute, the significance of which I did not fully appreciate until later.

Browsing through *CCC* and tracing their sources, I was also able to identify several articles describing the creation of separate ESL writing courses between 1945 and 1956, including those written by Gretchen Rogers (1945) at George Washington University, Herbert Schueler (1949) at Queens College, Sumner Ives (1953) at Tulane University, and William Marquardt (1956) at the University of Washington. My hypothesis was confirmed. Contrary to the popular belief, ESL students did not suddenly increase in the 1960s; their presence was already an issue at the conclusion of World War II in 1945. Creating separate ESL courses was a solution that was becoming increasingly popular.

As the arguments for separation became louder, ESL sessions at CCCC began to attract fewer and fewer composition specialists. In 1965, when Robert B. Kaplan chaired the ESL workshop, there was nobody in the room except for the presenters. Again in the following year, his workshop attracted only a small group of L2 specialists. Discouraged, Kaplan and "the small but loquacious group" of L2 specialists published the following recommendation:

1. That, given the small attendance at this workshop for several years under the aegis of CCCC, the group should meet hereafter only at NCTE meetings; the group thanks CCCC for its hospitality past and present.

2. That a TEFL [Teacher of English as a Foreign Language] be appointed to investigate needed research projects in our area, and that CCCC and NCTE give thought to sponsoring such research.[2]
3. That CCCC appoint a liaison person to maintain contact with ATESL and TESOL.

(Teaching English as a Second Language, 1966, p. 198)

I checked the conference reports for the next few years and confirmed that there was indeed no ESL session at CCCC between 1967 and 1970. However, I did not know what happened between 1971 and 1979 because *CCC* had stopped publishing the workshop reports after 1970, and the oldest CCCC program to which I had access was 1980. To fill the gap between 1971 and 1979, I called the National Council of the Teachers of English (NCTE), the umbrella organization for CCCC. On a rainy day in December 1997, I drove from West Lafayette, Indiana, to NCTE headquarters in Urbana, Illinois, to access its archives. There I examined all the programs between 1959 and 1979. I was able to confirm that there was indeed no session on L2 writing until 1976, when ESL issues came back to CCCC because of the increase of resident ESL students at open admissions institutions (Matsuda, 2003a, 2003b). Although the term *second language* appeared in the title of a workshop in 1971 ("Demonstration on Standard English as a Second Language"), it was not about second language writing per se; rather, it was a case of metaphorical borrowing to explain the difficulties encountered by NES basic writers—a development that I later described in different articles (Matsuda, 2003b; Matsuda & Jablonski, 2000).

Another source I found useful was a series of reports from CCCC Executive Committee meetings, also published in *CCC*. Initially, I did not expect to find anything in those reports, but I went through all of them just in case and found some of the most important pieces of information for my purpose. I discovered that CCCC had actually followed up on Kaplan's recommendation by appointing Joseph H. Friend of Southern Illinois University to serve as the liaison between CCCC and TESOL. The dialogue between Friend and Gordon Wilson of Miami University, who chaired CCCC in 1967, was especially useful in showing the immediate effect of the disciplinary division. When Friend asked "whether problems of teaching composition to non-English speakers should not be included in the program," Wilson responded by saying that the "competition of TESOL might prevent a sufficient number of people from attending a workshop."

Sitting on the hard, cold concrete floor in Periodical Stacks, I felt a chill go down my spine. It was the creation of TESOL in 1966 that institutionalized the disciplinary division of labor.

---

[2]TEFL in this context refers to an ESL specialist.

This disturbing realization became the basis of a new hypothesis for further inquiry. That is, the disciplinary division of labor was created as a result of the professionalization of ESL between the 1940s and 1966. This hypothesis led me to additional questions. When did the professionalization begin? Why did it happen during this particular period? To answer these questions, I turned to James Alatis' historical account of the TESOL organization and noticed that his discussion of the early years drew heavily on the work of Harold B. Allen (1973)—the name that had become familiar to me by then. Allen was involved in the creation of both CCCC and TESOL; he served as the chair of CCCC in 1952, the founding president of TESOL in 1966, as well as the president of NCTE in 1961.

I went back to the HSSE Library to find Allen's historical chapter and to browse through early issues of *TESOL Quarterly*, where I found two articles on the professional status of TESOL written by Allen (1967a, 1968). To my disappointment, however, the first issue of *TESOL Quarterly*—the most crucial one for my purpose—was missing. I went to the Interlibrary Loan office, wondering how I might request something that may or may not exist. Fortunately, the librarian had a solution for me: She suggested that I request a copy of the table of contents. A few weeks later, I received the table of contents, in which I found another statement on the professional status by Allen (1967b).

According to Allen (1973), the professionalization of second language teaching began with the creation of the English Language Institute at the University of Michigan in 1941. His explanation seemed to make sense, but I could not accept his claim at face value because, in 1941, Allen was affiliated with Michigan ELI. Corroboration also became problematic because just about everyone seemed to be connected to Michigan back then. (In the 1999 article, I ended up "corroborating" Allen's claim with Alatis' received history, which was based largely on Allen's account.) I finally decided that it would be reasonable to accept Allen's claim because the dominant presence of Michigan ELI at CCCC workshops and the sheer number of ESL professionals who were connected with the Institute seemed indicative of the significant impact the ELI had had on the profession. This premise led to additional questions such as: What drove Fries and his colleagues at Michigan to the path of professionalization? How did Michigan ELI become so influential? To what extent was their effort successful? To answer these questions, I tried to learn everything there is to know about this development by familiarizing myself with the writings of those key players such as Charles C. Fries, Robert Lado, Albert Marckwardt, Leonard Bloomfield, and others.

The question of the driving force was not so hard to answer because Fries and his colleagues were not so subtle with their agenda. The professionalism at Michigan was driven largely by the disciplinary needs of descriptive linguistics; they wanted to demonstrate the usefulness of linguistics by showing its real-life applications, especially in the area of language teaching. I was also able to account for the spread of Michigan's influence by identifying several means of reproduction, including the creation of the first ESL teacher preparation program, the development of textbooks and professional books, and the publication of *Language Learning: A Quarterly Journal of Applied Linguistics* in 1948. Not everything I learned in this process found its way into the 1999 article, but it became the basis of another historical article focusing on audiolingualism and the genesis of second language writing (Matsuda, 2001).

My historical narrative was shaping up nicely—perhaps too nicely. How could it be that there was no resistance to the dominance of Michigan ELI? Or to the division of labor? I became increasingly wary of what seemed to be a sweeping narrative that I had developed, and I decided to go through both primary and secondary sources again to search for counterevidence. I was aware of the creation of college ESL programs at the University of Michigan in 1911 by Joseph Raleigh Nelson (Allen, 1973; Howatt, 1984; Kandel, 1945; Klinger, 1958; Norris, 1966) and at Columbia University in 1923 (Kandel, 1945), but these developments responded primarily to local concerns. Although they were influential, they did not seem to have had the same kind of impact on the professionalization of second language teaching as Michigan ELI had.

Even after reanalyzing the sources, I did not find anything that would seriously challenge my arguments. One exception was Darian (1972), who claimed that the first college ESL program was established at Columbia in 1911. Because he did not provide any evidence for his claim, I checked it against other sources and found a statement by Kandel (1945), who was also affiliated with Columbia, that Columbia did not have an ESL program until 1923. Because Darian did not also mention Michigan's program, I decided to dismiss his claim as his error.

I did, however, manage to find a few signs of dissent. In the historical accounts provided by William Moulton (1961) and A. P. R. Howatt (1984), I sensed the feeling of resentment among language teachers toward Fries' view of applied linguistics, which literally sought to "apply" linguistics. I also found Allen's (1968) cautionary note against the arbitrary and complete separation of L1 and L2 instruction: "To say this [argue for the status of TESOL as a profession] is not to advocate the *reductio ad absurdum* that no one should legally be entitled to teach a single English word to non-English speaking persons without having obtained a license to practice" (p. 114). I made a conscious effort to incorporate these dissenting voices in my narrative to avoid the risk of overinterpretation and to show the complexity of these historical developments.

TOWARD COMMUNAL DIALECTIC

Even after I had developed my historical narrative, my work was not finished. As North (1987) points out, for a historical study to be acceptable, it has to make sense in light of existing narratives. The new narrative either has to fit existing ones or the historian has to challenge the status quo by identifying new evidence or providing new interpretations that are more plausible. For this reason, I went back to secondary sources (i.e., other historical studies) in both composition studies and second language studies to check my narrative against them. However, examining published historical studies was not sufficient. As a historian studying a relatively recent period, it was also important for me to account for the undocumented, lived sense of history held by people who were personally involved in those historical developments.

At the 1998 meeting of the American Association for Applied Linguistics, I mustered the courage to approach Bob Kaplan, who had been a key player in the creation of the disciplinary division of labor. We stood outside the convention hotel, and I watched him light up his pipe as I recounted my construction of the historical development and his role in it. To my relief, he did not object to my arguments; he even told me that I had "done my homework." He also shared with me his story of how he began to attend CCCC at the encouragement of Harold Allen, and how disappointed he was when nobody attended the 1965 workshop partly because of another session that was going on at the same time featuring Noam Chomsky.

Even after my article was accepted for publication, I continued the process of testing my historical arguments. At the Ohio State Conference on Reading-Writing Connections in August 1998, I approached John Swales, then the director of Michigan ELI. He generously invited me to visit Ann Arbor to explore the ELI Library and to present my historical study to the ELI staff. During my first visit, he introduced me to Joan Morley, who encouraged me to apply for the Morley Scholarship, which enabled me to visit Ann Arbor again to continue my archival work. During my second trip, John also introduced me to Peter and Nan Fries, who kindly invited me to spend a week at their house to explore the personal archives of Charles Fries, part of which has been donated to the Bentley Historical Library at the University of Michigan.

Much of what I found in these archives did not end up in my 1999 article because the article was already too far into production (it was published just before I had the chance to visit the Fries') and because I was primarily looking for counterevidence, which I did not find. Conversations with these people did not challenge my arguments in significant ways either, but they made my understanding of the history richer and, in some ways, more real. For that I am enormously grateful. Still it was important that I did not talk to these people before I had the chance to develop my own narrative. Just as I took care not to accept received history uncritically, I tried not to let other people's stories take over mine. I wanted my narrative to be one that was supported by carefully corroborated historical evidence, a balanced representation of various perspectives, and a critical examination of my own biases.

Ultimately, the development of historical knowledge relies on communal dialectic, the sharing of various historical narratives that would contribute to the construction of socially shared narratives. The field of second language writing needs more studies that are informed by careful historiography, not just personal hunches based on second-hand information or institutional lore. To develop a richer and more thorough understanding of important historical developments that have shaped the field, each of us as a member of the field needs to contribute to this communal dialectic by engaging in historical inquiry—by developing a narrative of one's own.

REFERENCES

Allen, H. B. (1967a). Challenge to the profession. *TESOL Quarterly, 1*(2), 3–6.

Allen, H. B. (1967b). TESOL and the journal. *TESOL Quarterly, 1*(1), 3–9.

Allen, H. B. (1968). Pros have it. *TESOL Quarterly, 2*(2), 113–120.

Allen, H. B. (1973). English as a second language. In T. A. Sebeok (Ed.), *Current trends in linguistics: Linguistics in North America* (Vol. 10, pp. 295–320). The Hague: Mouton.

Atkinson, D., & Ramanathan, V. (1995). Cultures of writing: An ethnographic comparison of L1 and L2 university writing/language programs. *TESOL Quarterly, 29*(3), 539–568.

Berlin, J. A. (1987). *Rhetoric and reality: Writing instruction in American colleges, 1990–1995*. Carbondale, IL: Southern Illinois University Press.

Braine, G. (1996). ESL students in first-year writing courses: ESL versus mainstream classes. *Journal of Second Language Writing, 5*, 91–107.

Brooks, N. (1960). *Language and language learning: Theory and practice*. New York: Harcourt, Brace.

Connors, R. J. (1992). Dreams and play: Historical method and methodology. In G. Kirsch & P. A. Sullivan (Eds.), *Methods and methodology in composition research* (pp. 15–36). Carbondale, IL: Southern Illinois University Press.

Darian, S. G. (1972). *English as a foreign language: History, development, and methods of teaching*. Norman, OK: University of Oklahoma Press.

Diller, K. (1978). *The language teaching controversy*. Rowley, MA: Newbury House.

Erazmus, E. T. (1960). Second language composition teaching at the intermediate level. *Language Learning, 10*, 25–31.

Gibian, G. (1951). College English for foreign students. *College English, 13*, 157–160.

Howatt, A. P. R. (1984). *A history of English language teaching*. New York: Oxford University Press.

Ives, S. (1953). Help for the foreign student. *College Composition and Communication, 4*, 141–144.

Johns, A. (1993). Too much on our plates: A response to Terry Santos' "Ideology in composition: L1 and ESL." *Journal of Second Language Writing, 2*(1), 83–88.

Kandel, I. L. (1945). *U.S. activities in international cultural relations*. Washington, DC: American Council on Education.

Klinger, R. B. (1958). The International Center. In W. A. Donnelly (Ed.), *The University of Michigan: An encyclopedic survey in four volumes* (Vol. 4, pp. 1843–1849). Ann Arbor: University of Michigan Press.

Marckwardt, A. H. (1961). Linguistics and English composition. *Language Learning, 2*, 15–28.

Marquardt, W. F. (1956). Composition and the course in English for foreign students. *College Composition and Communication, 7*, 29–33.

Matsuda, P. K. (1998). Situating ESL writing in a cross-disciplinary context. *Written Communication, 15*(1), 99–121.

Matsuda, P. K. (1999). Composition studies and ESL writing: A disciplinary division of labor. *College Composition and Communication, 50*, 699–721.

Matsuda, P. K. (2001). Reexamining audiolingualism: On the genesis of reading and writing in L2 studies. In D. Belcher & A. Hirvela (Eds.), *Linking literacies: Perspectives on L2 reading-writing connections* (pp. 84–105). Ann Arbor: University of Michigan Press.

Matsuda, P. K. (2003a). Basic writing and second language writers: Toward an inclusive definition. *Journal of Basic Writing, 22*(2), 67–89.

Matsuda, P. K. (2003b). Second language writing in the 20th century: A situated historical perspective. In B. Kroll (Ed.), *Exploring the dynamics of second language writing* (pp. 15–34). New York: Cambridge University Press.

Matsuda, P. K., Canagarajah, A. S., Harklau, L., Hyland, K., & Warschauer, M. (2003). Changing currents in second language writing research: A colloquium. *Journal of Second Language Writing, 12*(2), 151–179.

Matsuda, P. K., & Jablonski, J. (2000). Beyond the L2 metaphor: Towards a mutually transformative model of ESL/WAC collaboration. *Academic. Writing, 1*. Available: http://aw.colostate.edu/articles/matsuda_jablonski2000.htm.

McKay, S. (1981). ESL/remedial English: Are they different? *English Language Teaching Journal, 35*(3), 310–315.

McKay, W. F. (1965). *Language teaching analysis*. Bloomington, IN: Indiana University Press.

Moulton, W. G. (1961). Linguistics and language teaching in the United States 1940–1960. In C. Mohrmann, A. Sommerfelt, & J. Whatmough (Eds.), *Trends in European and American linguistics 1930–1960* (pp. 82–109). Utrecht: Spectrum.

Musumeci, D. (1997). *Breaking tradition: An exploration of the historical relationship between theory and practice in second language teaching*. New York: McGraw-Hill.

Norris, W. E. (1966, April). *ELI: A causal chronology*. Ann Arbor, MI: University of Michigan, English Language Institute. Mimeographed.

North, S. M. (1987). *The making of knowledge in composition: Portrait of an emerging field*. Portsmouth, NH: Boynton/Cook Heinemann.

Raimes, A. (1991). Out of the woods: Emerging traditions in the teaching of writing. *TESOL Quarterly, 25*(3), 407–430.

Rogers, G. L. (1945). Freshman English for foreigners. *School and Society, 61*, 394–396.

Santos, T. (1992). Ideology in composition: L1 and ESL. *Journal of Second Language Writing, 1*, 1–15.

Schueler, H. (1949). English for foreign students. *Journal of Higher Education, 20*, 309–316.

Silva, T. (1990). Second language composition instruction: Developments, issues and directions in ESL. In B. Kroll (Ed.), *Second language writing: Research insights for the classroom* (pp. 11–23). New York: Cambridge University Press.

Silva, T. (1993). Toward an understanding of the distinct nature of L2 writing: The ESL research and its implications. *TESOL Quarterly, 27*(4), 657–677.

Spolsky, B. (1995). *Measured words: The development of objective language testing*. Oxford: Oxford University Press.

Studies in English as a second language. (1956). *College Composition and Communication, 7*, 163–165.

Swales, J. (2001). EAP-related linguistic research: An intellectual history. In J. Flowerdew & M. Peacock (Eds.), *Research perspectives on English for academic purposes* (pp. 42–54). New York: Cambridge University Press.

Thomas, M. (1998). Programmatic ahistoricity in second language acquisition theory. *Studies in Second Language Acquisition, 20*, 387–405.

II

CONCEPTUALIZING L2 WRITING RESEARCH

4

Situated Qualitative Research and Second Language Writing

Dwight Atkinson
Temple University Japan

My purpose in this chapter is not so much to profess or advocate for a methodology as to critique one. In fact one of the themes I would like to develop here is that relentless questioning should be a continuing condition in *all* approaches to writing research. This is true, in one sense, simply because methodologies are imperfect, human-designed tools—tools that allow writing researchers to provide, at best, mere hints of static fragments of lives and realities that are unfathomably complex, fluid, and ongoing. But in a somewhat different, stronger sense, I would like to suggest that *built in* specifically to the methodology I discuss here is something we might consider building into all our research endeavors: reflexivity—the notion that one is not using correctly what one uses uncritically, without a constant sensitivity to blind spots, weaknesses, changing conditions affecting ecological validity and viability, and (of course) improvement. The methodology therefore becomes a *living* methodology, reanimated, reconstructed, and renewed each time it is used, and therefore always changing, ever evolving—in keeping (and this is critical) with the object of study itself. To go perhaps even farther, it becomes a form of *anti-methodology*, or at least a methodology without strict methods (Atkinson, 2003). If I advocate for anything at all in this chapter, it is for such a methodology.

DEFINING SITUATED QUALITATIVE RESEARCH

As my title suggests, the methodology (or anti-methodology) I focus on here is *situated qualitative research*. To start things off, let me define this term as I understand it, given that there seems to be substantial variation in the way different researchers use it, as well as the related terms *ethnographic, participant observation*, and *thick description* (Atkinson, Delamont, & Hammersley, 1988; see also Ramanathan & Atkinson, 1999)—terms that I also briefly define in relation to the main one.

First, *qualitative* describes a number of different research approaches that focus on the *particular quality of the phenomena being studied*, rather than on their frequencies of occurrence—their *quantity*.[1] By *particular quality* here, I mean that many qualitative researchers take the specific actors and scenes they are studying substantially as *particulars rather than as "generals,"* their first priority being to try to describe the intricacies of these lives and scenes in something approximating their own terms (Geertz, 1973). For many readers, this definition may shade perilously close to that of the term *ethnographic*—a sense that I also share (see e.g., Ramanathan & Atkinson, 1999). For its part, the term *thick description* is usually taken to describe the (impossibly ideal) *goal* of this kind of qualitative research: getting at the quality of what is being studied from the actors' points of view.

Second, *situated* describes a kind of qualitative research that is maximally grounded in the everyday social world of those being studied. Although all qualitative research gives at least some attention to the life worlds of its participants, certain researchers attempt to go substantially farther in this regard. They do so, for example, by existing among those being studied for extended periods of time while participating in their everyday worlds—i.e., "participant observation," which we can therefore think of as a main method or (preferably) *technique* of situated qualitative research—or by studying themselves and their own social milieux.

There has naturally been much questioning of how situated a researcher can actually become in this respect—of how well one can know a cultural scene like an insider when one is still fundamentally an outsider (but see Narayan, 1997, for a questioning of the insider–outsider dichotomy). Such questioning can be seen either as intrusive critique or—the position I have begun to argue—as a major constitutive feature of the situated qualitative approach. If this is in fact one important feature of this approach, then a second important feature is devising reasonable, if always partial and provisional, answers to such questions. Thus, to the question

---

[1]This does not mean that situated qualitative researchers necessarily ignore quantities or statistics, but they are likely to use them for somewhat different purposes.

of whether one can actually understand in any serious way a cultural scene that is not one's own—posed prominently by works such as Edward Said's (1978) *Orientalism*—the anthropologist Sherry Ortner (1984) has responded:

> Studying culture "from the actor's point of view" . . . does not imply that we must get "into people's heads." What it means, very simply, is that culture is a product of acting social beings trying to make sense of the world in which they find themselves, and if we are to make sense of a culture, we must situate ourselves in the position from which it was constructed. . . . *Try*. The effort is as important as the results, in terms of both our theories and our practices. . . . It is our capacity, largely developed in fieldwork, to take the perspective of the folks on the shore that allows us to learn anything at all—even in our own culture—beyond what we already know. . . . Further, it is our location "on the ground" that puts us in a position to see people not simply as passive reactors to and enactors of some "system," but as active agents and subjects in their own history. (pp. 130, 143; italics added)

The notion of *situatedness* has also been given a more philosophical—dare I say epistemological—interpretation by Donna Haraway (1988), a feminist critic of science. Haraway argues that the dominant theory of knowledge of what I call *strong science* has been "the view from nowhere," or "God's Eye view." The view from nowhere is the ideology of absolute scientific objectivity—the grand attempt to take humans out of the loop, so to speak, through the development of perfectly objective technologies and methodologies. Haraway argues that this ideology of knowing/seeing is one that emphasizes knowledge as power and control—ultimate knowledge in this framework is knowledge that allows Godlike control of the phenomena under study. Control over nature is thus built into the notion of the God's eye objectivity practiced by strong science.

In contrast, Haraway advocates a "view from somewhere" alternative—part of what I call *weak science*. The view from somewhere always acknowledges and indeed takes full advantage of its situatedness and partiality, the notion being that because individual researchers are always already somewhere in particular when doing their research, that that situatedness and partiality must therefore always powerfully inform and guide their science, and that they are consequently deeply connected and therefore ethically responsible to the people they are studying.

To put it differently, the particular qualities of the research situation—who the participants are, what they are saying and doing, what is going on around them, who *we* the researchers are, and what *we* are saying, thinking, doing, and so on—rather than being factored out or neutralized to arrive at universally generalizable findings, should instead be *factored in* in ways that make our findings locally and situationally valid, and the researcher locally and situationally responsible. According to Haraway, this is a much more humane and viable science because it stays close to the ground of human experience rather than trying to abstract away from it as much as possible. Weak science then is weak in a good way, in that it acknowledges the partial, provisional character of all knowing—that all researchers are actually always somewhere in particular—as well as the experiential and human side of knowledge, instead of opting for objective, distanced knowledge as power and control. Here, in a deeper philosophical sense, serious efforts to understand the views of the participants have a crucial role to play.

THE STUDY: TEXTUAL OWNERSHIP IN A COLLEGE CONTEXT IN INDIA

For the past 5 years, I have been working in English-medium colleges in India trying to understand the role of English in them, particularly in regard to the sorting and filtering mechanisms that are important parts of all educational institutions—the mechanisms by which people get put into, or have their places confirmed in, different social categories (e.g., Bourdieu, 1982; Gee, 1996). Clearly, English as the ex-colonial language functions powerfully in this regard in India; my goal is to develop a more concrete and lived understanding of how it does so.

One offshoot of this research program has been a smaller study, which is the only part that deals explicitly with L2 writing. It focuses on the widely reported practice in the college in which I am currently working of "booklifting" (an "insider" expression)—of appropriating published texts for the purpose of completing academic writing assignments in ways that might be considered "plagiarism" in some academic contexts.

Although this specific study is *situated* in the sense already described—so far I have spent about 1 year living on campus, during which time I have participated in many of the educational and social activities open to me as part of the college community—its main method of systematic data collection has been the oral interview. To be precise, I have conducted in-depth interviews with five current and former M.A. students and five current and former professors in the college's Department of English Language and Literature, attempting to ascertain their views and practices in regard to writing assignments and "booklifting" and its alternatives.

As those who regularly use it to get at the particular qualities of particular situations are often painfully aware, the situated qualitative interview is a highly complex activity (Kvale, 1996). It is a unique way, with unique problems, of getting unique kinds of information from participants. Thus, it has connections and resemblances with casual conversation (Spradley,

1979), yet it is *anything but* casual no matter how it may appear on the surface. As a major means of data collection for people who take their research on the whole quite seriously, it cannot be casual. It is also, no matter how "open ended," a highly guided speech event—researchers most typically nominate topics, ask detailed questions, and follow these with other (usually even more detailed) questions, all in the interest of focusing on *their* research problems.

In their classic methodology text, *Ethnography: Principles in Practice*, Hammersley and Atkinson (1995) note the double (and often conflicting) functionality of many ethnographic interviews—both to get at what happens (in order to develop a factual, more or less *etic* description of the situation) and to get at what the participant *thinks* about what happens (to develop an experiential, more or less *emic* description of the situation). A real problem here, of course, is that human beings don't typically distinguish between these two kinds of knowing: Values and attitudes play an integral part in perception, cognition, and description, and the resulting accounts are therefore heavily influenced by them. Interviews of multiple participants can to some extent be used to solidify findings in terms of what people think and what they actually do in regard to social practices, but even so a healthy skepticism toward the exact nature and status of the information resulting from such interviews is always necessary. In other words, interviews produce anything but simple, full, truthful accounts of participants' thought processes and activities, perhaps especially in situations (as research interview situations tend to be) where the researcher and the researched have differential status in terms of social power and position. Rather, situated qualitative research interviews tend to reflect the intricacies and complexities of individuals—as well as the complex social nature of the interview event itself.

For these and many, many other reasons (see e.g., Kvale, 1996; Mishler, 1986), situated qualitative researchers have learned to approach interviews and their resulting transcripts with a fair amount of caution and circumspection—as *texts*, basically, and as underdetermined, multiply interpretable, and multivocal as any other (Bakhtinianly or postmodernistically conceived) text. Such texts are typically read and interpreted in tandem with other forms of data and experience collected during the project, yet they are in no sense self-evident or self-validating speech events. It is this kind of indeterminacy—and the unique forms of methodological modesty, irony, and ceaseless self-questioning that should go along with it—that I foreground in what follows.

In the course of my research for this particular project, I conducted two interviews that the participants kindly permitted me to videotape. My original purpose for videotaping was to provide the students in a course on qualitative research I would soon teach with a concrete yet complex view of how interviewing works (or doesn't work) in situated qualitative research. This was part of a larger effort to record and problematize the research activities and decisions taking place during this study—exemplified especially in a set of methodological notes I took while it was ongoing. I draw on these notes in the following brief descriptions of the contexts of the two interviews, or at least the first one: each description is followed by a partial transcript of the interview.

The first interviewee was a 24-year-old woman, PV, who a year and a half earlier had finished her M.A. in English at the college and was now completing her M.Phil. degree.[2] Like several of the other participants I interviewed for this project, PV was someone with whom I had spent a lot of time and therefore knew fairly well—she had worked off and on as my research assistant during my three extended visits to the campus, and we had struck up a friendship. I felt it was particularly important to interview people I had established strong rapport with for this project because it concerned a topic that was ethically sensitive. Thus, in no sense did I construct a random sample—to get at particular kinds of understandings I needed to talk to particular kinds of people.

On first arriving some 2 weeks earlier, I had announced to PV that I intended to videotape several research interviews, and had asked whether she would consent to take part. Surprisingly, she had agreed without much persuading—I attributed this to both her experience as an on-stage performer (she was a member of the college's rather high-profile choir, and participated habitually in collegiate singing, poetry reading, and elocution contests) and her occasionally expressed desire to communicate with my students back in Japan. In the period between the time she consented and I actually interviewed her, however, PV expressed reservations about participating. In one case, she came to visit me for the express purpose of finding out what questions I would ask, her stated reason for doing so being that virtually all the academic writing she had done had been direct "booklifting," and so she wanted to carefully prepare her responses to the questions beforehand. I replied that I was not interested in making value judgments and that if I told her the questions it would completely change the nature of the interview speech event and resulting data.

The immediately following transcript covers the first 7 or so minutes of the approximately 50-minute interview I conducted with PV. In perusing both this and the transcript of the second interview given later, I would ask the reader to focus on the interactional structure, amount of talk and length of turns by each party, content of talk, and expression of affect (in-

[2]The M.Phil. degree is intermediate between the M.A. and the Ph.D. in the Indian education system. About 12 students were enrolled in this departmental program along with PV for the 2 years it took to complete the coursework and thesis.

asmuch as the latter is captured in the transcripts) both within and across interviews in order to prepare the ground for my own brief comparative discussion. I should remind the reader again, however, that my main reason for including this material is to provide concrete indications of the complexities and nonsystematicities that are endemic to situated qualitative research, and equally to provide examples of the kinds of questioning that I am arguing should accompany all such research activity.[3]

D: So my first question to you is um, you're now an M.Phil. student, um we're now talking about your M.A. career, two years ago, um, but my question is when you uh were an M.A. student what kind of assignments did you write, and um, what can you tell me about those assignments. By assignments I mean NOT examination papers [P: Ok (whispering)] but the writing assignments your professors gave you.

P: Ok (whispering) um (.) so um, can I introduce myself or [D: No uh no just go ahead and answer the questions if you will] Ok now uh (.) hope you'll um hope the listeners will count the good (laughingly) and uncount the mistakes [D: Don't listen to her] Hope it'll be useful to you all (laughingly) if not maybe I'll try to improve myself next time. Ok now, um I remember writing uh, an assignment paper, in European Fiction it was Anna Karenina and Madame Bovary, by our former HOD[4] Dr. Bhat. Um I enjoyed myself writing an assignment that was because, uh it was he who tickled me, uh: to be, a good initiator in the class (like) for example he he always used to ask me the ask me to write or, encapsulate, uh those, uh

---

[3]The following transcription conventions were used in transcribing interviews for this project:

, = short pause

(.) = longer pause

(.....) = pauses very roughly counted as seconds

. = falling intonation followed by a pause

? = rising intonation followed by a pause

: = vowel lengthening

CAPITAL LETTERS = Emphasis marked by stress, volume, voice quality, or raised intonation (note: when the first person personal pronoun *I* receives special stress it is bounded by asterisks)

( ) = (1) transcriber doubt (parentheses can be filled or unfilled); (2) "stage directions," e.g., (laughingly), (airplane flies noisily overhead), (tape recorder is turned off)

[ ] = Overlapping, latching, short turns, or back-channeling speech within another speaker's longer turn; e.g., A: And I tell them [B: I see] that well broadly I give them the area on which they could write.

[4]"HOD" stands for "Head of Department."

um Anna Karenina or Madame Bovary so I used to do it regularly in my class so he was (the), the main I mean he was the uh, he: tickled that interest in me so coming to this question, uh, it was quite a positive response I would say because in my earlier days I found writing a difficult task, so so, NOW um that was because I was thorough (with) the text and I enjoyed reading Anna Karenina and Madame Bovary I was able to, uh go through the voluminous, pages of Anna Karenina and, Madame Bovary so I was able to, *I* chose the topic for myself, I was able to compare and contrast the character of both the woman character Madame, and Anna, and it was quite interesting, and I was able to, y'know, draw a parallel between those two characters.

D: How many so this was one assignment. [P: Yes] Over the two years, [P: Ok] how many assignments do you remember doing.

P: Uh I remember doi:ng (.) but this is fresh in my mind I don' remember [D: Ok] but I I I think I've, done three or four of them.

D: So you didn't do one assignment for each paper [P: Yes I did] So you did altogether you did [P: Yes] eight about eight, because you had four [P: Yes] four papers per [P: Yes] semester. (Ok.) So altogether you did eight assignments [P: Yes]. Ok. And and generally speaking, I do want to know about the details as well but generally speaking, um tell me something about those assignments how did you, how did the teachers um get you started, um and then what did you do. Generally speaking [P: Uh you mean, uh teacher get started] How did they get you started did they give you a topic or did they say today uh in three weeks you have to write a this assignment [P: You mean the deadline?] Um whatever they told you at the beginning that made you do this.

P: Ok. When I first came uh joined as a PG[5] student uh: I was, I mean uh writing assignments was something uh, vague to me because I kept asking my professor as to what I should do and what are the topics that you want me to write and what they responded was that, they asked me to choose my own topic. [D: I see.] So that's how- I go about it. [D: Ok in all cases they they asked you to choose your own topic did they ever assign you a topic] Uh: sometimes they did (laughingly) but I don't remember anything

D: Ok ok I realize this is a little bit, in the past uh but but just as much as you can try to remember. Um (..) and once they either gave you a topic or you had your topic then what did you do did they tell you

[5]"PG" stands for "postgraduate."

exactly how to do it did they say go to the British Council Library and get some books or did they say, um come talk to me as (if a) yeah

P: No I don't think they, said all that. They just wanted to write an assignment submit it on the, given date.

D: Ok. Did they give you any instructions about page numbers or a length

P: Uh (..) yes, certainly they gave uh maybe asked us to write 10 pages or something

D: I see I see. So that depended on the particular professor. It wasn't a general understanding [P: No it, it was a general understanding] All these assignments [P: Yes] about 10 pages ok and how much time did they give you usually do you r- have any idea?

P: Uh (..) must be three weeks or five weeks or

D: Ok ok ok. And, in general terms, once they gave you the (.) original assignment go do this. Then what did you do how did you go about doing this. [P: (..) U:m can y' come again?] Yeah yeah. Um, so I'm interested in the process [P: No no can you repeat the question] Yes I am I am I'm gonna paraphrase the question ok um, (to DM and VB off-camera) are you going, are you coming back?[6] Ok. Um (.) what was the general process YOU went through [P: Ok] to do the assignment AFTER you received the original request to do the assignment by the professor that w- that's my question.

P: If I have time what I would do is I would go through the text. (But if it) if the text if the novel or the book is quite voluminous then it's impossible for me to write it down within the given time. Uh generally, um what I would do is collect some materials, either go to British Council read up, and then I summarize it and write it [D: I see I see. Ok] But the thing is if I'm not interested in the given text if the teacher or if the professor wouldn't allow me to choose the topic [D: Ok] for myself then I I don't have any interest in writing I just crib it from the books.

PV went on to explain in some detail how she typically went about writing different kinds of assignments. Then, about 6 minutes later in the interview, I became aware that she was discreetly referring from time to time to an envelope she held in her hand. I proceeded to question her with some sternness and urgency:

[6]DM and VB were two students who showed up unexpectedly while I was conducting this interview. They sat on a different part of the verandah from where PV and I were sitting and were apparently leaving when I spoke to them here "off camera."

D: That ok that's ok. Um, (pointing toward an envelope she held in her hand, which she was discreetly looking at) and what do you have there? [P: I just have some tips, I mean, as to what I should] Talk about, put them away, this is a spontaneous interview, I'm disappointed to know that you that you TRAINED for this interview. [P: It's not trained I actually wanted to] (in mock-horrified voice) Oh this is TERRIBLE terrible terrible. No that makes it a different kind of event I told you. (Looking at camera and waving his hand) Don't do what she did. Ok I'm joking. Um no but but so let's say uh just sort of imagine recreate in your mind you've done you've been assigned an ess- uh uh to write an essay on Pope [P: Ok] and Dryden um [P: Maybe an "Essay (on) Criticism" by Pope] Ok you even have the text ok. [P: Yes] So you would go to the British Council

The second transcript comes from an interview with a senior professor in the English department. Because I did not take notes on the planning and execution of this interview, I introduce the transcript only briefly and generally.

MP is a 48-year-old professor of English who ranks among the top five in seniority in his department. He specializes partly in modern drama, but his true love is a kind of intense Socratic-style questioning of his and his students' values and beliefs according to his panreligious philosophy—he often uses dramatic texts as a vehicle for this activity in the classroom. He is widely known as one of the most provocative and articulate professors on campus, and students often commented to me that his classes were high points in their college careers. As with PV, I have strong rapport with MP. In fact I consider him one of my two closest friends at this research site, and I have spent countless hours conversing, eating, and traveling with him and his family. A few days before the interview, MP had returned from a month-long trip to Europe and was still suffering the effects of the long trip and jet lag. Although he willingly granted my request to videotape the interview, he sat quite stiffly throughout, in marked contrast to his usually relaxed, rather jovial speaking style. The following partial transcript consists of the first 6½ minutes of a 53-minute interview:

D: So my first question to you is what kind of um, assignments do you professors ask students to do how many of them over a two-year period to get an MA um, and uh, what are your expectations for those assignments.

M: I believe the students have been asked are asked to write assignments on each paper.[7] [D: Ok] Uh sometimes in each on each

[7]"A paper" in the Indian educational context typically means a course (in the U.S. context).

genre, [D: Ok] uh and, this is a part this is a part of the, assessment system to see how they can work independently. I'm not quite certain the number of assignments they would write because I think that would vary, according to the number of teachers that meet them and the number of, subjects that are actually covered by them. But uh I think on an average they would probably do something like um, say about 10 assignments per semester I'm not quite certain of this though [D: Ok ok] I'm not quite certain of this though. It would depend upon the number of teachers and the number of subjects they would have to do. And uh, this is primarily to test their capacity to work independently.

D: Um uh do you do you happen to recall the um p- proportion of marks proportion of marks that that this might uh account, for in the overall marking?

M: I believe it covers around 10 marks 10 percent [D: Out of oh 10 percent] 10 percent.

D: Good. Um, what is the typical assignment as given by a teacher what would you or your colleagues say to the student to prepare them [M: (Yeah)] to to INITIATE this activity

M: When the assignment sys- should I say task began, uh when we started using this mode of assessment the students were permitted to choose their own topics. That CHANGED a bit for some reason or the other, and students were then TOLD on what topics they should write. I'm not quite certain why this change took place because I was not in the department at that time I was on deputation. And when I returned I found this change. I'm not really certain why but I can imagine that is probably due to the fact that, the students are probably taking the assignments, that had been done by prev- by students of previous years. And uh you know taking it down, and passing it off as their own and so one method might have been it might have been possible that it was felt that maybe if a topic was given to them, this could be avoided. However I must say that as far as I'm concerned (D gets up to adjust video camera) I let the students choose their own topics, [D: (Adjusting camera) Uh huh?] and uh, I must believe that they, would would do their work on their own I know that this is, for the most part not, the case but nevertheless I find it uh, somehow illogical or, not good I would say to choose a topic for the student and ask him to work, on something that he may not have sufficient interest in so I prefer that they choose their own topic, discuss it with me and then, or inform me of the topic and then begin.

D: So to to recap um e- u- uh you're saying that the majority practice is probably to give students a topic (M: I) a set topic

M: That I believe is the the the, the way the system functions now the teacher gives the student a topic and he writes on the topic uh I say this because not because I've checked with my colleagues but because the students come to me and say what should I write ON. And I tell them (D: I see) that well BROADLY I give them the area on which they could write, but uh the actual topic is usually decided by them.

D: Is that difficult for the students do they find that uh challenging or or um, [M: You see] unrealistic?

M: Uh (.) WELL I when I say I give them the choice I might decide for instance that they do an assign- I I generally ask them to do an assignment on MY paper. Either the detailed text [D:Ok right] or the nondetailed text but I don't give them the actual topic.[8] [D: Ok] I restrict them to my text (I say) I believe the students are also free to do texts that are being taught by other teachers. [D: Oh ok] I generally restrict them to to the subjects I'm doing, and uh then we sort of discuss a few things before we actually before I actually let them go ahead and choose their topic so I don't know whether it's really difficult and if they DO find it difficult they're always welcome to come back and you know, reassess the situation and take another topic. I think I'm generally fairly free with them when it comes to the assignments, (as with) the classroom.

D: Right. Um, you mentioned detailed portions and nondetailed portions um [M: Yeah] would you give them different kinds of writing assignments uh to cover both?

M: Well, by and large I give them assignments in the nondetailed texts. [D: Oh] Primarily because we're doing the detailed texts in class, and we try (it) in far as possible to cover all the aspects of the text in class. And therefore as far as possible I give them the nondetailed texts, OR other plays written by the: authors or playwrights that we are dealing with. For instance if I was doing an American play by a particular playwright, let's say Eugene O'Neill or Tennessee Williams I would ask them to take uh, a play OTHER than the detailed text that we are doing so this exposes them to another play of O'Neill and therefore a better understanding of O'Neill as a playwright, uh and, or I might

[8]"Detailed texts" (or "detailed portions") are the literary texts that are primarily focused on in a course, and that are therefore covered in detail in the classroom. "Nondetailed texts" (or "nondetailed portions") are texts that students are required to be familiar with for the purposes of examination, but that are not typically the focus of classroom teaching. The obvious discrepancy between the numbers of writing assignments described by PV and MP is in part due to whether one includes in this category writings about nondetailed texts, which tend to be considerably shorter and more summary-like in nature.

> for instance take a nondetailed text and take the playwright and ask them to do another play of that particular playwright or of the nondetailed text itself. One of the reasons is that we have so many texts prescribed I I believe far too many texts prescribed for our students, uh in the course of semester (and) sometimes they do find it extremely difficult to, to cope with the workload, and therefore by giving them an assignment on the nondetailed text I make things a bit easier for them and also help them prepare for the test.

There are many things to comment on in these two interviews. In keeping with situated qualitative research practice, I offer a brief interpretation of some aspects of these interviews that is in every sense provisional, and that I do not intend to impose on others. On the contrary, my reason for featuring these transcripts at length is largely to provide material for an active critique of the methodology, which—please remember—I am claiming is itself an important *part* of the methodology. At the same time, however—and this is part of the complexity of this kind of research—I do believe I have a certain amount of knowledge of the situation that a casual reader would not, and that my interpretation may therefore be informed in ways that others' are not. Naturally, of course, I also have special blindspots.

Comparatively speaking, the two interviews are quite different—in a sense, one could almost see them as different speech events. These differences are related in part to the different social positions and symbolic capital (i.e., historically accumulated social advantage [Bourdieu, 1986]) each of the participants holds. PV, for instance, is young, female, postcolonial, a student—relatively disempowered vis-à-vis the older Anglo-American male professor-researcher-interviewer. Her language skills, despite a general fluency and ease of expression, are also at a different level than MP's, or my own for that matter—this can be noted, I believe, in the fact that on occasion she seems to have trouble understanding me. Another obvious difference has to do with the fact that for PV, the experiences I am asking about are a year and a half removed from the present, whereas for MP they are not only part of his present life as a professor, but are issues he has experienced repetitively over many years as a faculty member. It may further be the case that PV feels somewhat insecure in this situation; as a young, unmarried woman in South India, being alone with a man in a semiprivate situation is at least unusual, at most close to taboo.

In contrast, MP is a highly privileged, highly articulate, middle-aged male with vast experience talking to groups and individuals both in India and beyond about his life. He is of course also a postcolonial, but from a background that placed his forebears in close contact with the overlords themselves.

But, it would not do to put the differences between these interviews down mostly to differences in social status or role. What I am personally most interested in, in fact, is the different ways the interviewees *position themselves* vis-à-vis the interview situation, rather than how they are positioned in it or in relation to me by their societies. Particularly interesting is how PV subverts the intent of the interviewer by first including some introductory comments in her answer to my first question, then a moment later by answering a somewhat different question than the one asked (i.e., markedly in the way *she* wants to answer it), and later once again by demonstrating that she has chosen to define the interview situation according to her own desires, by providing herself a "tips" sheet even though I had more or less forbidden it. There is clearly a lot of agency and a certain amount of power in what PV is doing in this interview, in direct contradistinction to her fairly disempowered social status and social role.

MP, on the other hand, offers an interesting contrast. He looks nervous, sits stiffly, and answers my questions in a rather flat, affectless voice. It is quite probable that his style of speaking is directly related to his uncomfortableness in front of the video camera—in fact it is important not to overlook the role of the video camera in defining the situation in both interviews—but I doubt that the video camera alone is determining MP's behavior. In fact, in an earlier interview with MP that was not videotaped, I recall him also being unusually stiff and "official" (as I remember thinking about it at the time), my assumption being that he felt himself to some extent placed in the role of the "voice of authority" or "voice of the faculty," and that it was primarily this which led to his markedly stiff, formal speaking style.

There are many other things that can be noted here—the list is in fact nearly infinite, I believe—including aspects of my own behavior, which of course must be closely attended to in any seriously situated, reflexive description. But in the interest of space, let me conclude.

CONCLUSION: *DOING* THE IMPOSSIBLE

I have presented segments of two different situated qualitative interviews, of two different individuals—these are two quite different situations, perhaps two different speech events even, in part or in whole. How can anyone in their right mind claim to be able to see these as anything more than two idiosyncratic events related to each other in any more than incidental ways?

Yet isn't this the way, in one sense or another, we *all* do research—in some sense, *all* our research? Any time anyone gives anybody a survey form to fill out, or visually observes their behavior, or takes experimental measurements under controlled conditions, or analyzes a text, or prompts or elicits reflection or recall, they jump into the ocean of messy, nonsystematic, individual human behavior. And what they come up with as they surface again, and then pull themselves back out of that ocean with (if this is indeed possible at all—see the earlier description of Haraway's [1988] work), is indelibly branded, tainted, soaked, and marked through and through with what it is and where it came from. This is part of the message, I believe, that has been coming for some years out of the sociology and anthropology of science—that context, in science as in other forms of life, matters—but it is also one, I believe, that all researchers must also know somewhere deep in their hearts all the time. Efforts to study human behavior by limiting its influence, variability, or naturalness are in this sense illusory and misguided (Atkinson, 2002).

In terms of the particular methodology I have been highlighting, however, there is a *special* charge to welcome human behavior in all its richness and diversity, even if doing so works against the smooth functioning of the methodology itself. This, I would argue, is the special contribution that situated qualitative research can make—as a research approach that is maximally flexible, maximally adaptive to the always-in-process, always-in-flux individuals-in-society and social situations that it attempts to study. And it can only do so, in some sense, by being almost antimethodological. Only by giving priority to individuals and their individual behavior are we able to do it. Only in this way—and this is just one of the many paradoxes endemic to situated qualitative research—are we able to understand how individuals lead social lives. This is because the individual and the social are not separate things, but rather two aspects of the same thing, each of which contributes to defining the whole (e.g., Gee, 1992; Rogoff, 1990).

My favorite slogan or metaphor for doing situated qualitative research has therefore in recent years become "*Doing* the impossible." Note that the emphasis here is on "doing" rather than on "the impossible." In some ways, I relate it closely to how humans succeed against all odds in living their daily lives—how, if we actually sat down and carefully calculated it and planned it out and thought about it, simply living our full, busy, and (always of necessity at least partly) unplanned lives would be a logical impossibility. Yet we do for the most part move forward, we do live our lives. I see situated qualitative research as something of that kind and that order.

We cannot know human beings in other than partial ways. We probably cannot even know *ourselves*, for goodness' sake, more than fleetingly and faultily. This is an important part of the point—the "impossible" part of my slogan. It is why we as researchers need to be constantly interrogating, doubting, hedging, and complexifying what it is we are doing and why we are doing it, even as we *are* doing it. Yet the point is also that we *can* know something about ourselves and others, we can—modestly, haltingly, perhaps even timidly—do our research. We can, with all our might and all our effort, do *weak* science. *Do. Try*. This is the (anti-)methodology of situated qualitative research.

REFERENCES

Atkinson, D. (2002). Toward a sociocognitive approach to second language acquisition. *Modern Language Journal, 86*, 525–545.

Atkinson, D. (2003). *Does using qualitative methods amount to doing qualitative research in TESOL?* Unpublished paper.

Atkinson, P., Delamont, S., & Hammersley, M. (1988). Qualitative research traditions: A British response to Jacob. *Review of Educational Research, 58*, 231–250.

Bourdieu, P. (1982). The school as a conservative force: Scholastic and cultural inequalities. In E. Bredo & W. Feinberg (Eds.), *Knowledge and values in social and education research* (pp. 391–407). Philadelphia: Temple University Press.

Bourdieu, P. (1986). Forms of capital. In J. G. Richardson (Ed.), *Handbook of theory and research for the sociology of education* (pp. 241–258). New York: Greenwood.

Gee, J. P. (1992). *The social mind: Language, ideology, and social practice*. New York: Bergen & Garvey.

Gee, J. P. (1996). *Social linguistics and literacies: Ideology in discourses* (2nd ed.). London: Taylor & Francis.

Geertz, C. (1973). *The interpretation of cultures*. New York: Basic Books.

Hammersley, H., & Atkinson, P. (1995). *Ethnography: Principles in practice* (2nd ed.). London: Routledge.

Haraway, D. (1988). Situated knowledges: The science question in feminism and the privilege of partial perspective. *Feminist Studies, 14*, 575–599.

Kvale, S. (1996). *InterViews: An introduction to qualitative research interviewing*. Thousand Oaks, CA: Sage.

Mishler, E. (1986). *Research interviewing: Context and narrative*. Cambridge, MA: Harvard University Press.

Narayan, K. (1997). How native is a "native" anthropologist? In L. Lamphere, H. Ragone, & P. Zavella (Eds.), *Situated lives: Gender and culture in everyday life* (pp. 23–41). New York: Routledge.

Ortner, S. (1984). Theory in anthropology since the sixties. *Comparative Studies in Society and History, 26*, 126–166.

Ramanathan, V., & Atkinson, D. (1999). Ethnographic approaches and methods in L2 writing research: A critical guide and review. *Applied Linguistics, 20*, 44–70.

Rogoff, B. (1990). *Apprenticeship in thinking: Cognitive development in social context*. New York: Oxford University Press.

Said, E. (1978). *Orientalism*. New York: Vintage.

Spradley, J. P. (1979). *The ethnographic interview*. Fort Worth, TX: Harcourt Brace Jovanovich.

5

A Multimethod Approach to Research Into Processes of Scholarly Writing for Publication

John Flowerdew
City University of Hong Kong, China

Any consideration of research method depends on research questions, which in turn are derived from an overall research problem or goal. In this chapter, I consider the research methods used in a project designed to tackle a specific problem. Consideration of this problem led to a set of research questions that could not be answered by a single research method for reasons set out later. The research project I describe was funded by the Research Grants Committee of Hong Kong and bore the title "Cantonese First Language Academics Writing for Publication in English." The research problem, as suggested by the title, was to find out how Hong Kong scholars, whose first language was not English, went about the process of writing and publishing in English. The topic was a problem for a number of reasons, which becomes clear in the course of the chapter.

BACKGROUND OF THE RESEARCH

For a considerable time, English has been accepted as the dominant language for publication of academic research findings. Reviewing a number of surveys (Arvantis & Chatelin, 1988; Baldauf & Jernudd, 1983; Garfield, 1978; Maher, 1986; Wood, 1997) concerning the use of English in scholarly publications over a decade ago, Swales (1990) concluded that, although there may have been some exaggeration in claims concerning the degree of its preponderance, ". . . there is no doubt that English has become the world's predominant language of research and scholarship . . ." (p. 99). Within the English language research literature, studies have shown that only a small percentage of publications emanate from countries where English is not the national or official language and from scholars whose first language is not English (Baldauf & Jernudd, 1983; Swales, 1985).

Swales (1990) has reported some of the difficulties encountered by NNES researchers in publishing in English, citing Jernudd and Baldauf's (1987) findings concerning Scandinavian researchers in the field of psychology. Although the Scandinavian researchers studied by Jernudd and Baldauf all published in English and the Scandinavian countries have successful educational policies that encourage polylingualism, the need to publish in English represented a constant challenge. Researchers' attitudes are represented by the following statements from Scandinavian scholars:

- It is constantly depressing to be confronted by one's shortcomings in (a) foreign language.
- It is meaningless to publish original research in psychology in Swedish.
- I regard the language barrier as a central problem for Norwegian researchers in my professional field.
- One year in England/USA—even as a street sweeper—would likely mean more to a scientific career than half a million crowns in the form of a research grant.
- It is important for those of us who are non-native speakers to create some understanding among many researchers that English is not our natural (or obvious) language of communication. (Jernudd & Baldauf, 1987, p. 150; cited in Swales, 1990, p. 102)

Swales adds two further problems to this list: (a) the need for non-native English speakers to devote time, which could otherwise be devoted to research, in maintaining and improving their English skills; and (b) the high rejection rates of scholarly journals, which means increasing pressure on manuscripts with evidence of nonstandard English.

In the years leading up to the writing of the research proposal (in 1996), Hong Kong had seen a massive expansion in the provision of university level education—an expansion that had seen a concomitant emphasis on and increase in the amount of scholarly research. To achieve such rapid expansion, tertiary level institutions had, to a large degree, relied on the employment of academics from overseas, especially at more senior levels. With the approach of 1997, when Hong Kong was to become a

Special Administrative Region of China, it was inevitable that efforts would be made to encourage local Hong Kong Chinese to move into both senior and junior academic positions.

Although it is probably true to say that the initial emphasis in the expansion of tertiary level provision in Hong Kong had been on curriculum development and teaching, the funding body of the Hong Kong universities had more recently turned its attention to the question of research and publication and the setting of quality assurance measures within this area. Institutions were beginning to set minimum target levels of publication as a basis for career development decisions.

Because of the relatively limited provision of university education in Hong Kong until the recent expansion, most Cantonese-speaking academics in Hong Kong were likely to have undertaken at least their postgraduate—if not undergraduate—study overseas in English-speaking countries. With the expansion of local tertiary provision, more young scholars today embark on an academic career having studied at both undergraduate and postgraduate levels in Hong Kong, and therefore not having benefited from living in an English-speaking society and not having had access to native-English-speaking members of their discourse community (Swales, 1990).

In view of the situation outlined earlier, research into the problems and strategies of Cantonese first language academics in writing for publication was timely. Research that could describe the then prevalent situation and identify likely trends with regard to publication in English, and that would describe and analyze the problems and strategies of Cantonese first language academics, would be of direct value to the Hong Kong academic community. At the same time, given the international interest in English for Academic Purposes and in academic discourse in general, the research had the potential to make a significant contribution to the international literature of these fields.

SPECIFIC RESEARCH OBJECTIVES

The specific objectives of the project were expressed as follows:

- to investigate overall publication rates, educational and professional background, and attitudes toward publishing in English of Cantonese first language academics in Hong Kong;
- to identify, from the perspective of writers, editors, and referees, key problems for Cantonese first language academics in Hong Kong in writing for publication in English;

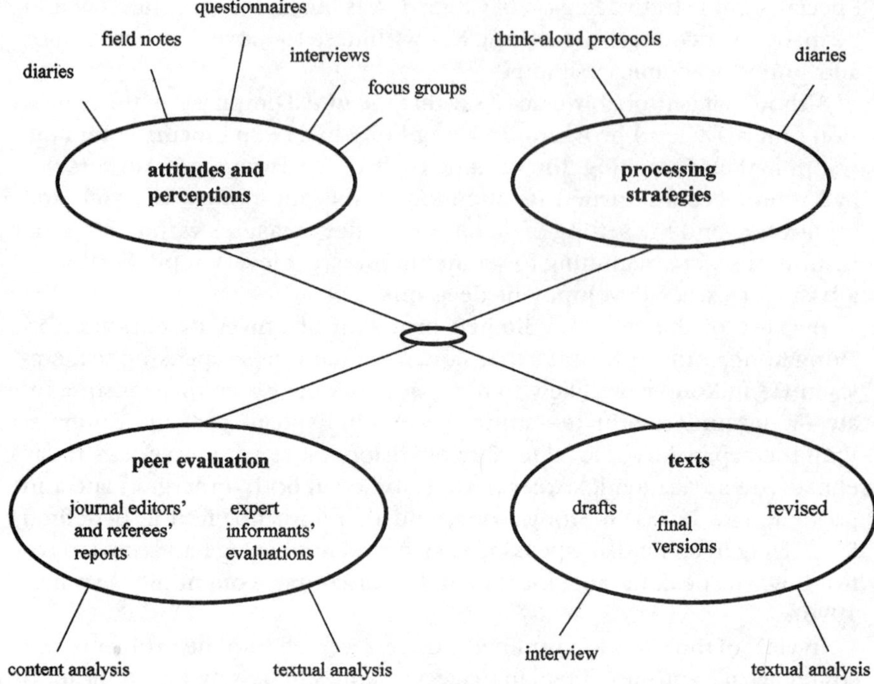

FIG. 5.1. Methods.

- to identify key strategies used by Cantonese first language academics in Hong Kong in writing for publication in English; and
- to investigate attitudes of journal editors and referees to submissions from non-native English speakers, especially from Hong Kong, and feedback given in the form of referees' reports.

Given these wide-ranging objectives, a variety of research methods was appropriate. Figure 5.1 shows methods at the disposal of the investigator interested in issues such as those expressed in the objectives listed earlier. They are organized around four types of investigative goal: attitudes and perceptions, processing strategies, texts, and peer evaluation. Due to various constraints, the main one of which was time, of these four goals, processing strategies were not examined. The other three, however, were all the subject of investigation, and all of the methods indicated were employed with lesser or greater success.[1] Given the wide range of methods

[1]Diaries proved to be problematic because it was difficult to persuade subjects to be disciplined in their writing. Focus groups were used in the early stages of the project in generating issues for further investigations by means of the other instruments.

available, the research project provided me with the opportunity to work in various theoretical and methodological paradigms. Thus, I viewed the project as a model of how a specific issue can be investigated from a multiplicity of perspectives using a range of methodologies.

The multimethod approach is represented in the publications emanating from the research project, which are briefly described (with the emphasis on methodological issues) in the following section.

THE RESEARCH OUTPUTS

The Quantitative Survey

The first output of the research was the quantitative survey (Flowerdew, 1999b). Following a literature review and initial informal discussion and focus groups with academics in Hong Kong's five universities, a questionnaire was developed and piloted with an institution in Hong Kong that was about to achieve university status, but that was not included as part of the main study. Based on the results obtained, the questionnaire was revised before being sent out to the five universities. The quantitative survey focused on the following questions: What exposure to English have these Hong Kong scholars had? What are their attitudes toward publishing in English? What are their problems? What are their strategies for successful publishing? What change, if any, do they see accompanying the reversion of sovereignty over Hong Kong from Britain to China?

Perhaps the most interesting finding was that, although the majority felt confident in being able to publish a paper in English, a (larger) majority also believed there to be prejudice against non-native speakers on the part of editors and referees. One methodological problem was that of return rate. Hong Kong university staff are subjected to a considerable number of surveys, and it was difficult to obtain a high response rate; 2,300 academics were sent a questionnaire. After a period of time, those not responding to this first questionnaire were sent another copy, with a cover letter encouraging them to participate; 717 completed questionnaires were received from these two mailings. This represents a response rate of 31%, which is considered to be good for surveys conducted in Hong Kong with academics (Social Science Research Centre, University of Hong Kong, personal communication). Although the return rate was low, which meant that the results had to be interpreted with caution, the sample that responded corresponded closely to the overall profile of the Hong Kong academic community. In addition, the respondents provided a good range in terms of publication success, including both senior and junior and successful and less successful scholars in terms of rank and publication rate, respectively.

The Qualitative In-Depth Interview Study

This study (Flowerdew, 1999a) was based on in-depth or semistructured interviews with 26 scholars from a representative range of disciplines and universities. The interviews were conducted by the researcher and an assistant. The approach was social constructivist (Berger & Luckmann, 1966; Gergen, 1985) insofar as it aimed at encouraging the participants to voice their own perceptions of the issues, rather than having them respond to an agenda established by the researcher. The approach can be described as *grounded* or emic rather than etic (Strauss & Corbin, 1990). Nevertheless, given my ongoing research and what I was learning from the quantitative survey, the assistant and I were able to, I hope, gently guide the interview participants to cover the key issues. These issues, as they were communicated in the interviews, were identified in a systematic fashion with the use of qualitative software.

Questions asked in the interviews were designed to elicit a large sample of utterances (Spradley, 1979). Participants were told at the beginning that the longer their answers were, the better; although the interviewer had a set of general areas for discussion, participants were encouraged to introduce any information or interpretation that they felt appropriate. Initial questions were mostly open ended and descriptive (Spradley, 1979). Typical descriptive questions included: "Can you describe your experience in getting published?"; "How would you describe your written English?"; "What do you think are your individual problems in writing in English for publication?" Structural questions (Spradley, 1979) such as "Could you give me other examples of problems you have had with editors?" and "What other types of assistance do you get from native speakers in preparing an article for submission to a journal?" were adapted to each individual participant to follow up on descriptive questions, to test hypothesized categories, and to elicit examples to fit into hypothesized categories. Contrast questions were used to compare participants across interviews.[2] Contrast questions included, for example, "Some people I have interviewed have said that there is more need for writing in Chinese in the arts and humanities. Do you agree?" and "Editors I have interviewed and some Hong Kong writers have said that grammar and spelling are not a real problem. What is your view on this?"

Analysis was conducted by means of ATLAS.ti qualitative research software (Scientific Software Development, 1997). ATLAS.ti allows research-

[2]My use of the term *contrast question* is different from that of Spradley.

ers to store, select, index/code, and annotate large amounts of research material such as interview data and notes. These data can then be sorted and retrieved according to the categories established.

Just as having the researcher and a research assistant conduct the interviews allowed for triangulation in data collection, so did having both people participate in analysis. Data were loaded onto the ATLAS.ti software and sorted and resorted into categories individually by the researcher and the assistant. Categories represent logically and situationally grounded constructs that the researcher has identified as meaningful within the context of the research. A category, therefore, need not be supported by any arbitrary number of mentions in the text. When an example of a category is noted in the data, it can be in the form of sentences, phrases, or even single words. In the process of analysis, categories may be created, renamed, deleted, and combined. Analysis also involves the organisation of categories into hierarchical logical structures.

The aim was to look for both commonalities and differences within the group of participants. Rather than just considering the uniqueness of the specific culture of NNES writers, differences such as discipline, educational and professional background, and amount of exposure to English were sought. During this analysis, opportunities were taken to return to the participants for confirmation of statements they had provided, for further elucidation of such statements, and for additional data. These supplementary data were also incorporated into the ATLAS.ti database. I emphasize that a deliberate effort was made to avoid forcing the experiences and perceptions of subjects into preestablished categories, although literature on second language writing and the knowledge gleaned from the quantitative survey were not ignored altogether. At all times, I was conscious of the need to avoid applying stereotypes of what the literature tells us about L2 writing and end up with a deficit model (although, as it turned out, this is to a large extent the picture that was painted). I was also conscious of Hong Kong's unique (postcolonial) situation and the likelihood that my findings would be unique in some respects, but similar to other NNES contexts in others.

Once the data were sorted and resorted, it was clear that scholars' problems concerning writing for publication in English made up a distinctive subset of categories. These categories are represented by the headings in the left-hand column of Table 5.1. They were selected from over 40 categories. The most interesting features from among this subset were identified and reported in this survey in the participants' own words. The middle column of Table 5.1 shows the range of scholars referring to a given problem, while the right-hand column gives the total number. In this way, the software allows a quantitative dimension to be included in the study, although given the small numbers, not too much can be read into these.

TABLE 5.1
Summary of Participants' Comments Regarding the Disadvantages of Publishing in English

The Disadvantages of Being an NNES	*Scholar Code*	*Number of Scholars Who Expressed Views on This Point*
Have less facility of expression	3 4 5 7 8 10 11 13 17 20 21 23 24	13
Take longer to write	2 3 7 8 11 13 17 22	8
Have a less rich vocabulary	3 4 5 7 8 10 11 19 23	9
Are less capable in the subtleties of argumentation	1 4 8 17 20	5
L1 may intervene in the composition process	2 5 7 19	4
Are more capable of writing quantitative articles	2 5 20 23	4
Often relegated to writing in a simple style	7 19 20	3
Introductions and/or discussions become the most problematic parts of research articles to write	2 3 4 5 7 13 19 20	8

The Editors' Interview Paper

In this study, I wanted to get the editors' perspective on NNES contributions to their journals. I interviewed a fair number of editors across a range of disciplines, but the publication was limited to those editors working in the field of Applied Linguistics and English Language Teaching. The purpose was to gain insights into how editors viewed NNES contributions and how the chances of NNESs being published might be enhanced. The sampling method was opportunistic insofar as I took advantage of attendance at conferences and seminars by editors to ask them to be interviewed. It is perhaps indicative of the seriousness with which editors consider this issue that no editor I approached refused to be interviewed. Twelve editors of leading international journals were interviewed. The approach to interviewing was the same as that in the qualitative study of the NNES writers (i.e., the interviews were semistructured, and editors were encouraged to voice their own perceptions of the issues rather than respond to an agenda established by the researcher). As with the earlier study, again, the ATLASti software was used in the analysis of the data and to assist in deriving the key categories. Both researcher and assistant separately coded the data to ensure researcher triangulation. The categories agreed on were as follows:

1. A questioning of the concept of the term *non-native speaker*.
2. The overall attitudes of editors and reviewers to NNES contributions.
3. Problematic aspects of NNES contributions:
   - "surface" errors
   - parochialism
   - absence of authorial voice
   - nativized varieties of English
4. Positive attributes of NNES contributors:
   - awareness of cross-linguistic and cross-cultural issues
   - objectivity of "outsider" perspectives
   - an international perspective
   - a testing mechanism for the dominant theories of the "centre"
   - access to research sites and data where NESs would be intrusive
   - alerting "centre" scholars to research undertaken on the "periphery"

During the data analysis, some of the editors were contacted again by e-mail to obtain their views on issues that other editors had mentioned, but which they had not. In this way, the reliability of the findings was strengthened by being able to quantify those in agreement with a given point. In addition, after a draft of the paper had been written up, a copy was sent to all of the interviewees with the object of obtaining participant verification (Ball, 1988). All of the editors acknowledged reading the paper and, indeed, a number had specific comments on how the paper might be improved. In addition, it became clear that for a number of editors, the paper achieved a certain degree of what Lather (1991) refers to as "catalytic validity"—how the research develops understanding in those it studies and encourages them to reassess the way they view the world.

The NNES Writer Case Study Paper

This paper (Flowerdew, 2000) is a case study of a non-native English speaking Hong Kong scholar and the difficulties he encountered in publishing a paper in an internationally refereed journal on his return from studying for a Ph.D. in the United States. The significance of this paper is that it demonstrates what it implies to be a non-Anglophone researcher seeking international publication in English, but living and researching in a non-Anglophone country. In this paper, there is an overt emphasis on social-constructivist theory, applying the Swalesian notion of "discourse community" and the concept of learning as legitimate peripheral participation (after Lave & Wenger, 1991). Nevertheless, in the tradition of grounded research, these concepts became relevant only once the data had started to be collected.

Many case studies were conducted by both the researcher and the research assistant, starting with a pilot study conducted by a student of the researcher. The particular case chosen for publication was selected, as a rather complete set of research data was made available by the research participant. The method used in this investigation was broadly speaking ethnographic, with a single case study format. To examine the issue from a number of different perspectives and achieve as much triangulation as possible, several sources of data were used for the study. The central focal point of the analysis and point of orientation of the other sources were the various drafts and the final version of a paper published in the *XYZ Journal* (not its real name). The author of this paper was the young Hong Kong scholar mentioned earlier who had recently returned from doctoral study in the United States. His field of study was mass communication. For the purpose of the study, he was referred to by the pseudonym of Oliver. Other data sources were interviews and e-mail communication with Oliver by the author; correspondence between Oliver and the journal editor, reviewers, and the in-house editor who worked on the paper; field notes and a report written by an NES in Hong Kong who provided editorial assistance to Oliver; and participant verification (Ball, 1988) of the final report by Oliver.

The case study was conducted in Hong Kong over several months during 1998. As part of the full-scale project, as described in this chapter, a research assistant worked with the author to assist in data collection and analysis. To conduct a case study of the type reported here, the research assistant made himself available to provide editorial assistance to Hong Kong Cantonese L1 academics in return for their agreement to serve as possible case study subjects. Oliver was one of those people who agreed to participate in this way. In return for editorial assistance, Oliver provided various drafts and final versions of academic papers he had written and was interviewed on a number of occasions by both the research assistant and the author. He also provided copies of correspondence he had conducted with editors in connection with papers he had submitted for possible publication. A preliminary analysis of the articles and correspondence provided by Oliver suggested that a manageable case study could be conducted focusing on just one article, which was an empirical public opinion survey study relating to Hong Kong's political transition from British to Chinese sovereignty.

In analysing the data, it became clear that the whole writing and publication process was a learning experience for the participant—hence the application of legitimate peripheral participation theory. At the same time, the participant was seeking access to the international discourse community of scholars, but from a disadvantaged position, Hong Kong—hence the application of discourse community theory.

Textual Analysis

The work conducted so far has not been published, and so I do not say much about it here. The focus of this work is on introductions because this is the aspect of the research article that (since the seminal work of Swales [1990]) has been most researched to date. The main issue for me is this: To what extent are the problems encountered by the participants in this study general writing problems (probably influenced by Cantonese transfer) or specific to the genre of the academic research article? Of course there is great variation in the quality of the writing of the participants. Some could not be distinguished from NESs, whereas others had serious problems. Focusing on those writers whom I would consider had serious problems, initial findings suggest that both types of problems exist. Of particular significance, however, is a problem with the distribution of information across the clause (in Hallidayan terms, *theme/rheme development*). This is probably typologically influenced, given that Chinese is a topic prominent language (Li & Thompson, 1981). However, a problem more directly related to the structure of the academic article is a failure to follow the typical move structure of introductions—the so-called *CARS model* (Swales, 1990). These problems are in addition to the seemingly universal problems of concord, voice, use of prepositions, and relative clauses.

CONCLUSION

In this chapter, I have tried to demonstrate how a multimethod approach can be taken to an applied linguistics issue—that of NNES scholars writing for publication in English. The main challenge (and success I would claim) of the project is, in using these various methods and developing publishable findings, insights are developed into the problem from different perspectives. One of the main challenges for scholars writing for publication "on the periphery" (myself included), this research has shown, is in producing research that is at once of relevance to the local setting, but also of interest to the international community. In overcoming this problem, I would claim that this project has been successful. As such, the value of the findings go beyond the immediate issues being researched. They are at the same time pertinent to broader issues such as the whole question of globalization of scholarship and the ownership of English.

ACKNOWLEDGMENTS

The research reported in this chapter was funded by Hong Kong University Research Council under the project reference CityU 769/96H. I would like to express my gratitude to my research assistant, Daniel Reeves, for his contribution to the work reported in this chapter.

REFERENCES

Arvantis, R., & Chatelin, Y. (1988). National scientific strategies in tropical soil sciences. *Social Studies of Science, 18*, 113–146.

Baldauf, R. B., & Jernudd, B. H. (1983). Language of publications as a variable in scientific communication. *Australian Review of Applied Linguistics, 6*, 97–108.

Ball, S. J. (1988). Participant observation. In J. P. Keeves (Ed.), *Educational research methodology and measurement: An international handbook* (pp. 310–314). Oxford: Pergamon.

Berger, P., & Luckmann, T. (1966). *The social construction of reality*. London: Allen Lane.

Flowerdew, J. (1999a). Problems in writing for scholarly publication in English: The case of Hong Kong. *Journal of Second Language Writing, 8*(3), 243–264.

Flowerdew, J. (1999b). Writing for scholarly publication in English: The case of Hong Kong. *Journal of Second Language Writing, 8*(2), 123–145.

Flowerdew, J. (2000). Discourse community, legitimate peripheral participation, and the nonnative-English-speaking scholar. *TESOL Quarterly, 34*(1), 127–150.

Garfield, E. (1978). The science citation index as a quality information filter. In K. S. Warren (Ed.), *Coping with the biomedical literature explosion: A qualitative approach* (pp. 68–77). New York: Rockefeller Foundation.

Gergen, K. J. (1985). The social constructionist movement in modern psychology. *American Psychologist, 40*, 266–275.

Jernudd, B. H., & Baldauf, R. B. (1987). Planning science communication for human resource development. In B. K. Das (Ed.), *Communicative language teaching* (pp. 144–189). Singapore: RELC.

Lather, P. (1991). *Getting smart: Feminist research and pedagogy with/in the postmodern*. London: Routledge.

Lave, J., & Wenger, E. (1991). *Situated learning: Legitimate peripheral participation*. Cambridge, England: Cambridge University Press.

Li, C. T., & Thompson, S. (1981). *Mandarin Chinese: A functional reference grammar*. Berkeley and Los Angeles: University of California Press.

Maher, J. (1986). The development of English as the international language of medicine. *Applied Linguistics, 7*, 201–218.

Scientific Software Development. (1997). *ATLAS.ti: Visual qualitative data analysis model building. New Version 4.1*. Berlin, Germany: Author.

Spradley, J. P. (1979). *The ethnographic interview*. New York: Holt, Rinehart & Winston.

Strauss, A., & Corbin, J. (1990). *Basics of qualitative research*. Newbury Park, CA: Sage.

Swales, J. (1985). ESP—The heart of the matter or the end of the affair? In R. Quirk & H. Widdowson (Eds.), *English in the world: Teaching and learning the language and the literatures* (pp. 212–223). Cambridge, England: Cambridge University Press, in association with the British Council.

Swales, J. (1990). *Genre analysis: English in academic and research settings*. Cambridge, England: Cambridge University Press.

Wood, A. (1997). International scientific English: Some thoughts on science, language and ownership. Science Tribune. Retrieved September 14, 2003, from http://www.tribunes.com/tribune/art97/wooda.htm

6

Hypothesis Generation and Hypothesis Testing: Two Complementary Studies of EFL Writing Processes

Miyuki Sasaki
Nagoya Gakuin University, Japan

In this chapter, I reflect on my inquiry process for two complementary studies (Sasaki, 2000, 2002); the former represents a hypothesis-generating exploratory study and the latter a hypothesis-testing confirmatory study. Both of these studies fall under the category of *quantitative* research "where generalizability from the sample to the population is the aim" (Newman & Benz, 1998, p. 10). In terms of content, they deal with Japanese EFL (learning English in a non-English-speaking environment) learners' English writing processes.

My inquiry process for these two studies is typical of the one I have often employed when the target of research has not previously been extensively studied. In such a case, it may be difficult to formulate specific hypotheses to be tested, but researchers may still want to find out whether some patterns exist in the given situation of interest. Researchers can then explore the collected data and formulate some operational hypotheses, which could later be confirmed or disconfirmed using another sample from the same population.

I first learned to use such an exploratory-to-confirmatory sequence when I was trained to use factor analysis for my doctoral dissertation (Sasaki, 1991, 1996). According to Kim and Mueller (1978), *exploratory* factor analysis is used when "the researcher may not have any idea as to how many underlying dimensions there are for the given data," whereas *confirmatory* factor analysis is used "as a means of testing specific hypotheses" (p. 9)—for instance, regarding possible numbers and relations of underlying factors.[1] Exploratory factor analysis is often used as a preparatory step for a following confirmatory factor analysis (Bollen, 1989).

Later when I had to plan other types of quantitative research, I realized that this exploratory-to-confirmatory sequence could be applied to studies that did not involve factor analysis. Sasaki (2000, 2002) represent one of those sequences I have used for the study of L2 writing. They followed a typical quantitative research procedure of planning—data collection–data analysis—writing up the paper (Isaac & Michael, 1981). In this chapter, however, I describe not only such a procedure for each study, but also the problems (both expected and unexpected) I encountered while conducting the study and how I managed to solve them. By doing so, I hope to encourage some of the readers not to give up their research projects just because they are faced with such problems.

SASAKI (2000): AN EXPLORATORY STUDY

Preparatory Steps

From 1992 to 1994, I was involved in several studies that investigated factors affecting the quality of Japanese university students' English writing (e.g., Hirose & Sasaki, 1994; Sasaki & Hirose, 1996). While I was conducting these product-oriented studies, I also became interested in the *processes* of how these students produced their L2 texts and how these processes might change over time. I looked at previous studies and found that a number of studies had already examined the composition processes of ESL (learning English in an English-speaking environment) learners with heterogeneous educational and cultural backgrounds. However, few studies at that point had examined Japanese EFL learners' L2 writing processes both cross-sectionally and longitudinally. Consequently, I decided to conduct an exploratory study using a relatively small sample. From the results of the previous studies that examined mainly ESL learners, I tried to select as the targets of analysis as many aspects as possible of the participants' writing behavior that might potentially be important for characterizing their writing processes.

There was also a methodological problem I needed to solve before conducting this exploratory study. Traditionally, it has been common to use concurrent think-aloud protocols while participants are writing a composition for the purpose of collecting microlevel writing process data in the

[1]A *factor* in this context means a hypothetical common trait shared by several observed variables. For example, several listening comprehension test scores may share a common trait of listening ability.

fields of both L1 and L2 composition studies (e.g., Emig, 1971, for L1 studies; Cumming, 1989, Raimes, 1985, for L2 studies). Thus, I tried this method with some of my potential participants, but they found it difficult to talk and write in their L2 at the same time. I realized that the think-aloud method may not be the best for collecting writing process data when participants' L2 writing ability is low and when they are not accustomed to verbalizing their thinking process.

Fortunately, my former co-author, Keiko Hirose, introduced me to a promising method developed by Anzai and Uchida (1981) for L1 Japanese writers. Having realized that it was difficult to collect concurrent think-aloud data from Japanese child participants, Anzai and Uchida conducted a well-designed empirical study and developed a method for collecting *retrospective* protocol data that could provide detailed information about what a participant was thinking about while writing. Because the participants were asked to talk just after they finished writing while looking at the composition they had just written, their writing process was not greatly disturbed. They were asked to explain what they had been thinking about at each pause longer than 2 seconds. These pauses had been hand recorded by a research assistant sitting beside the participants while they were writing. Because a writing process is a continuous but unpredictable act, I thought that asking the participants what they had been thinking about every time they stopped writing would be an effective way of probing their thinking process.

A Pilot Study

At this point, I conducted a small-scale pilot study using five participants from a sample population similar to the one I intended to use for the exploratory study. I wanted to know whether Anzai and Uchida's (1981) method would be truly applicable to my potential participants. Overall, it was a great success. All of the participants, including a few shy ones, contributed ample composing process data for analysis.

Based on the results of the pilot study, I also revised Anzai and Uchida's method to better fit my own study. First, I decided to ask participants to talk about their writing processes when they stopped writing for longer than 3 seconds instead of the original two because I had discovered that the period of 3 seconds was the shortest I could correctly measure. Second, I decided to limit the writing session to about 30 minutes because I noticed that the participants would get too tired to think properly if the total time for writing and the subsequent question-and-answer sessions exceeded 2 hours. Finally, I decided to use a video camera to record the participants' writing behaviors, including their hand movements, instead of just recording their writing behaviors while sitting beside them. Watching the videotapes of their own writing behaviors helped the participants remember what they were thinking about at each pause better than just looking at the compositions they had written.

Conducting Sasaki (2000)

Having gained confidence in the effectiveness of the main method I would use, I proceeded to plan the basic research design of the exploratory study at the beginning of 1996. The first thing I had to do was select the participant groups. For the same reasons I had selected as many targets of analysis as possible for this study, I selected as many target participant groups as possible that seemed important for eventually building a comprehensive model of Japanese EFL learners' writing processes. I thus ended up comparing three paired groups: experts versus novices, more versus less skilled student writers, and novices before and after two semesters of instruction (see Fig. 6.1). I wanted to include the *expert group* (defined as those whose "professional work included regularly writing English re-

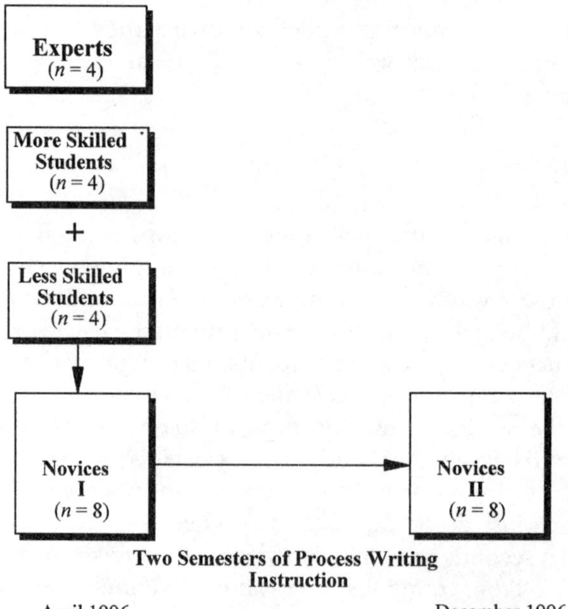

FIG. 6.1. The basic research design of Sasaki (2000) that compared three paired groups of experts versus novices, more and less skilled student writers, and novices before and after two semesters of process writing instruction.

search papers while their life was anchored in Japan," Sasaki, 2000, p. 265) in this study because I believed that their writing ability, not that of native speakers, should be the ultimate goal to be aimed at by EFL students, my target student groups. I decided to have two student groups with different writing ability because similar groups had behaved differently in the previous product-oriented studies (Hirose & Sasaki, 1994; Sasaki & Hirose, 1996). Finally, I wanted to find out the effects of process-writing instruction because I was interested in possible longitudinal changes in the students' writing processes and how they might still differ from the experts' writing processes. Unfortunately, however, I could not obtain a control group to compare with the novice group regarding improvement in L2 writing ability because at that time all freshmen at the university where I was planning to collect data were supposed to receive two semesters of process writing instruction. It was ethically impossible to ask for a control group that did not receive the instruction. This was a problem caused by my using intact groups, but I had to give up the idea of checking the true effects of the process writing instruction, and I resolved to simply observe the novice students' changes over the two semesters because my participants were, after all, real human beings who were entitled to receive a good education.

The next thing I had to decide before actually conducting Sasaki (2000) was the sample sizes of the selected participant groups. When I was conducting the pilot study, I learned that collecting data for this type of study was quite time-consuming (it took about 2 hours to collect data from one participant and about 10 to 15 hours to transcribe the tape-recorded participants' protocols for one session), so I decided to have only four expert writers, four more skilled writers, and four less skilled writers for this exploratory study. Based on the results of a writing assignment that was different from the task used for this main study, the more skilled writers were selected from the top one third of a sample of 45 students and the less skilled writers from the bottom one third. I also collapsed the more and less skilled writer groups into one novice group to be compared as a whole with the expert group at the beginning of the study because the more and less skilled writer groups were similar in that neither had received much L2 writing instruction, including instruction on matters such as "organizing a paragraph centered on one main idea" (see Sasaki, 2000, p. 265). In other words, these two student groups could be collectively called *novices* in terms of their L2 writing instruction history, although their L2 writing ability was quite different (see Fig. 6.1).

In 1996, Keiko Hirose helped me collect the experts' data, and I collected the novices' data both before and after the instruction. We asked each participant to write an English composition in a quiet room. The four experts and the eight novice students wrote an argumentative composition according to Prompt 1 about the issue of school uniforms. The eight student writers then wrote in response to Prompt 2 about the Japanese people's celebrating Christmas after the two-semester instruction period ended (see Appendix B of Sasaki, 2000).

Before the participants started to write, we obtained permission to videotape them while they were writing. We then began to videotape them with the camera focused mainly on their hand and pencil movement. As in Anzai and Uchida (1981), we waited until the participants started to write the first words of the composition before asking them several questions about their planning, such as what they were trying to write at that time and whether they had decided what they were going to write in the beginning, in the middle, and in the end. When they answered the questions, they were told that their answering time would not be included in the 30 minutes allocated for writing. After the first question session, we let them continue writing until they finished. Right after they had finished, the participants were again asked, in slightly different words, whether they had planned the beginning, the middle, or the ending part of their composition before they started to write down the first word. This second question session was conducted to check the reliability of the data for the first session. After this second question session, the researcher and each participant watched the participant's writing process on videotape together. On the videotape, every time the participants stopped writing for longer than 3 seconds, we asked them to explain, in either Japanese or English, what they had been thinking about. This continued until they finished the entire process of writing shown on the tape. The participants' accounts were all tape recorded and subsequently transcribed.

Using the data obtained from these writing sessions, I compared the three paired groups of participants (experts vs. novices, more vs. less skilled student writers, and novices before and after the instruction) in terms of writing fluency, quality/complexity of their written texts, their pausing behaviors while writing, and their strategy use. As was typical with an exploratory study, I did not intend to use any inferential statistics to test the significance of the results, so I did not have to consider restrictions related to applying inferential statistics such as adjustment of the alpha level by a Bonferroni correction for multiple comparison (Tabachnick & Fidell, 1996). I examined all groups of participants and all aspects of writing behaviors that seemed worth examining.[2]

[2]I ended up using some nonparametric procedures when appropriate and necessary (e.g., I used the Wilcoxon Mann Whitney test to compare the experts' composition subscores with those of the novices; see Sasaki, 2000), following the advice of one of the reviewers for *Journal of Second Language Writing*, where the paper was eventually published.

Results of Sasaki (2000)

Among the seven results obtained from Sasaki (2000), the last two ("both global and local planning guided the experts' and novices' writing processes" and "the experts' global planning and partial adjustment of such planning while writing was based on their elaborate but flexible goal-setting and assessment of the characteristics of the given task," p. 282) were a product of my searching through the data for behavioral differences among the different groups. These behavioral characteristics were not quantifiable, but seemed important to distinguish among the groups. I judged that I was justified in presenting these as additional and legitimate results because this was an exploratory study. As in the "specification search" process used in confirmatory factor analysis after it has been found that "the hypothesized model does not fit" (Long, 1983, p. 68), I explored the data without being guided by an explicit, predetermined theory or hypothesis. Of course, however, I was aware that all the findings presented in the prior summary "must be viewed as tentative, in need of verification, with a second, independent sample" (Long, 1983, p. 68).

GETTING SASAKI (2000) PUBLISHED

I finished writing the first draft of the study and submitted it for publication to the *Journal of Second Language Writing* (*JSLW*) in January 1999. At the end of July of the same year, I received a letter from the editors saying that one reviewer rejected my paper and the other accepted it with revisions. It further said that the editors would give me a chance to revise and resubmit the paper under the condition that this would not guarantee that they would publish it. I had to respond to six pages (single spaced) of the editors' and reviewers' comments. They included such questions as, "What exactly is new in this paper?" and a number of detailed reasons why my paper was not worth publishing. I have to confess here that I could not start to revise the paper for 2 months because I was so shocked by those comments.

In August 1999, I returned to these comments once again, having remembered that reviewers' comments, no matter how harsh they might have sounded, had always improved my past papers in some way. After reading the comments several times, I determined that I could probably address all of them if I spent enough time on them. I decided to resubmit the paper to the *JSLW* and revised it following the editors' and reviewers' advice (see also Sasaki, 2001, 2003). I thus improved the literature review section, changed some terms (e.g., from *more efficient writers* to *more skilled writers*), gave more detailed explanation where necessary, rewrote the parts that were misleading, corrected the grammatical errors, and addressed the limitations of the study more clearly. Finally, I removed the section called "A Model of L2 Writing Processes" because I agreed with the editors and one of the reviewers in that it was much too early to present an empirical model of L2 writing processes based on the temporary findings that might have fit only the small sample used in this exploratory study (although one of the reviewers liked it very much).

I submitted the revised version in March 2000. On June 28, 2000, I received an e-mail letter from the editor of the *JSLW* again with comments, as well as two additional reviewers' comments. This time both reviewers accepted the paper with revisions. Many of these revisions were minor, but some required me to conduct nonparametric statistical procedures where applying them was possible (recall Note 2). I finished all the necessary revisions and resubmitted the final draft on July 7, 2000, the deadline set by the *JSLW* editors. The paper was published in the last issue of the 2000 volume of the journal.

SASAKI (2002): A CONFIRMATORY STUDY

Preparatory Steps

Before I could conduct the confirmatory study following Sasaki (2000), I needed to determine its exact research design. The first step I had to take was to determine the hypotheses to be tested. The main purpose of this study was to confirm the findings of the previous exploratory study (i.e., Sasaki, 2000), but I had to restate them in the form of several hypotheses so they could be individually tested for statistical significance. I accordingly formulated the following eight hypotheses (Sasaki, 2002):

1. EFL writing experts write longer texts at greater speed than EFL writing novices.
2. After two semesters of process writing instruction, neither the quantity nor the speed of the novices' writing improves.
3. The experts spend a longer time before starting to write than the novices.
4. After the instruction, the novices spend a longer time before starting to write.
5. While writing, the experts stop to reread or refine their expressions more often than the novices, whereas the novices stop to make local plans or translate from L1 to L2 more often than the experts.

6. After the instruction, the novices stop to reread more often while making fewer local plans. However, they still have to stop to translate from L1 to L2 as often as before.
7. The experts tend to plan a detailed overall organization (i.e., Global Planning), whereas the novices tend to make a less detailed plan (i.e., Thematic Planning).
8. After two semesters of process writing instruction, the novices learn to do global planning, but it is qualitatively different from the experts' global planning. (pp. 54–55)

These eight hypotheses basically determined the entire research design of Sasaki (2002). They indicated that I needed to collect data consisting of: (a) the participants' compositions, (b) time that the participants spent before starting to write and time that they spent writing the whole composition, and (c) the participants' retrospective accounts of what they were thinking about when they stopped writing. Unlike the exploratory study, I decided not to compare more and less skilled writers partly because I did not want to make the research design of the confirmatory study too complex for the application of statistical procedures (the design was already complex enough with so many variables to be investigated) and partly because I found in Sasaki (2000) that the differences between the more and less skilled writers were similar to those between the expert and novice writers, which were to be examined in this confirmatory study (see Fig. 6.2).

After having settled on this basic design, however, I still needed to determine several other details before conducting the actual study. First, I

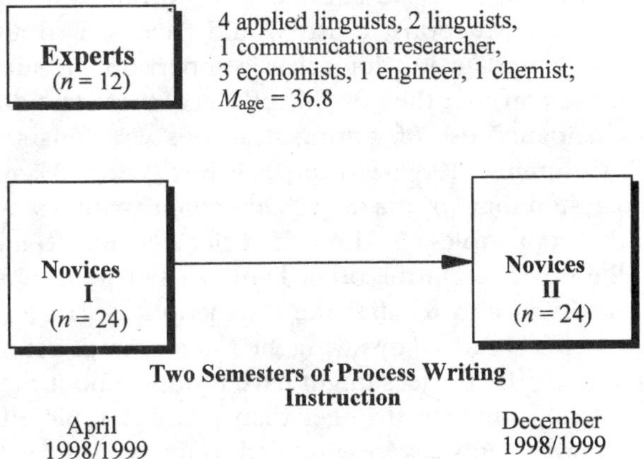

FIG. 6.2. The basic research design of Sasaki (2002) that compared two paired groups of experts versus novices and novices before and after two semesters of process writing instruction.

had to decide on the sample sizes of the target participant groups: novices and experts. Of course the larger the sample sizes, the better for applying parametric statistical procedures (Hatch & Lazaraton, 1991). However, as in the case of Sasaki (2000), it was not easy to collect the data from a large sample. In the end, I concluded that 12 experts and 24 novices would be the maximum number of participants I could collect data from even if I spent the next 2 years doing so. I also concluded that these sample sizes would be large enough (though not ideal) to apply inferential statistical procedures to if I collected the data carefully.

A third issue I needed to consider was whether to revise the data-collection procedure I had used for the exploratory study. Because it had been revised once based on the results of a pilot study (see the study cited earlier), there was not much to be improved. However, I decided to use two video cameras instead of one for recording the participants' writing behaviors. Because it was sometimes difficult for the participants to see which part of the texts they were working on in the exploratory study, I judged that using two video cameras with one focusing on the participants' hand/pencil movement and the other focusing on the overall writing behavior, including their eye/head movements, would provide additional clarity.

A fourth point I needed to determine before actually conducting Sasaki (2002) was whether I should alternate the two prompts with half of the 24 novices before and after the instruction (i.e., half of them receiving Prompt 1 before the instruction and Prompt 2 after the instruction, with the other half receiving Prompt 2 before the instruction and Prompt 1 after the instruction). If I did so, I could have avoided possible topic effects on the students' composition scores and their use of writing strategies. In fact one of the *JSLW* reviewers claimed that I should have done so for Sasaki (2000). However, if I had alternated the prompts for the novice I group (before the instruction), I also would have had to alternate the prompts for the expert group for a fair comparison. In such a case, I would have had to consider the possible effects of these two different topics on the participants' use of writing strategies. Previous studies (e.g., Carter, 1990; Cumming, 1989; Flower, Schriver, Carey, Haas, & Hayes, 1992) had suggested that writers may change their writing strategy use in response to different topics. In the end, I decided not to alternate the prompts for the novices. On the other hand, I used similar but different prompts for novices I and II (after the instruction) because I was afraid that maturation effects caused by giving the same prompt before and after the instruction (e.g., the novices might have thought about the topic over the two semesters) might be stronger than possible topic effects (especially when Prompts 1 and 2 were intended to induce similar argumentative writing; see Sasaki, 2000; Sasaki & Hirose, 1996). This compromise was a real dilemma, but I concluded that topic effects, if they existed at all, would be larger for the expert–novice (intergroup) comparison than for the novices I and II (intragroup) comparison. Of course, I was aware that comparing novices I and II could be problematic because of possible topic effects, and I mentioned this as one of the limitations of Sasaki (2002) in the Results and Discussion section.

Finally, I had to determine appropriate statistical procedures for testing the eight hypotheses. At this point, I consulted with Yasuko Nogami, a psychometrician. She suggested that as an important preliminary step I should check the normality of the data distributions, which is one of the most critical conditions for applying parametric statistical procedures (Bohrnstedt & Knoke, 1988; Hatch & Lazaraton, 1991). She especially emphasized the fact that time-ratio values and strategy token-ratio values, like the ones I was planning to use in Sasaki (2002), tend to have skewed distributions, and that these values can acquire more normal distributions by logarithmic transformation (Iwahara, 1997). Only after the data satisfied the condition of normal distribution could I consider applying parametric procedures. If not, I had to use nonparametric procedures, although they were not as powerful (Hatch & Lazaraton, 1991). As parametric procedures for testing Hypotheses 1 through 6, which dealt with continuous data, Yasuko suggested that I use *t* tests with adjusted alpha levels based on a Bonferroni correction (Tabachnick & Fidell, 1996). For testing Hypotheses 7 and 8, which dealt with frequency data, she suggested using a chi-square test for comparing the experts and novices and using McNemar's test for comparing the novices before and after the instruction.

Conducting Sasaki (2002)

It took me 2 full years (1998 and 1999) to collect the necessary data for Sasaki (2002). For the expert group, I found 12 EFL expert writers (10 men and 2 women) as I had planned. Unlike in the exploratory study, I was able to find expert writers in different professional fields (with a mean age of 36.8 years; see Sasaki, 2002). For the novice group, I lost two candidates who dropped out of the university, which decreased the sample size of the novice group to 22. They were all 18-year-old college freshmen majoring in British and American studies when the study started. Fortunately, the overall characteristics (e.g., age, L2 proficiency, L2 writing ability) of both the expert and novice groups were similar to those of the exploratory study.

I finished collecting all the necessary data in January 2000. Following Yasuko Nogami's advice, I checked the normality of the distributions of the time-ratio and strategy-frequency ratio data by comparing them with those of their corresponding logarithms by the Shapiro–Wilks distribution-normality test (SPSS Incorporated, 1994). Because the values after logarithmic transformation in both ratio cases were more normally distributed, and because they satisfied the normal-distribution condition for applying *t* tests, I consequently used these values for the statistical tests. Among the eight hypotheses set up in the beginning, six were confirmed and two were partially confirmed with some writing strategies used unexpectedly by the participants (see Sasaki, 2002, for a summary of the findings).

Getting Sasaki (2002) Published

I finished writing the first draft at the end of 2000. I had been invited to submit a chapter for a book entitled, *New Directions for Research in L2 Writing: Volume II of the Studies in Writing Series*, to be published by Kluwer Academic, and I decided to submit this draft as a candidate for this chapter. Fortunately, the editors accepted it as the chapter, but here again I had to go through what the editors called a *multilayer* review process: I had to revise the draft first according to three internal reviewers' (i.e., those whose chapters would be included in the same book) comments, second according to two external reviewers' comments, and finally the editors' and the series editor's comments. I received the internal reviews in the middle of February 2001, and I had to finish the revision by the end of March of the same year. Just as when I had to revise Sasaki (2000) in response to the *JSLW* reviewers' comments, I expanded the literature review, added more examples and explanation, corrected some mistaken descriptions, clarified some descriptions, and removed unnecessary parts while responding to 72 comments.

I subsequently received the two external reviewers' comments in the middle of May 2001. This time the reviewers focused mainly on the content and organization of the chapter except for one suggestion to improve statistical validity of the intercoder agreement. Although I basically followed the reviewers' advice, I sometimes disagreed with them and did not change the draft as they had suggested. In particular, I did not follow one reviewer's suggestion that I should "leave out the pre–posttest comparison" because I had not alternated the two prompts before and after the instruction. As I mentioned earlier, I had my own principled reasons for not alternating the prompts. I decided to keep the comparison, but added the acknowledgment in the Results and Discussion section that "comparing novices I and II could be problematic because of possible topic effects" (Sasaki, 2002, p. 58).

QUESTIONS FOR FURTHER STUDIES

I submitted the final version of the draft on September 2, 2001, and the book containing my chapter was published early in the following year. This should be the end of my story in this chapter. However, as many researchers experience with their studies, even the confirmatory study's results left me with more questions unresolved than I had originally asked. At a macrolevel, the results "cover only part of the complex mechanism of L2 writing processes" (Sasaki, 2002, pp. 76–77). As I stated in the Conclusion section, they should be complemented by the results of future studies that investigate other sample populations of different L1/L2 and educational/cultural backgrounds using different types of writing under different conditions.

At a microlevel, I became interested in answering some of the questions I had come across when analyzing the data of Sasaki (2002). For example, I found that the novice students significantly changed after two semesters of process writing instruction in terms of writing ability and strategy use. Then I wondered how they would further change or remain unchanged 1 more year after or even 3 years after the initial study when they are ready to graduate from the university. From the same data, I also found that the novices learned to do global planning after the instruction. Then I wondered how they felt about such a writing style change. Did they like it or not like it? Would they continue to keep that style 1 year later or even 3 years later?

Such an extended length of observation and the participants' own internal emic perspectives are characteristic of qualitative research (Miles & Huberman, 1994), but are not typical of quantitative studies. A follow-up study with such an additional qualitative perspective, however, would be helpful for understanding more deeply the results I obtained in Sasaki (2002). In this sense, I agree with Newman and Benz' (1998) claim that quantitative and qualitative approaches are on an "interactive continuum" (p. 20), and that they should complement each other to achieve higher quality research. On this qualitative–quantitative research continuum, "the qualitative analysis with its feedback loops can easily modify the types of research questions that will be asked in quantitative analysis research; and the quantitative analysis results and its feedback can change what will be asked qualitatively" (p. 25). According to Newman and Benz, my two prior questions are located in a typical "feedback loop" going from quantitative to qualitative approaches. Thus, I am currently conducting such a follow-up study[3] of Sasaki (2002) while again facing numerous problems. My hope is that this one step further will eventually lead to a comprehensive L2 writing process model that will be useful for both researchers and teachers in the L2 writing field (Cumming, 1998).

REFERENCES

Anzai, Y., & Uchida, N. (1981). *Kodomo wa ikani sakubun o kakuka* [How children produce writing]. *Japanese Journal of Educational Psychology, 29*, 323–332.

Bohrnstedt, G. W., & Knoke, D. (1988). *Statistics for social data analysis* (2nd ed.). Itasca, IL: F. E. Peacock.

Bollen, K. A. (1989). *Structural equations with latent variables*. New York: Wiley.

[3]This study has now been published as Sasaki (2004).

Carter, M. (1990). The idea of expertise: An exploration of cognitive and social dimensions of writing. *College Composition and Communication, 41*, 265–286.

Cumming, A. (1989). Writing expertise and second-language proficiency. *Language Learning, 39*, 81–141.

Cumming, A. (1998). Theoretical perspective on writing. *Annual Review of Applied Linguistics, 18*, 61–78.

Emig, J. (1971). *The composing processes of twelfth graders*. Urbana, IL: National Council of Teachers of English.

Flower, L., Schriver, K. A., Carey, L., Haas, C., & Hayes, J. R. (1992). Planning in writing: The cognition of a constructive process. In S. P. Witte, N. Nakadate, & R. D. Cherry (Eds.), *A rhetoric of doing: Essays on written discourse in honor of James L. Kinneavy* (pp. 181–243). Carbondale, IL: Southern Illinois University Press.

Hatch, E., & Lazaraton, A. (1991). *The research manual: Design and statistics for applied linguistics*. New York: Newbury House.

Hirose, K., & Sasaki, M. (1994). Explanatory variables for Japanese students' expository writing in English: An exploratory study. *Journal of Second Language Writing, 3*, 203–229.

Isaac, S., & Michael, W. B. (1981). *Handbook in research and evaluation: A collection of principles, methods, and strategies useful in the planning, design, and evaluation of studies in education and the behavioral sciences* (2nd ed.). San Diego: EdITS Publishers.

Iwahara, S. (1997). *Kyouiku to shinri notameno suikeigaku* [Inferential statistics for education and psychology]. Tokyo: Nihonbunkakagakusha.

Kim, J., & Mueller, C. W. (1978). *Introduction to factor analysis: What it is and how to do it*. Newbury Park, CA: Sage.

Long, J. S. (1983). *Confirmatory factor analysis*. Newbury Park: Sage.

Miles, M. B., & Huberman, A. M. (1994). *Qualitative data analysis* (2nd ed.). Thousand Oaks, CA: Sage.

Newman, I., & Benz, C. R. (1998). *Qualitative-quantitative research methodology: Exploring the interactive continuum*. Carbondale, IL: Southern Illinois University Press.

Raimes, A. (1985). What unskilled ESL students do as they write: A classroom study of composing. *TESOL Quarterly, 19*, 229–258.

Sasaki, M. (1991). *Relationships among second language proficiency, foreign language aptitude, and intelligence: A structural equation modeling*. Unpublished doctoral dissertation, University of California, Los Angeles.

Sasaki, M. (1996). *Second language proficiency, foreign language aptitude, and intelligence: Quantitative and qualitative analyses*. New York: Peter Lang.

Sasaki, M. (2000). Toward an empirical model of EFL writing processes: An exploratory study. *Journal of Second Language Writing, 9*, 259–291.

Sasaki, M. (2001). *An introspective account of L2 writing acquisition*. In D. Belcher & U. Connor (Eds.), *Reflections on multiliterate lives* (pp. 110–120). Clevedon, England: Multilingual Matters.

Sasaki, M. (2002). Building an empirically-based model of EFL learners' writing processes. In S. Ransdell & M.-L. Barbier (Eds.), *New directions for research in L2 writing* (pp. 49–80). Amsterdam: Kluwer Academic.

Sasaki, M. (2003). A sholar on the periphery: Standing firm, walking slowly. In C. P. Casanave & S. Vandrick (Eds.), *Writing for scholarly publication: Behind the scenes in language education* (pp. 211–221). Mahwah, NJ: Lawrence Erlbaum Associates.

Sasaki, M. (2004). A multiple-data analysis of the 3.5-year development of EFL student writers. *Language Learning, 54*, 525–582.

Sasaki, M., & Hirose, K. (1996). Explanatory variables for EFL students' expository writing. *Language Learning, 46*, 137–174.

SPSS Incorporated. (1994). *SPSS 6.1 Base System User's Guide, Macintosh version*. Chicago, IL: Author.

Tabachnick, B. G., & Fidell, L. S. (1996). *Using multivariate statistics* (3rd ed.). New York: HarperCollins.

7

Talking About Writing: Cross-Modality Research and Second Language Speaking/Writing Connections

Robert Weissberg
New Mexico State University, USA

If one were to make a survey of the landscape of second language (L2) writing studies, the general outline might look something like Cumming (2001) has described, consisting of three principal areas of research: studies done on the qualities of learners' texts, learners' composing processes, and the sociocultural contexts of their writing. It is the sociocultural area that is of interest to me and in which I have worked. In this chapter, I examine this area from a singular perspective. In so doing, I rearrange the topography of L2 writing research to some degree.

There is a large segment of this sociocultural way of studying L2 writing that I refer to here as *cross-modality research*. Although it is concerned principally with writing, it also takes a long and serious look at oral language. It is oral language, after all, that is instrumental in establishing the social context for writing. I wish to suggest that the intersection of writing and speech is not only a clearly definable category of L2 writing research, but a productive one. I argue that it is a line of research that has much to tell us about the nature of L2 writing—how people do it, what they say about it while or after they do it, how it is taught, and how it is learned. In addition, by looking closely at those areas of the field where L2 writing and L2 speech intersect, we can gain some useful insights into the ways research questions are formulated, how research methods are chosen, how data are interpreted, and how we connect our work with composition theory.

First, I survey the general terrain of cross-modality research as a subset of L2 writing research. Second, I summarize and critique my own approach to research in this area, with emphasis on methodological issues. Finally, I examine a candidate theory as it relates to this area of second language writing research to see how it might function both as a framework for critiquing cross-modality work already done and as a guide for future studies.

TYPES OF CROSS-MODALITY STUDIES

Cross-modality research is defined here as any study of language in use in which the researcher investigates a point of juncture where speech and writing intersect and interrelate. Those of us who engage in this type of research are asking the general question, "What can we learn about the processes, products, and pedagogy of L2 writing by looking at the oral discourse that surrounds their writing activities?" Cross-modality research in L2 writing includes a considerable number of published studies, only a small portion of which are surveyed here.

There are four general research approaches taken toward answering the question posed above. Some studies (Cumming, 1989; Hansen-Strain, 1989; Weissberg, 2000) have looked at the speech/writing intersect from the point of view of learners' L2 development and proficiency. Here oral data from L2 writers have been used to establish benchmark proficiency estimates or, in the case of Weissberg (2000), to trace development of learner language over time in comparison with data from the same learners' writing.

Another approach to the oral/writing intersect is taken by researchers attempting to develop models of L2 composing processes; Qi and Lapkin (2001), Woodall (2002), and Zimmerman (2000) are only three of the most recent. Here speech data in the form of think-aloud protocols are used as a kind of oral window through which to view the cognitive processes of L2 writers.

A third area of interest to cross-modality researchers is the role that instructional talk plays in classroom writing instruction. Both Cumming (1992) and Weissberg (1994) looked at teacher talk in college ESL composition classes; Edelsky (1983) and Fillmore (1977), among others, have looked at the talk that surrounds younger L2 writers in their classrooms. (This has been a lively area of research in first language composition as well—see, e.g., Anne Dyson [1987, 1991] and Martin Nystrand [1997].) These studies examine the talk that occurs in writing classrooms and describe how teachers and students together create (or fail to create) instructional conversations, and what this might mean for the quality of students' eventual writing.

Finally, a fourth group of studies examines the role of talk in providing feedback for L2 writers (Connor & Asenavage, 1994; Tsui & Ng, 2000; Zhu, 2001). These researchers focus on the talk that occurs in peer revision groups, writing center tutorials, and student–teacher conferences. Oral feedback studies are a central part of L2 cross-modality research because they examine and describe the social organization of writing instruction, at least as it is presently practiced in the United States.

Taken as a whole, this is a fairly large body of work, and some of the research approaches are more central than others to the question raised earlier. For example, two peripheral cross-modality areas are studies that look at speech-related, although not strictly speaking oral, phenomena: dialogue journal writing and the instructional technique known as *reformulation*. I have argued elsewhere (Weissberg, 1998) that, because journal writing is interactive, informal, highly personal, situated, and addressed to a specific audience, it is in fact *written conversation*. I claimed, in fact, that journal writing sits directly on the cross-hairs of the writing/speaking intersection. Although some L2 journal writers go to great lengths to avoid oral-based writing, for others the person-to-person discourse of the dialogue journal provides them with an opportunity to engage in conversation, and consequently language development, at a safe distance (Fazio, 2001; Peyton, 1990; Peyton et al., 1993).

It is more of a stretch to include studies of reformulated writing (see e.g., recent work by Qi & Lapkin, 2001) as lying on the speech/writing intersection. However, if one looks at students' attempts to replicate the written style of their tutors from a sociocultural point of view (Lantolf, 2000; Prior, 2001; Wertsch, 1991), what one sees is essentially a case of *multiple voices*—one writer, an expert, leading a novice to a higher level of written output by lending her or him a new voice, a temporary set of new linguistic clothes. This is essentially *scaffolding*—a very oral-like activity. Thus, although researchers who work with L2 learners' dialogue journal writings and reformulations are not dealing directly with oral data, they are to some degree studying written analogs of speech.

It can be seen from this survey that cross-modality studies account for a significant portion of current and past L2 writing research. It is worth asking why so much of the research in our field should be concerned in one way or another with spoken language. I believe there are three main reasons for this. First and most obvious is that much of the writing that L2 researchers encounter is produced within a social, if not an institutional, context, whether it be a classroom, a writing center, among a small group of student peers, or in an instructor's office. These are the contexts for writing that teacher researchers like myself work in daily, and we assume that these instructional settings (and thereby our students' writing) will be enhanced if we are better able to understand and manage the talk that occurs there.

A second possible reason that there has been so much study of talk in L2 writing research is the realization that by examining what people say about their writing, we are able to take advantage of one of the few points of access available into L2 writing processes. In fact if we are interested in researching *how* L2 learners write (as opposed to *what* or *how well* they write), speech data are no less privileged than learners' written texts; both are indirect evidence or "trace data" of writing processes (Bracewell & Breuleux, 1994).

A final and more problematic motive behind this area of research is the assumption, carried over from L1 literacy studies, that L2 writing is developmentally contingent on speech. This is the notion that lies behind much of the popularity of dialogue journal writing as an instructional technique (Peyton et al., 1993; Shuy, 1987). I have previously shown (Weissberg, 2000) that, although this is undoubtedly true for L1 writers and may be the case for some L2 learners, it does not hold for all. Other problematic aspects of cross-modality research are covered in the following section.

PROBLEMS IN CROSS-MODALITY RESEARCH

Cross-modality studies in L2 writing are problematic both methodologically and theoretically. First, research methods in these studies, like the field itself, are hybridized. Some (Cumming, 1989; Fazio, 2001; Tsui & Ng, 2000; Weissberg, 2000) are an eclectic mix of statistical, quasi-experimental (sometimes with quite low sample sizes) designs and descriptive, qualitative data-gathering techniques. This methodological eclecticism is not necessarily a flaw, although sometimes "soft" data are used where quantitative measures would be more appropriate and vice versa. For example, in my work on morphosyntactic development (Weissberg, 2000), I used qualitative data to establish baseline measures of students' proficiency and then traced developmental trends quantitatively. The two techniques could well have been reversed.

How speech data are elicited in cross-modality studies can also be problematic. Although some researchers have used well-established instruments, such as Zimmerman's (2000) use of the "Pear Stories" films, others have been more inventive, not always with the most satisfactory results. McCafferty (1992), for example, claimed to observe the use of *private speech* by L2 students, but apparently obtained his oral samples in direct, face-to-face dialogue with his subjects. Similarly, I have used monologue samples of learner speech where conversational data would have better addressed my research question (Weissberg, 1998).

The number of subjects used in these studies is also an issue. As Cumming (2001) noted, published L2 writing research in general is heavily represented by case studies. This is undoubtedly related to the fact that our often data-heavy collection procedures (such as think-aloud protocols) make working with larger sample sizes impractical. Whatever the reason(s) may be, sample size has an important influence not only on the extent to which results from a single study can be generalized, but also, and more fundamentally, on how researchers come to view the language behavior that they study.

Put bluntly, the issue here is to what extent sampling decisions predetermine research results and the ways in which researchers interpret them. Earlier, relatively large-scale studies (Cumming, 1989; Hansen-Strain, 1989; Valdes et al., 1992) hypothesized universals in writing development, whereas case studies like my own (Weissberg, 1994, 2000) and many others have focused on individual differences. As cross-modality research turns from large studies to case studies of five writers or fewer, we simultaneously see the growing acceptance of the notion that there are few, if any, universals in L2 writing; that it is very much an individualized phenomenon (Cumming, 2001; Lantof & Appel, 1994; Zimmerman, 2000).

Whatever truth there may be in this notion, we must recognize that it is as much an artifact of the size of samples used in L2 writing research as it is a consequence of an objective reading of the studies' outcomes. There may be no way out of this dilemma, but it is important to recognize, as John-Steiner and Mahn (1996) have said, that "[T]he method is simultaneously prerequisite and product, the tool and the result of the study" (p. 195).

Finally, on the topic of cross-modality research methods, I want to critique what has been, in my own studies at least, a most problematic issue—selecting the most appropriate units of analysis for use with a particular set of oral data. One alternative is to adopt an existing system as Woodall (2002), Zimmerman (2000), and Boyd and Rubin (2002) have done. This has the distinct advantage, as Byrd and Rubin point out, of allowing for meaningful comparisons of results across different studies. The problem arises when no existing analysis tool directly answers the requirements of one's research question. This is the problem I faced when I investigated patterns of teacher talk in composition classes, specifically as they related to instructors' uses of written text materials in class (Weissberg, 1994).

In that instance, as in my later study on oral and written syntactic development (Weissberg, 2000), I developed a set of analytical categories based directly on the data at hand through a qualitative research procedure called *analytic induction* (LeCompte & Preissle, 1993):

> This strategy involves scanning the data for categories of phenomena and for relationships among categories, developing working typologies and hypotheses on an examination of individual cases, and then modifying and refining them on the basis of subsequent cases. (p. 254)

When this procedure is followed, the result is an analytic tool that fits the data set at hand exceedingly well. The problem is, as mentioned earlier, that if each new study uses analytic induction, there is no methodological basis for comparisons across studies. This can eventually inhibit the development of further work in the area.

Another problem with ad hoc categories is that, as Boyd and Rubin (2002) point out, although they help the researcher see what there *is* in the oral data, they are of no help in identifying what salient categories may be missing. One solution to this problem is to strike a compromise—essentially what Cumming (1992) did in his study of composition teacher talk. One makes a first pass at the data set using analytic induction and then checks the categories one has identified initially against established analytical schemes from the literature. This ensures against missing a salient category simply because it did not show up in a particular set of speech data. Finally, one validates the scheme with the help of independent raters who take a second pass at the data.

The second general area posing problems for cross-modality researchers is the lack of an adequate theoretical basis to explain speech-writing connections for L2 writers. When we limit our analyses of L2 writing to the examination of written texts, we can rely on a well-developed, if not entirely coherent, theoretical tradition on which to base our work. But when we cross over to oral data, we not only shift language production modalities, we also make a theoretical leap that these data, whether they be concurrent protocols, peer comments on a student's first draft, or the classroom discourse of writing lessons, are somehow relevant to L2 written products and/or processes. So far, however, there has been no attempt to articulate precisely what the nature of this relevancy might be or how it might be established.

The speech–writing intersection in L2 writing research is therefore something of a theoretical Bermuda triangle—an undefined territory further obscured by unexamined assumptions about its nature. One such assumption (mentioned earlier, and one with no theoretical basis that this author is aware of) is that L2 learners' writing is necessarily based on or derived from their oral L2 knowledge. Another assumption that deserves to be examined is the notion that a highly social composition classroom, one marked by frequent, on-task oral exchanges between teacher and students, and students with each other, has any positive impact on the quality of students' eventual writing. (In this regard, I think of Oscar, one of the adult university ESL students in my case study of cross-modality syntactic development, for whom conversing in English was an unpleasant chore, perhaps even physically difficult, and for whom pair and group work were intimidating, but who nonetheless developed quickly into a competent writer of academic English [Weissberg, 2000].)

Furthermore, we are no closer to establishing a theoretical stance from which to judge the relationship between oral and written proficiencies in L2 learners. Are they two expressions of one unitary, underlying proficiency, as the findings of Valdés et al. (1992) suggest, or are they distinct and independent, as Cumming's (1989) results seemed to indicate? To my knowledge, there have been no recent attempts to readdress this important question.

It is also not known how the two modalities are related developmentally for L2 learners. It has not been established whether there are any universal tendencies governing L2 learners' progress through the writing/speaking intersection, such as Barry Kroll (1981) has suggested for L1 learners. Kroll describes a process called *differentiation*, in which children's oral language eventually gives rise to written speech, and later on, with exposure to written language, to the development of a differentiated written register. Still later, according to Kroll, highly skilled writers are able to reintegrate certain elements of their speech register back into their writing to create a livelier, less stilted written style (Fig. 7.1).

The problem for L2 researchers is that a model like Kroll's L1 representation takes no account of the variety of circumstances in which L2 writing can develop, nor of the fact that many novice L2 writers are already experienced writers in another language in which they may even have had formal composition training. Can a model like Kroll's explain the development of L2 literacy in ESL L1-literate adults? It appears that it may apply to some learners, but not to others (Weissberg, 2000). It may be that learning to write in an L2 is so specific to each individual writer's circumstances that no single model can be posited.

From a theoretical perspective, then, the entire cross-modality enterprise in L2 writing research appears to be less a coherent project with

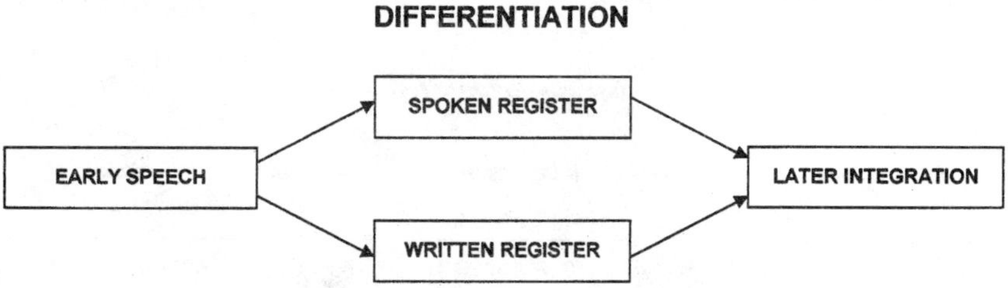

DIFFERENTIATION

FIG. 7.1. An interpretation of Kroll's (1981) Differentiation Model of speech and writing for L1 speakers.

stated assumptions and goals and more a collection of disparate studies about writing unified only by a common interest in oral language data. If a more coherent view of the speaking/writing connection is to be achieved, L2 writing researchers would benefit from an explicit theoretical stance on which to base decisions about the kinds of research questions to be asked, the numbers of subjects to be studied at a time, and the most appropriate units of analysis to be used in organizing speech data. The learning theory developed by Vygotsky and his Soviet colleagues may provide some help in this direction, and it is the subject of the next section.

SOCIOCULTURAL THEORY AND THE L2 SPEECH/WRITING CONNECTION

Sociocultural theory as developed by Vygotsky (1986) and the Soviet school of developmental psychology provides an alternative way to look at literacy development—one that also deals explicitly with the intersection of oral language and writing, but that may prove more adaptable to the needs of L2 writing teachers and cross-modality researchers than other models based on work with native speaker writers. Briefly, sociocultural theory holds that for the individual learner, social interaction precedes and drives the development of cognitive abilities. Oral language is the mediator—the driving force that transforms the young learner's social world of interpersonal communication into the interior, intrapersonal world of thought and the development of higher cognitive processes. This "folding" (Luria, 1969, p. 143) inward of social language and its transformation into cognition is accomplished through the mediation of inner speech (sometimes termed *speech for self* or *verbal thought*), which the learner uses for guidance and self-regulation when faced with difficult cognitive problems to solve. Writing is one such high-level cognitive operation, and inner speech is instrumental in its development (Fig. 7.2). In fact socioculturalists use the term *written speech* to describe the learner's early attempts at writing (Luria, 1969).

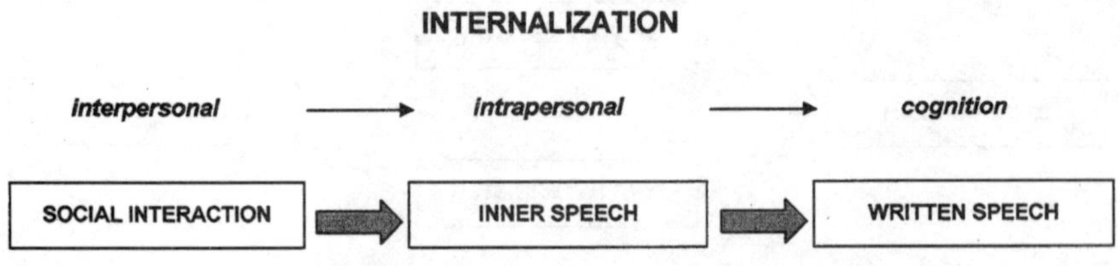

FIG. 7.2. Sociocultural view of the oral/writing connection.

Although sociocultural theory, like the differentiation model discussed earlier, is problematic when applied to L2 writers, it is a useful framework for cross-modality researchers for a number of reasons. First, it makes the speaking/writing developmental link explicit, like Kroll's model, but it goes further and operationalizes the role of spoken language in the process of learning to write through its identification of inner speech as mediator. In fact Leont'yev (1969), one of Vygotsky's Soviet followers, gave particular attention to the inner speech of L2 learners. Based on his research with language minorities in the Soviet Union, he suggested a model for L1/L2 language switching in bilinguals' inner speech that anticipates Woodall's (2002) work with bilingual think-aloud protocols.

Sociocultural theory also helps clarify methodological problems in cross-modality research design. For example, regarding the problem of sample size discussed earlier, socioculturalists point out that a person's written language development is situationally dependent on a particular social, historical, and cultural setting (Zebroski, 1994). Because social settings are constantly in flux, literacy development must be a highly idiosyncratic phenomenon—a claim that justifies case study research as an entirely appropriate method for studying L2 writing and writing development.

Second, sociocultural theory can help us choose the best kind of oral samples to be collected for cross-modality research. For example, by looking through the sociocultural filter we can appreciate anew the value of working with think-aloud protocols. Concurrent protocols not only provide a window on the internal composing processes of L2 writers, they may also be evidence of their use of inner speech—a point Woodall (2002) made recently. Zimmerman's (2000) careful analysis of specific writing process functions in his subjects' protocols supports the notion that oral language, through the medium of inner speech, is an important resource available to adult L2 writers as they generate their texts.

Sociocultural theory also helps us evaluate specific speech elicitation techniques. For instance, if we are interested in tapping a learner's inner speech through the use of think-aloud protocols, we may wish to rethink elicitation schemes in which students work together in pairs as they write (Zimmerman, 2000) or work face to face with an experimenter (McCafferty, 1992).

Sociocultural theory can also inform our search for the most appropriate units of analysis. Consider again the case of think-aloud protocols. Protocol analyses used to date have not always separated planning and editing/revising functions of writing from the actual generation of text or pretext (i.e., from the propositional content of the protocol that forms the raw material for the writer's eventual written text). By reconceptualizing protocols as manifestations of inner speech, researchers can identify cognitive functions within the oral data just as they would parse a transcription of conversational discourse for its communication functions. This would help researchers tease apart segments of a protocol in which the writer is formulating text from other segments in which the writer is planning, editing, or engaging in other executive functions. (See Prior, 2001; Zimmerman, 2000, for more extensive discussions of the need for fine-grained categorizing systems when looking at protocols.) Once this is accomplished, the researcher can link the text-generating segments of the protocols to the subjects' eventual written texts, creating a single cross-modality data set for further analysis, as Bracewell and Breuleux (1994) have done with native speaker writers.

As mentioned earlier, sociocultural theory is not without its problems when applied to L2 writing research. Although it is unarguable that grounding decisions about research methodology on a strong theoretical basis makes for better research design, questions about the ultimate appropriateness of sociocultural theory remain. Despite the work of Leont'yev referred to earlier, the theory may still be too closely linked to L1-child research to be of use to cross-modality researchers, who are primarily interested in the L2 writing processes of L1-literate adults.

It is especially questionable whether sociocultural theory will be able to explain cases of L2 students whose writing proficiency far outstrips their oral proficiency. What does this kind of writer imply for a theory of writing that posits inner speech as the mediator for the composition of written texts? Is sociocultural theory flexible enough to explain writers like Oscar (mentioned earlier), or will it be necessary to broaden our definition of inner speech to account for writers who are relying on an oral base for their writing, but whose oral base may at times be their L1, like Woodall's (2002) language-switching subjects. It may turn out that some L2 writers' access to inner speech is modality specific. For example, writers like Oscar may be able to access a highly developed English "voice" when writing, but be unable to tap it when speaking.

CONCLUSION

Despite these reservations, L2 writing research stands to gain by adopting a framework like sociocultural theory for cross-modality studies—not only to achieve greater coherence and comparability across studies, but also to guide methodological decisions made by researchers in their individual studies. Setting a provocative research question suggested by an interesting classroom problem or an earlier study is not sufficient; such motivations may provide the initial impetus for a study, but they do not ensure that defensible decisions will be made concerning sample selection, elicitation techniques, and data analysis. Similarly, a popular pedagogical approach can provide a pragmatic, unifying framework among writing researchers in the short run, but teaching fashions change, and what today generates dozens of research projects may be of little interest to writing teachers and researchers tomorrow. A larger, more durable, and more flexible theoretical framework is needed to develop a coherent and productive research tradition in the area of cross-modality L2 writing studies. Sociocultural theory may not be the ideal answer, but it is a good candidate for the job.

REFERENCES

Boyd, M., & Rubin, D. (2002). Elaborated student talk in an elementary ESOL classroom. *Research in the Teaching of English, 36*, 495–530.

Bracewell, R., & Breuleux, A. (1994). Substance and romance in analyzing think-aloud protocols. In P. Smagorinsky (Ed.), *Speaking about writing: Reflections on research methodology* (pp. 55–88). Thousand Oaks, CA: Sage.

Connor, U., & Asenavage, K. (1994). Peer response groups in ESL writing classes: How much impact on revision? *Journal of Second Language Writing, 3*, 257–276.

Cumming, A. (1989). Writing expertise and second-language proficiency. *Language Learning, 39*, 81–141.

Cumming, A. (1992). Instructional routines in ESL composition teaching: A case study of three teachers. *Journal of Second Language Writing, 1*, 17–35.

Cumming, A. (2001). Learning to write in a second language: Two decades of research. *International Journal of English Studies, 1*, 1–23.

Dyson, A. (1987). Individual differences in beginning composing. *Written Communication, 9*, 411–442.

Dyson, A. (1991). The word and the world: Reconceptualizing written language development. *Research in the Teaching of English, 25*, 97–123.

Edelsky, C. (1983). Segmentation and punctuation: Developmental data from young writers in a bilingual program. *Research in the Teaching of English, 17*, 135–156.

Fazio, L. (2001). Effect of corrective feedback on dialog journal writing. *Journal of Second Language Writing, 10*, 235–249.

Fillmore, L. (1977). *The second time around: Cognitive and social strategies in second language acquisition*. Unpublished doctoral dissertation, Stanford University (UMI #77-77085).

Hansen-Strain, L. (1989). Orality/literacy and group differences in second-language acquisition. *Language Learning, 39*, 469–496.

John-Steiner, V., & Mahn, H. (1996). Sociocultural approaches to learning and development: A Vygotskian framework. *Educational Psychologist, 31*, 191–206.

Kroll, B. (1981). Developmental relationships between speaking and writing. In B. Kroll & R. Vann (Eds.), *Exploring speaking-writing relationships: Connections and contrasts* (pp. 32–54). Urbana IL: National Council of Teachers of English.

Lantolf, J. (Ed.). (2000). *Sociocultural theory and second language learning*. Oxford, England: Oxford University Press.

Lantolf, J., & Appel, G. (Eds.). (1994). *Vygotskian approaches to second language acquisition*. Norwood, NJ: Ablex.

LeCompte, M., & Preissle, J. (1993). *Ethnographic and qualitative design in educational research*. San Diego: Academic Press.

Leont'yev, A. (1969). Inner speech and the processes of grammatical generation of utterances. *Soviet Psychology, 7*, 11–16.

Luria, A. (1969). Speech development and the formation of mental processes. In M. Cole & I. Maltzman (Eds.), *A handbook of contemporary Soviet psychology* (pp. 121–162). New York: Basic Books.

McCafferty, S. (1992). The use of private speech by adult second language learners: A cross-cultural study. *Modern Language Journal, 76*, 179–189.

Nystrand, M. (1997). *Opening dialog: Understanding the dynamics of language and learning in the English classroom*. New York: Teachers College Press.

Peyton, J. (1990). The influence of writing tasks on ESL students' written production. *Research in the Teaching of English, 24*, 142–171.

Peyton, J., Staton, J., & Shuy, R. (1993). *Dialog journals in the multilingual classroom: Building language fluency and writing skills through written interaction*. Norwood, NJ: Ablex.

Prior, P. (2001). Voices in text, mind, and society: Sociohistoric accounts of discourse acquisition and use. *Journal of Second Language Writing, 10*, 55–81.

Qi, D., & Lapkin, S. (2001). Exploring the role of noticing in a three-stage second language writing task. *Journal of Second Language Writing, 10*, 277–303.

Shuy, R. (1987). Dialog as the heart of learning. *Language Arts, 64*, 890–897.

Tsui, A., & Ng, M. (2000). Do secondary L2 writers benefit from peer comments? *Journal of Second Language Writing, 9*, 147–170.

Valdés, G., Haro, P., & Echevarriarza, M. (1992). The development of writing abilities in a foreign language: Contributions toward a general theory of L2 writing. *Modern Language Journal, 76*, 333–352.

Vygotsky, L. (1986). *Thought and language*. Cambridge, MA: MIT Press.

Weissberg, R. (1994). Speaking of writing: Some functions of talk in the ESL composition class. *Journal of Second Language Writing, 3*, 121–139.

Weissberg, R. (1998). Acquiring English syntax through dialog journal writing. *College ESL, 8*, 1–22.

Weissberg, R. (2000). Developmental relationships in the acquisition of English syntax: Writing vs. speech. *Learning and Instruction, 10*, 37–53.

Wertsch, J. (1991). *Voices of the mind: A socio-cultural approach to mediated action*. Cambridge, MA: Harvard University Press.

Woodall, B. (2002). Language switching: Using the L1 while writing in an L2. *Journal of Second Language Writing, 11*, 7–28.

Zebroski, J. (1994). *Vygotskian perspective on the teaching of writing*. Portsmouth, NH: Boynton/Cook.

Zhu, W. (2001). Interaction and feedback in mixed peer response groups. *Journal of Second Language Writing, 10*, 251–276.

Zimmerman, R. (2000). L2 writing: Subprocesses, a model of formulating and empirical findings. *Learning and Instruction, 10*, 73–99.

8

Researching Teacher Evaluation of Second Language Writing via Prototype Theory

Richard Haswell
Texas A&M University, Corpus Christi, USA

I begin with a puzzle, a famous puzzle, one that I will solve in two ways. A pair of bicyclists, A and B, are 20 miles apart. They are moving toward each other in a straight line, each at 10 miles an hour. A fly takes off from the front rim of bicycle A and heads in a straight line toward bicycle B, flying at 15 miles an hour. As soon as it touches the front rim of bicycle B, it heads back to bicycle A, then back to bicycle B, and so on. (It may help to picture the fly as an industrious dean.) When the two bicycles meet and presumably the fly is squashed between the front tires, how far has it flown?

As I say, there are at least two ways to arrive at the answer, which happens to be 15 miles. One is to measure each leg of the fly's journey, taking into account the diminishing distance between bicycles with each leg, and to sum the infinite series—a method assisted greatly by calculus. The other way can be accomplished by people such as myself who never mastered calculus. It's an armchair method that reasons as follows. If the two bicyclists are 20 miles apart, each will have traveled 10 miles when they meet. If they are traveling at 10 miles an hour, they will meet in 1 hour. If the fly is flying at 15 miles an hour, then in 1 hour it will have traveled 15 miles.

I will return to this puzzle at the end of the chapter with an estimate of how far I have traveled. In the meantime, this puzzle gives me a place to start. Moving to the second way of solving it entails what cognitive scientists used to call a *frame shift*, or what creativity theorists used to call a *re-*

orientation. A mental blink switches us from miles covered to hours spent. I want to argue that today research into evaluation of student writing in general and teacher research into evaluation in particular could use a blink. Researchers are frame stuck and could use a re-orientation to change the way they solve problems. I am speaking of both evaluation of first language writing and evaluation of second language writing. Both fields are stuck in the same frame—not a surprise because both cycled through the last century so much in tandem, at least in terms of research methodology.

In this chapter, I am going to look directly at that uncomfortable and sometimes seamy side of L2 and L1 composition called *proficiency testing*. One instance of my topic is Linda Blanton's (chap. 11, this volume) student, Tran, and the examination hurdle he had to jump to get his degree. I am further focusing in on one practice of such testing—the construction and use of evaluative categories—categories such as "holistic level 2," "proficient," "band 3," and "ready for advanced composition." Actually, I will focus twice: once to critique these kinds of categories and again to recommend a quantified method by which to research them. Perhaps my procedure fits Tony Silva's (chap. 1, this volume) definition of *critical rationalism*. Certainly my critique extends beyond standardized testing and includes teachers, researchers, and students because all of them, every day, use value-laden categories in connection with student writing.

Dwight Atkinson (chap. 4, this volume) asks researchers to try to know people "on their own terms." But do people themselves know their terms, and do researchers know the terms by which they try to know people? These "terms" are almost always categories. The bind is that categories are normally obscure to the user of the categories, certainly the inner workings of them. This chapter is simply recommending to researchers "a tool for seeing the invisible," more exactly for seeing "the role of invisibility in the work that categorization does in ordering human interaction" (Bowker & Star, 2000, p. 5). The tool it recommends is not the only way out of the frame-stuck position of L1/L2 evaluation research, but it should be better known. As a tool of current critical rationalism, it is familiar to nearly every social science field except for composition studies. In gist the research method will help shift attention from the *application* of writing criteria to the *grounds* for writing criteria—a shift enabled with categorization theory, and a shift requiring a turn from the standardized to the local. It is a simple mental click, but every part of it turns out to be very complex. This chapter covers two somewhat separate steps of the shift. Part I looks at the way standardized testing categorizes essay writing criteria, and Part II looks at the way faculty could differently, and perhaps better, categorize essay writing main traits.

PART I: HOW BIG TESTING OPERATIONS CATEGORIZE ESSAY WRITING SKILLS

Historically, commercial testing firms have had a major hand in constructing the evaluative frame current among teachers and researchers. Consider the scoring sheet from Jacobs, Zinkgraf, Wormuth, Hartfiel, and Hughey's (1981) *Testing ESL Composition: A Practical Approach* (Fig. 8.1). The authors call it the "ESL Composition Profile." Since this scoring guide was published in 1981, it has proved very popular. It, or its offspring, will be familiar from workshop handouts or Xeroxes left behind in faculty coffee rooms. In its main features, it is no different than dozens of similar guides by which raters have decided, and continue to decide, the academic fate of thousands upon thousands of second language students. These main features are:

1. A limited number of basic criteria or main traits (e.g., content, organization, vocabulary, language use, and mechanics).
2. A fitting of each trait into a proficiency scale, the levels of which are also small in number and usually homologous or corresponding (e.g., 1, 2, 3, or 4 for each trait).
3. A breakdown of each trait into subtraits, which are also small in number and homologous or corresponding. See Table 8.1, which teases out the subtraits of the main trait *content* in Jacobs et al. There are four subtraits each with corresponding levels: knowledge of the topic, substance, development of the topic, and relevance. The homology, it should be noted, does not allow for a writer who has "a limited knowledge" of the topic, yet applies what little she or he knows in a way that is "relevant" to the topic.

This hidden feature of homology, very significant, has been little discussed by composition researchers. The "ESL Composition Profile" is lauded because it is just that—a *profile* of the student, not a *categorization* of the student. It encourages an evaluation of student proficiency that is complex, perhaps recording high accomplishment in content, but low in mechanics—a complexity that befits writers who often show uneven writing skills in a second language. In this the profile contrasts with holistic scoring methods, which erase this possible unevenness of writing accomplishments in reporting a single score. But, in fact the kind of rating that underlies the "ESL Composition Profile" is identical to holistic rating. The "Profile" just asks the rater to perform the holistic five times. In short—this is the emphasis I put on it—both methods of scoring ask the rater to apply the same *kind of categorization*.

ESL COMPOSITION PROFILE

STUDENT DATE TOPIC

	SCORE	LEVEL	CRITERIA	COMMENTS
CONTENT		30-27	EXCELLENT TO VERY GOOD: knowledgeable • substantive • thorough development of thesis • relevant to assigned topic	
		26-22	GOOD TO AVERAGE: some knowledge of subject • adequate range • limited development of thesis • mostly relevant to topic, but lacks detail	
		21-17	FAIR TO POOR: limited knowledge of subject • little substance • inadequate development of topic	
		16-13	VERY POOR: does not show knowledge of subject • non-substantive • not pertinent • OR not enough to evaluate	
ORGANIZATION		20-18	EXCELLENT TO VERY GOOD: fluent expression • ideas clearly stated/supported • succinct • well-organized • logical sequencing • cohesive	
		17-14	GOOD TO AVERAGE: somewhat choppy • loosely organized but main ideas stand out • limited support • logical but incomplete sequencing	
		13-10	FAIR TO POOR: non-fluent • ideas confused or disconnected • lacks logical sequencing and development	
		9-7	VERY POOR: does not communicate • no organization • OR not enough to evaluate	
VOCABULARY		20-18	EXCELLENT TO VERY GOOD: sophisticated range • effective word/idiom choice and usage • word form mastery • appropriate register	
		17-14	GOOD TO AVERAGE: adequate range • occasional errors of word/idiom form, choice, usage *but meaning not obscured*	
		13-10	FAIR TO POOR: limited range • frequent errors of word/idiom form, choice, usage • *meaning confused or obscured*	
		9-7	VERY POOR: essentially translation • little knowledge of English vocabulary, idioms, word form • OR not enough to evaluate	
LANGUAGE USE		25-22	EXCELLENT TO VERY GOOD: effective complex constructions • few errors of agreement, tense, number, word order/function, articles, pronouns, prepositions	
		21-18	GOOD TO AVERAGE: effective but simple constructions • minor problems in complex constructions • several errors of agreement, tense, number, word order/function, articles, pronouns, prepositions *but meaning seldom obscured*	
		17-11	FAIR TO POOR: major problems in simple/complex constructions • frequent errors of negation, agreement, tense, number, word order/function, articles, pronouns, prepositions and/or fragments, run-ons, deletions • *meaning confused or obscured*	
		10-5	VERY POOR: virtually no mastery of sentence construction rules • dominated by errors • does not communicate • OR not enough to evaluate	
MECHANICS		5	EXCELLENT TO VERY GOOD: demonstrates mastery of conventions • few errors of spelling, punctuation, capitalization, paragraphing	
		4	GOOD TO AVERAGE: occasional errors of spelling, punctuation, capitalization, paragraphing *but meaning not obscured*	
		3	FAIR TO POOR: frequent errors of spelling, punctuation, capitalization, paragraphing • poor handwriting • *meaning confused or obscured*	
		2	VERY POOR: no mastery of conventions • dominated by errors of spelling, punctuation, capitalization, paragraphing • handwriting illegible • OR not enough to evaluate	

TOTAL SCORE READER COMMENTS

FIG. 8.1. ESL Composition Profile (Jacobs et al., 1981).

TABLE 8.1
Breakdown of Subtrait Levels for the Main Trait of Content in Figure 1 (Jacobs et al., 1981, p. 30), Showing Homology of Levels

Level	*Subtrait 1*	*Subtrait 2*	*Subtrait 3*	*Subtrait 4*
Points	*Knowledge*	*Substance*	*Development*	*Relevance*
30–27	Knowledgeable	Substantive	Thorough development of thesis	Relevant to assigned topic
26–22	Some knowledge of subject	Adequate range	Limited development of thesis	Mostly relevant to topic, but lacks detail
21–17	Limited knowledge of subject	Little substance	Inadequate development [of topic]	Inadequate [relevance to] topic
16–13	Does not show knowledge of subject	Nonsubstantive	Not enough to evaluate	Not pertinent

I will return to this fact later in this chapter, but first it is worth observing how the features of holistic or profile scoring lend themselves to the kind of evaluation research that has dominated L2 and L1 composition studies for decades. The limited number of traits allows comparison of group rating behavior, perhaps contrasting the way native and non-native faculty evaluate ESL essays. The scaling of traits and subtraits allows study of rater reliability along with the development of training methods that produce high interrater reliability coefficients needed to defend commercial testing or research studies. The reduction of uneven and otherwise complex writing proficiency to units, and the internal ordering of traits or subtraits as homologous and mutually exclusive, allow the generation of empirical outcomes useful in research, placement, and program validation.

Here comes the blink. What happens when the "ESL Composition Profile" sheet is re-oriented with a new question? The five main traits, whose names in fact are oriented differently than the rest of the words on the sheet (see Fig. 8.1)—where did they come from? The question does not ask how well they function as parts of a performance-evaluation mechanism. I am asking who put these main traits into the mechanism and why, not how well they work once put there. Factor analysis of scores produced by this mechanism, for instance, might eliminate one of these traits if it contributes no unique information to the profile, but it could not find another and better trait for replacement. The question asks why content, organization, vocabulary, language use, and mechanics and not creativity, logic, suspense, tradition, shock-appeal, humor, cleverness—and the list could go on.

The question is not trivial or irrelevant. The criteria not chosen shape the outcomes as much as those that are chosen. Now it happens that the origin of these five main traits of the "ESL Composition Profile" is known, and the providence may be surprising. They came from grades and marginal comments written on student homework. The graders and commenters included a few teachers, but most were social scientists, natural scientists, workplace editors, lawyers, and business executives. None of them had TESOL experience. The writers were first-year students at Cornell, Middlebury College, and the University of Pennsylvania, probably none of them second language students. This was in 1958 (Diederich, 1974; Diederich et al., 1961). Three researchers at Educational Testing Services (ETS) factored the commentary, passed the factoring on to a colleague of theirs at ETS, Paul Angelis, who passed it on to the authors of the "ESL Composition profile" (Jacobs et al., 1981). In the relay, one of the original five factors, flavor, got dropped, and another, wording, got divided into vocabulary and language use, but no new factors were added. So the main criteria of a popular L2 essay rating method were derived not from L2 essays, nor from L2 teachers, nor much from teachers at all.

Main traits of other long-lived second language writing tests probably have equally troubling and mysterious histories (Table 8.2). I do not know the archaeology of these categorizations. To find out would make a fascinating study, but I suspect many of them originated with a certain amount of blithe. Certainly the following rationale by David P. Harris is blithely expressed. Harris was the project director of the TOEFL exam from 1963 to 1965, and his comment appears in his 1969 book, *Testing English as a Second Language*: "Although the writing process has been analyzed in many different ways, most teachers would probably agree in recognizing at least the following five general components: Content, Form, Grammar, Style, Mechanics" (pp. 68–69).

TABLE 8.2
Main Traits of Scoring Rubrics for Six Tests of ESL Writing

Test	*Trait*
Test in English for Educational Purposes (Associated Examining Board)	*Content* *Organization* *Cohesion* *Vocabulary* *Grammar* *Punctuation* *Spelling*
Certificate in Communicative Skills in English (Royal Society of Arts/University of Cambridge Local Examinations Syndicate)	*Accuracy* [of mechanics] *Appropriacy* *Range* [of expression] *Complexity* [organization and cohesion]
Test of Written English (Educational Testing Service)	*Length* *Organization* *Evidence* *Style* *Grammar* *Sentences*
Michigan English Language Battery	*Topic development* *Sentences* *Organization/coherence* *Vocabulary* *Mechanics*
Canadian Test of English for Scholars and Trainees	*Content* *Organization* *Language use*
International English Language Testing System	*Register* *Rhetorical organization* *Style* *Content*

PART II: HOW RESEARCHERS AND TEACHERS MIGHT CATEGORIZE ESSAY WRITING SKILLS

In fact most teachers do not agree, certainly not ESL teachers, and certainly not on the assumption, which Harris implies, that these five components are equally important. The question is how can teacher researchers find out what they do agree on? I am turning to teacher researchers because I do not have much faith that the giant testing firms will ever change their ways. There are many inquiry methods, "tools for seeing the invisible," to ferret out main traits, ranging from rater think-aloud protocols to participant/observer ethnography of rating groups. Some of this inquiry is and has been going on, some of it both massive and complex—calculus solutions. The International Association for the Evaluation of Educational Achievement project of the early 1980s explored 28 criteria (Purves & Takala, 1982), and Grabe and Kaplan's (1996) taxonomy of language knowledge erects 20 main categories encompassing 41 distinct traits, to mention one old and one recent study. The remainder of this chapter offers a less onerous method, an armchair procedure, if you will. It is a procedure based on prototype categorization theory.

To start, let me review the sociocognitive prototype model of categorization. Prototype categorization stands in opposition to classical notions of category definition that centuries of Aristotelian logic have formed and that seem almost too obvious to question. A classical category of writing evaluation—say "writing mechanics"—has a fixed set of defining features that provide the category with absolute boundaries. Things—say a failure to spell conventionally the word *America*—fall into the category or not. Members within a category, then, belong there equally. An incorrect full stop is no less good an instance of writing mechanics than a misspelling of *America*. Compared to this *classical* categorization, *prototypical* categorization operates quite differently. It does not fix a set of defining features, but rather organizes itself around a best example or prototype. Members of the category stand closer or further from this prototype. Members or parts of a category are not equal—they have different degrees of centrality or "goodness of part" (this quality of prototype categories is sometimes called *graded structure*). Some members are so marginal that they may be closer to the prototype of another category. Hence, prototypical categories do not have boundaries. They overlap with other categories, and instances may belong equally to two different categories. The title of Kafka's novel, which spells *America* with a "k," may belong equally to mechanics, style, or creativity. Other kinds of categorization have been explored, of course, and argument continues over their use and interrelationships in the evaluation of human performance (for reviews of the theory, see Hampton, 1993; Haswell, 1998; Lakoff, 1987).

But there should be little argument that commercial essay testing must treat prototypical categorization as anathema. Consider again the "ESL Composition Profile" (Fig. 8.1). At no less than three points, the procedure is structured classically: the overall categorization of "writing proficiency" with its five defining features, content, organization, vocabulary, language use, and mechanics; the "mastery levels," again with absolute boundaries, as the scale points make clear; and the subtraits, separate but homologous (Table 8.1). Prototypical categorization would destroy this system of evaluation. It would certainly scrap the overall configuration of the "ESL Composition Profile" as all compartments and right angles, a fearful symmetry that, among other things, expresses a fear of overdetermination and overlap. To note just one fear, conceptual slippage would lead directly to a slip in the interrater reliability coefficient.

What's wrong with the Profile's classical way of categorizing as a means of evaluation? Two generations of categorization researchers, who have explored the way prototype categorizing affects evaluation of human performance in nearly every area imaginable, offer a clear and even unforgiving answer. The trouble with classical categorization is that it doesn't account for the way people normally categorize. People do judge some misspellings of *America* as worse than others, some even as clever and a matter of style, not mechanics, some even as thoughtful and a matter of content and not a matter of mechanics at all. "Every category observed so far," summarizes Lawrence Barsalou (1987), "has been found to have graded structure" (p. 111).

Some researchers in second language acquisition have participated in this robust inquiry into typicality effects. Lindstromberg (1996) worked with the teaching of prepositions as graded categories, and Taylor (1995) masterfully treated grammatical and lexical concepts as prototypical. But as far as I know, no one has studied how the human rating or grading of L2 essays categorizes in prototypical ways. Yet so much of what a writing teacher does is categorizing. To put a "B" on a paper is to pigeonhole it in the category of "B work." To read a placement essay and assign the writer to the second level of an ESL curricular sequence is to categorize the writing as "intermediary work." To judge an ESL writer's exit portfolio from first-year composition as successful is to place it in the basket labeled "ready for advanced composition." These are all acts of categorization, and the last 30 years of psychological and sociological research into the way people categorize would argue that only by a miracle would these acts follow Aristotelian rules, would not show prototype effects.

Let me take the last example—end-of-first-year proficiency—and use it to show what one piece of writing evaluation research based on prototype theory might look like. For this chapter, I ran a preliminary, online study to demonstrate the method. My research question was this: In making decisions about end-of-first-year writing proficiency, do L2 teachers categorize writing traits differently in their evaluation of L2 writers than do L1 teachers L1 writing? For traits, I selected 10 from the Council of Writing Program Administrator's (2000) recent Writing Outcomes document, the 10 that can be most readily inferred from written text (Table 8.3). I applied a matched guise design, with two groups of teachers evaluating the same essay under difference preconceptions. One group, L1 teachers, believed it was written by an L1 writer; the other group, L2 teachers, believed it was written by an L2 writer. Finally, and most crucially, I had each participant first rate each trait (on a 7-point Likert scale) in terms of its centrality in their evaluation of first-year writing accomplishment. Note that this teacher-rater generalized judgment of the 10 traits preceded their specific rating of an essay in terms of the traits. In this way, although the procedure ended up generating a profile of one student's essay along a set number of writing traits, just as in the "ESL Composition Profile," it produced further information—namely, how central the raters thought those traits were.

This experiment did not escape some of the problems of online research. Control of participant selection was weak, and the conditions under which participants performed the evaluation could not be regularized. Also the number of participants (43 L2 teachers and 57 L1 teachers) was too low to support thorough inference testing of 10 traits. Therefore, although the experiment was conducted with all the rigor the conditions allowed, I offer the findings only as illustrative. They do argue the feasibility of prototypical inquiry in L1/L2 research and suggest the method's potential in challenging traditional evaluation research, little of which is based on any other assumptions than those of classical categorization.

Let me first look at the second step of the evaluation, in what seems like rather astonishing support for traditional evaluation (Table 8.4). At this

TABLE 8.3
Ten Essay Writing Traits Selected From the Writing Program Administrators Outcomes Statement for First-Year Composition

Short Form	*Description*
Audience	Responds to the needs of the readers
Documentation	Uses appropriate means of documenting the writing
Inquiry	Shows the use of inquiry, learning, thinking
Integration	Integrates their ideas with the ideas of others
Purpose	Focuses on and conveys the purpose for the writing
Situation	Responds appropriately to the rhetorical situation
Sources	Uses sources conventionally and well
Structure	Arrangement or format fits the rhetorical situation
Surface	Is in control of surface features (spelling, etc.)
Voice	Adopts an appropriate voice, tone, formality

TABLE 8.4
Rating of One Essay Under Two Preconceptions ("ESL" and "Native"*) by Two Sets of Readers ("ESL," N = 43, L2 Teachers; "Native," N = 59, L1 Teachers) on a Likert Scale (7 = *high proficiency*, 1 = *low proficiency*)

ESL		*Native*	
Scale $\bar{X}$ (SD)	*Trait*	*Scale $\bar{X}$ (SD)*	*Trait*
5.54 *(1.05)*	Voice	4.44 *(1.61)*	Documentation
5.35 *(1.43)*	Documentation	4.41 *(1.46)*	Voice
4.65 *(1.73)*	Purpose	3.73 *(1.74)*	Purpose
4.61 *(1.53)*	Inquiry	3.66 *(1.46)*	Inquiry
4.30 *(1.34)*	Audience	3.60 *(1.26)*	Audience
3.98 *(1.63)*	Sources	3.53 *(1.48)*	Structure
3.95 *(1.45)*	Structure	3.53 *(1.71)*	Sources
3.88 *(1.62)*	Situation	3.34 *(1.21)*	Situation
3.88 *(1.31)*	Surface	3.27 *(1.57)*	Integration
3.84 *(1.63)*	Integration	3.05 *(1.56)*	Surface

*ESL readers assumed the writer was NNS, from South Korea; native readers assumed the writer was NS, from the U.S. midwest.

point in the experiment, all teachers had been shown the same student essay and asked to rate it in terms of the 10 WPA Outcomes traits. As I have said, the 43 teachers with L2 teaching experience had been led to believe that the essay was written by an ESL student. They understood that the writer was born in Korea and immigrated to the United States 3 years ago. The other 57 teachers, with little or no L2 teaching experience, were led to believe that the essay was written by an NES student, born and raised in the midwest of the United States. Yet the two groups generated evaluation profiles—rankings of the accomplishment of the essay along the 10 WPA traits—that are remarkably similar. On 10 traits and at any point, the group means do not differ by more than one rank. L1 and L2 writing teachers, as rating groups, seem to concur on this essay's writing success regardless of their differing presuppositions about the writer's language status.

Another finding shown here (also shown in Table 8.4) is even more consistent, although it has been reported before in ESL research (see Silva, 1989, for a review). With every WPA trait, the ESL-assumed writer is rated more highly than the native language-assumed writer. In the online discussion among the participants that followed my presentation of this finding, several L1 teachers suggested that the finding shows the generosity of L2 teachers in rating L2 writing. But it is more reasonably explained in terms of the possible parameters of accomplishment imagined by the two rater groups. The L1 teachers were locating the essay within the typical range of end-of-first-year writing performance of L1 writers and the L2 teachers within the range of L2 writers. In effect the two groups were applying the Likert scale (*least proficient* at one end, *most proficient* at the other) to two different imagined populations of student writers. But however the difference in leniency is explained, Table 8.4 seems to show L1 and L2 teachers agreeing on the 10 WPA traits in terms of essay accomplishment with remarkable consistency.

But when we look at the way the two teacher groups judged these 10 traits in terms of centrality or goodness of part, we see that maybe this L2–L1 teacher concordance is deceptive and hides some deep disagreements. The disagreements are over the internal categorization of these traits vis-à-vis language status. As I mentioned earlier, the two groups had rated the same 10 traits according to their centrality as measures of end-of-first-year proficiency. One group rated them for L2 writers, the other for L1 writers. Table 8.4 shows the group means for each trait on a 7-point Likert scale, with 7 being the *most central*, 1 the *least central*. The main prompt for participants is a standard one in prototype research (adapted from Tversky & Hemenway, 1984): "How central is the trait in terms of judging first-year writing accomplishment of the ESL writers [or NES writers] at your university?" After an illustration of "centrality," the prompt ended: "Keep in mind that you are judging the goodness of each trait in showing an ESL [or NES] writer's readiness to exit first-year writing instruction." Comparison of the group means on these 10 traits finds the two groups agreeing on the three most central traits. Whether the student is writing in a first or second language, the prototype or best example of first-year writing proficiency is a well-organized essay with a definite purpose appropriate to the rhetorical situation. At this point, the two groups appear to diverge. Three traits that might fall under Jacobs et al.'s (1981) rubric of mechanics—documentation, surface conventions such as spelling, and appropriate use of sources—are taken as next most central with L1 writers, but as most marginal with L2 writers. Two traits that reflect depth of thinking—integration of the ideas of others and demonstration of inquiry and learning—are more central in the L2 writers and more marginal in the L1.

But rank alone does not show what I think is the most striking finding here. Rather, it is comparative centrality or goodness of part. Notice in Table 8.4 how each trait is judged more central to first-year writing proficiency for L1 writers and less central for L2 writers. In fact for L2 writers, L2 faculty judged 7 of the 10 traits as less central than L1 faculty judged all 10 of the traits for L1 writers. Figure 8.2, which maps the difference in a way sympathetic to the concept of prototypicality, raises disturbing questions. Here is the most dramatic way of putting the findings: On every trait used to judge a particular essay, the presumed L2 writer was rated more

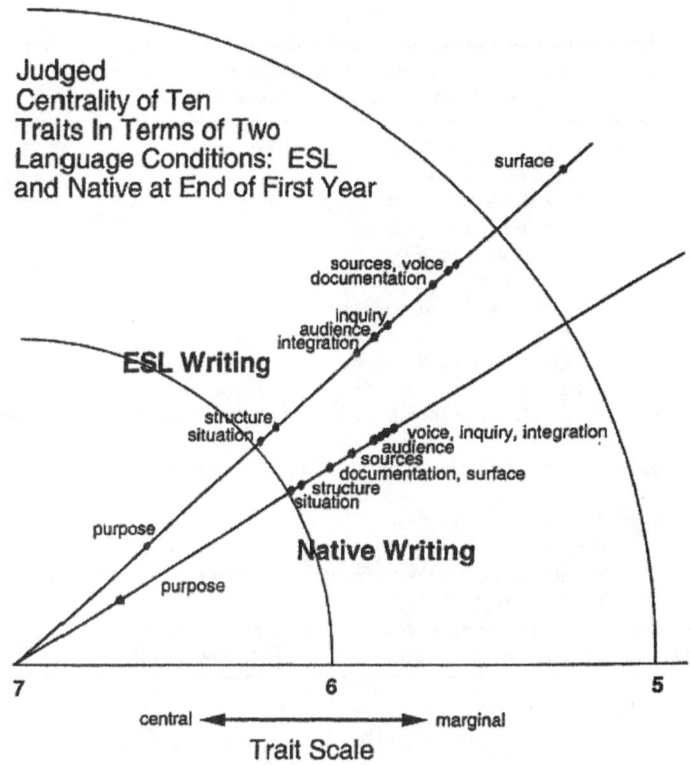

FIG. 8.2. Judged centrality of ten traits in terms of two language conditions: ESL and NES at the end of the first year.

highly than the presumed L1 writer; yet on every trait used to judge student writers as a group, the L2 proficiency was judged more marginal than the L1 proficiency. What prototypical categorization giveth, prototypical classification taketh away.

Or maybe it seems that way only at first. Prototypical inquiry returns—as it always will—to my re-orienting question. Where do these main traits come from? How does one interpret this preliminary finding that traits selected by the WPA Outcomes group, all of whom were L1 teachers, do not well fit L2 teachers' conception of L2 proficiency? Do these selected traits, sanctioned by a major organization of U.S. writing program administrators, marginalize second language students? Or does proficiency at a certain point in time, in this case at the end of the first year of college, occupy a less central place in the minds of L2 teachers when they think of L2 students and their writing growth? Or does this set of traits fit the second language teachers' notion of end-of-first-year accomplishment in writing, but just not fit as well? In that case, what more central traits are missing? Table

TABLE 8.5
Traits Judged by College Writing Teachers (L1 N = 43; L2 N = 59) as Useful to the Evaluation of First-Year Writing Proficiency and Missing From the 10 Research Traits

Suggested Traits Common to Both L1 and L2 Teachers	
Syntax	Variation and complexity
Development	Of a thesis statement
Support	With detail and specifics
Cohesion	Transitions, etc.
Revision	Evidence of
Vocabulary	Sophistication and variety
Suggested Traits Unique to L1 Teachers	
Fluency	Putting ideas into words
Ideas	Complexity, elaboration, sophistication, meaningfulness, larger relevance
Interpretation	Of the assignment, or thoughtful response to the research question
Suggested Traits Unique to L2 Teachers	
Fluency	Sustained length
Affectivity	Enthusiasm, curiosity, engagement with the topic, positive attitude toward writing
Argumentation	Multiple perspectives, covering opposing arguments
Originality	Creativity, departures from standard essay structure

8.5 provides an initial answer to this final query. I asked research participants—both L1 and L2 teachers—to provide traits that they felt were important in judging first-year proficiency, but were missing from the WPA 10. In several areas, L2 teachers identified proficiencies that contrast with those mentioned by L1 teachers: depth of ideas as opposed to depth of affect or sophistication of argument, interpretation of the issues as opposed to originality of essay construction. The contrasts hint at directions that prototype research models might take the study of ESL evaluation.

At this point, let me insert a comment on inference testing of the centrality data (Table 8.4, Fig. 8.2). Problems in the collection of those data preclude the validation of this particular study with such testing, but I performed some of it anyway, again as a demonstration of method. As an omnibus testing of group performance, a simple t test can be used for significant difference between the grand mean of the Likert scale ratings for all 10 traits. Because for each of these traits the mean rating of my L2 raters was more marginal than that of the L1 raters, it is not surprising that the grand mean difference between the two groups was statistically significant (L2 raters, X 5.55, SD 0.78; L1 raters, X 5.84, SD 0.65; T 2.02; $p < .046$). t tests can also be applied separately to the Likert scale ratings on each of the 10 traits. With this study, two showed significant differences: documentation (L2 raters, X 5.30, SD 1.36; L1 raters, X 5.78, SD 1.19; T 1.96; $p <$

.053), and surface (L2 raters, *X* 4.74, *SD* 1.65; L1 raters, *X* 5.80, *SD* 1.03; *T* 3.96; $p < .000$). Finally, intraclass correlations can be run among raters of each group along the 10 trait ratings to judge the degree to which faculty agree in their prototypical structuring of the category "end-of-first-year proficiency." Here concordance among raters in both groups (L2, median *r* .26; L1, median *r* .32) fell within but toward the bottom of the range that has been found in other goodness-of-part studies (cf. Tversky & Hemenway, 1984).

I have just enough space to turn from this exploratory study back to the larger issue—the timelines of prototype research in L2 writing evaluation. Most important, prototype inquiry can help explore unacknowledged presuppositions not only of teachers, but of students and even commercial test designers. Nor is its potential confined to questions of evaluation. Everywhere there are terms, and the terms are categorizations that could use some deconstruction. To mention just one research question raised in this volume, methods of exploring structures of centrality could well provide the grounding that Rosa Manchón (chap. 14, this volume) argues ethnographers need for the codes through which they analyze participant transcripts. As just noted, prototype inquiry does not require high-end statistics, either descriptive or inferential. Although it demands the same rigor as any other research, it is a method that can locate new and striking results and do so with armchair calculations.

This brings me back to the puzzle of the bicycles and the fly. As I noted, it can be solved with a complex equation entailing the summing of an infinite series, or it can be solved with a simple division of distance by time. A student once challenged John von Neumann with the puzzle. Mathematically, von Neumann, it may be remembered, had one of the swiftest calculating minds of the last century. He gave the correct answer within a couple of seconds. "Oh, you knew the trick," said the disappointed student. "What trick?" said von Neumann, "I just summed the infinite series." There will always be people who find the difficult way easy. Prototype analysis is for them, too.

REFERENCES

Barsalou, L. W. (1987). The instability of graded structure: Implications for the nature of concepts. In U. Neisser (Ed.), *Concepts and conceptual development: Ecological and intellectual factors in categorization* (pp. 101–140). Cambridge, England: Cambridge University Press.

Bowker, G., & Star, S. (2000). *Sorting things out: Classification and its consequences*. Cambridge, MA: MIT Press.

The Council of Writing Program Administrators. (2000). *Outcomes statement for first-year composition*. http://www.english.ilstu.edu/Hesse/outcomes.html. Accessed Oct. 2002.

Diederich, P. B. (1974). *Measuring growth in English*. Urbana, IL: National Council of Teachers of English.

Diederich, P. B., French, J. W., & Carlton, S. T. (1961). *Factors in judgments of writing ability* (ETS Research Bulletin RB-61-15). Princeton, NJ: Educational Testing Service (ERIC *Document Reproduction Service*, ED 002 172).

Grabe, W., & Kaplan, R. B. (1996). *Theory and practice of writing: An applied linguistic perspective*. London: Longman.

Hampton, J. A. (1993). Prototype models of concept representation. In I. van Mechelen, J. A. Hampton, R. S. Michalski, & P. Theuns (Eds.), *Categories and concepts: Theoretical views and inductive data analysis* (pp. 67–95). London: Academic Press.

Harris, D. P. (1969). *Testing English as a second language*. New York: McGraw-Hill.

Haswell, R. H. (1998). Rubrics, prototypes, and exemplars: Categorization theory and systems of writing placement. *Assessing Writing, 5*, 231–268.

Jacobs, H. L., Zinkgraf, S. A., Wormuth, D. R., Hartfiel, V. F., & Hughey, J. B. (1981). *Testing ESL composition; A practical approach*. Rowley, MA: Newbury House.

Lakoff, G. (1987). *Women, fire, and dangerous things: What categories reveal about the mind*. Chicago: University of Chicago Press.

Lindstromberg, S. (1996). Prepositions: Meaning and method. *ELT Journal, 50*, 225–236.

Purves, A. C., & Takala, S. (Eds.). (1982). *An international perspective on the evaluation of written communication*. New York: Pergamon.

Silva, T. (1989). A review of research on the evaluation of ESL writing. ERIC *Document Reproduction Service, ED* 409 643.

Taylor, J. R. (1995). *Linguistic categorization: Prototypes in linguistic theory* (2nd ed.). Oxford: Oxford University Press.

Tversky, B., & Hemenway, K. (1984). Objects, parts, and categories. *Journal of Experimental Psychology: General, 113*, 169–193.

9

Composing Culture in a Fragmented World: The Issue of Representation in Cross-Cultural Research

Xiaoming Li
Long Island University, USA

Lester Faigley (1992), in his *Fragments of Rationality: Postmodernity and the Subject of Composition*, traces the trajectory of the emergence and fast ascendance of postmodern theory in an era of postmodernity.[1] It is an era, he asserts, that glorifies uninhibited "self-gratification and hedonism to keep the economy expanding" (p. 10), an era in which the desire of consumers, nevertheless, can never be completely fulfilled, and only by purchasing and using a consumer object can insatiable consumers "occupy an imagined identity," an identity inherently both temporary and unstable (p. 13). This relentless economic expansion is also the chief engine driving globalization, which has evoked deep resentment and open hostility in some parts of the world, yet in other parts is seen as a direct path to prosperity and democracy, it is welcomed and embraced. Postmodernity, Faigley concludes, is an age of fragmentation, multiplicity, drifting, plurality, and intensity.

After the publication of so many monographs, journal articles, and conference papers in the last decade or so, postmodern theory has become a

[1]In his book, Faigley (1992) identifies three metadiscourses on postmodernism: "(1) aesthetic discussions of postmodernism; (2) philosophical discussions of postmodern theory; and (3) sociohistorical assertions that Western nations, if not indeed all the world, have entered an era of postmodernity" (p. 6). He further explicates that postmodernity, the last of the three, is about "a more general cultural condition" of our time (p. 9). Such a condition creates a postmodern sensibility, and the effects of these "major economic and cultural shifts" are the concern of postmodern theory.

fixture in the intellectual landscape of the West. By now, many, myself included, have come to accept the premise of postmodernism that language is not a transparent, innocent, or disinterested mediator between the world and our consciousness. And most of us have responded to, if not been totally persuaded by, Foucault's (1975) powerful argument that links all forms of "the will to knowledge" and all modes of cultural representation of "the Other," more or less explicitly, to the exercise of power. As he puts it in *Discipline and Punish*, discourse "produce[s] reality; it produces domains of objects and rituals of truth" (p. 194). By now few of us would employ words like *self*, *reason*, *knowledge*, *objectivity*, *truth*, *universal*, or *natural* without first acknowledging or pausing to contemplate their problematic implications and applications. Thanks to the pervasiveness of postmodern theory over the last two decades in Western academic institutions, where most of us reside, we have come to be aware that truth is opaque, that knowledge is rhetorical and socially constructed, and, probably most relevant to my chapter here, that all categories of identity are instable, permeable, and multiple.

All this poses a special challenge to the study of contrastive rhetoric, which is based on the premise that "language and writing are cultural phenomena" (Connor, 1999, p. 5). If the very label of *Chinese writers*, for instance, is a rhetorical and social construct that, according to one respected scholar, "sanction[s] an ethnocentric stance" that "can lead us to stigmatize, to generalize, and to make inaccurate predictions" (Spack, 1998, p. 765), what is the justification or legitimacy for research that aims to understand and characterize them as a stable and bounded entity at least when we fix our gaze on them? If we erase the borders of all group identities, splintering culturally identified and grouped ESL students into unique individuals (i.e., just as unique as any native speakers), how do we acknowledge, still less attend to, the special needs of our students who come from non-English-speaking linguistic and educational backgrounds? If we have learned anything about language and discourse from postmodern theory, we have also learned this: no name, no representation. Ironed flat of their group identity, these students will blur into an undifferentiated blanket of individuals and fall into a cognitive black hole.

In my chapter, I focus on the question of representation—an issue I first encountered when working on my doctoral dissertation, which I later revised and published under the title, *"Good Writing" in Cross-Cultural Context* (1996), and continued to wrestle with in another project that has been published recently as a chapter in the book, *Writing and Learning in Cross-National Perspective* (2002). I reflect on how my grappling with the issue of representation shaped the modes of inquiry and specific designs of those projects, although the final answer about representation still eludes me. I then come back to the challenges confronting us by briefly pondering the meaning of two key terms in the debate: culture and essentialism. Finally, I suggest that, as we continue to pursue contrastive rhetoric—an enterprise that has yielded a great many insights into the cultural dynamics of ESL writing classes and will offer still more—we should not continue business as usual, but rather should engage in a rigorous examination of the philosophical and political underpinnings of our research methodology as this book calls us to do.

From the beginning, the issue of representation was thrust on me as a highly political and philosophical matter, as I entered the doctoral program in what was then known as Composition Studies and Literature at the University of New Hampshire in 1987. In the same year, Stephen North (1987) published his *The Making of Knowledge in Composition*, in which he declares, "There is a methodological war being fought, but it takes place, as it were, behind the scenes" (p. 352). He warns if we avoid this war, the field of composition "will lose any autonomous identity altogether" (p. 365). It was no coincidence that it was also the time that postmodern theory started to make headway in composition studies, following its tremendous gains in literary criticism. The paradigm shift was the talk of the town. A host of publications at this time questioned the validity of the so-called "scientific" mode of inquiry—the very means, North reminded us, that had elevated composition to a respected discipline only two decades before.

This "scientific" mode of inquiry was critiqued simultaneously on two fronts, the political and philosophical. The former was represented by James Berlin's momentous essay in 1988, "Rhetoric and Ideology in the Writing Class." In that piece, Berlin criticized Linda Flower's use of protocol analysis, a methodology borrowed from the cognitive psychology, as "eminently suited to appropriation by the proponents of a particular ideological stance, a stance consistent with the modern college's commitment to preparing students for the world of corporate capitalism" (p. 482). His thesis, which posits that cloaked in the pursuit of objective truth, science is implicated in perpetuating the oppressive and unjust status quo, has since been echoed in a vast number of publications.

On the philosophical front, the differences among the modes of research were delineated in equally stark dichotomous terms. Lincoln and Guba (1985), for example, draw the field into two sharply divided paradigms, the naturalistic and the traditional scientific, and argue that the two paradigms are based on opposing epistemology, the positivistic and the phenomenological, which differ on such basic philosophical assumptions as the nature of reality, the subject–object relationship, and the nature of "truth." According to Lincoln and Guba, formalist and experimental studies are traditional methods born out of the scientific paradigm, whereas case studies and ethnography, with their attention to contextuality, best embody the naturalistic paradigm.

Maybe because I was brought up in a culture that believes in the intertwining and codependency of opposites instead of their sharp division and mutual exclusion, I was suspicious of such good-versus-evil or right-versus-wrong arguments. Yet I was quite receptive, or susceptible, one might say, to narratives steeped in the complexity of real-life experience. The small book, *The Double Helix* (Watson, 1968), for example, captures the atmosphere of the early postwar years in England, where the discovery took place and many of the often accidental encounters and relationships of the people involved. It shows, as its Nobel Prize-winning author writes in the beginning, that "science seldom proceeds in the straightforward logical manner imagined by outsiders. Instead, its steps forward (and sometimes backward) are often very human events in which personalities and cultural traditions play major roles" (p. ix).

Jane Tompkins' (1986) "Indians," a shorter narrative, recounts her futile search for an objective history of the Puritan's relations with Native Americans. What she found were accounts that were "not simply contradictory," but some "completely incommensurable, in that their assumptions about what counted as a valid approach to the subject and what the subject itself was, diverged in fundamental ways." Her project, which started as a search for what happened at one historical time, changed "to the question of how knowledge is arrived at" (p. 103). If Berlin (1988) was careful not to place subjects "within a seamless web of inescapable, wholly determinative power relations" (p. 478), Tompkins seems to carry his arguments straight to their logical conclusion, where she found an "epistemological quandary" that entraps all. She concludes with a mea culpa, typical of the postmodern ethos whose epistemological confidence is all but gone: "The historian can never escape the limitations of his or her own position in history and so inevitably gives an account that is an extension of the circumstances from which it springs" (p. 115). So the issue is not whether researchers are being truthful in reporting facts or whether they are friendly to those they observe, but that all researchers are confined by their own historical and cultural situatedness and can only see what that position allows them to see even when they are looking carefully and earnestly at the "other."

With all this reading and thinking, I had an outline map of dos and don'ts as I started contemplating my doctoral dissertation. When I decided to examine teachers' comments on student papers in China and the United States, I knew searching for a set of objective and "fair" criteria for good writing would be as futile as chasing a mirage, so I decided to focus instead on teachers' perspectives on good writing. I knew that I would not just report on writing teachers in action, on how they respond to and evaluate student writing, as a good journalist would do, but that I would also study what is not immediately apparent (i.e., the cultural and historical forces that propelled them to act one way or another, as well as their particular locale in each country, their educational and literary background, personal beliefs, teaching environment—all the materiality that informed and shaped each teacher's views and praxis on "good writing"). I also knew that only an ethnographic study like Shirley Brice Heath's (1983) could accurately capture "the material conditions of a particular time and place" (Therborn, 1980; cited in Berlin, 1988, p. 478). Yet I also understood that if I wanted to make any claims about a cultural practice, I needed, as North advised, to check the typicality of my findings against a larger sample. So I envisioned the shape of the project to be like a pyramid built from the top, starting from a few "key" participants, whose praxis I would examine in full contextuality, and then have their judgments checked against a larger number of writing teachers in each country. Finally, I also knew that arriving at "truth," although a lofty and worthy goal, was beyond my reach, and that the best I could do was approximate the reality. Therefore, the "thick slice of reality" I captured in my ethnographic study, no matter how meticulously and thoroughly I might report and analyze it, would be neither conclusive nor final, but partial and contingent on the material conditions as well as the historical moment at which the project was to be carried out.

But how to reach even that modest goal? I did have some advantages. I had spent the bulk of my educational years in China and had versed myself in American composition theories for years, which granted me a broader perspective, and I had acquired linguistic competence in both Chinese and English, allowing me easy access to both cultures. All those were important reasons that I chose to do a cross-cultural study, but that alone could not give me an epistemological free pass because it is impossible for a researcher to fully understand, let alone break free from, one's limited and limiting positionality. Should I just take my positionality as a given and move ahead as usual, as suggested by Tompkins (1986) at the end of her monograph? If that is the case—that is, we can do nothing about our situatedness but acknowledge it—what is the point of all this hand wringing about epistemology? At that juncture, it just so happened that Joseph Tobin, an anthropologist by training and a professor of education from the University of Hawaii, came to UNH as a visiting professor, and I was introduced to his work, *Preschool in Three Cultures* (1989), at one of his video presentations. I was immediately attracted to his work not only because what he and his colleagues had just completed was a successful cross-cultural and ethnographical study, but, more important, because of the truly unique "multivocal" approach they devised for the study, which to me offered a possible way out of the "epistemological quandary" that I had been mired in. I invited Professor Tobin to serve on my dissertation committee, and he kindly accepted.

Under his direct guidance, I turned a rough outline map into a detailed blueprint. To put it simply, the study consisted of three rounds of discussion. First, four "principal" teachers, two from the United States and two from China, each recommended three to four pieces of what they considered the best personal narratives by the students they were teaching and explained to me their criteria for the selection. The discussion was thus between the principal teachers and me, the researcher. Second, the principal teachers commented on six pieces of student writing I selected from the pool of papers they recommended. I then invited them to discuss the comments of the other teachers on the same set of student papers and, when they disagreed, explain their criteria to others. The discussion at this stage was among the four principal teachers. Third and last, I selected four from the six pieces of student writing and distributed them to a wider audience. Results of 60 teachers' ranking of the four pieces were tabulated, and their comments written to buttress their judgment were categorized and reported. These rounds of dialogue, what I called "the telling and retelling of the same story," were intended to generate a multitude of perspectives on "what is good writing." More important, it was designed to share the selective and interpretive power between the author and the authored, the observer and the observed, to breach the limited positionality of the researcher.

The study, I would assert, yielded a wealth of perspectives and opened up our understanding of the cultural situatedness of all criteria for "good writing," but the goal of achieving parity of power between the observer and the observed is still beyond my reach. Although the participating principal teachers did have their say in deciding how their worlds should be represented by selecting the initial set of student papers according to their own criteria, and I gave equal or more reportage space to their interpretations of their own pedagogical practices than to my own, I still set the agenda. That is, I chose the research topic, I selected the four principal teachers, I made the final decision as to which six and then four pieces of students' writing would form the basis of discussions, and I asked interview questions, which directed the discussion in one direction instead of others. Finally, as the sole author of the final report, I edited in what I considered significant and edited out what I considered irrelevant. I also streamlined rounds of messy, multifaceted, many-layered dialogues into a linear, palatable, and publishable narrative. Power came in the forms of selection, editing, the narrative convention, as well as the theoretical framework I chose to believe. The inquiry never strayed from the compass of my chosen theory, and there was never any doubt in my mind that another researcher with a different theoretical orientation would have led the project to a different place and written a different report even if he or she followed the same procedures that Tobin and I designed.

It is this theoretical framework that should be made explicit to subject it to continuous reexamination and revision in light of new theories. The underlying premise of the study of "Good Writing" is the belief that all individuals, including those self-proclaimed rebels, are subject to the influence of the culture they are enmeshed in. That belief oriented the study in both its design and eventual findings. I was careful to present the four principal teachers as unique individuals, and they are, and I could have concluded just that. At the beginning of the last chapter, "One Researcher's Perspective," I ponder aloud: "So, what is good writing? It is tempting, after glancing at the results of the survey according to which each piece receives at least three different rankings from the participants of either country, to conclude that 'good writing' is a just a matter of personal taste" (Li, 1996, p. 111). But I didn't take the bait. Instead I immersed myself in the data and was able to construct distinct patterns of evaluation.

The question now is: Is culture a valid objective for inquiry when globalization is making ruthless advances all over the world, when borders become porous and permeable as youngsters chat across the oceans via the Internet, when some people regardless of race or nationality rally with fierce resolve around certain religions and others around the ideal of democracy? Where does culture reside in such a quickly realigned and infinitely malleable world? I agree with Said (1993) that "all cultures are involved in one another, none is single or pure, all are hybrid, heterogeneous, extraordinarily differentiated, and unmonolithic" (p. xxix). Any researcher close to the ground cannot ignore that reality, and that was what I sensed acutely during my visit to China to interview teachers for the "Good Writing" project.

Therefore, when I had the opportunity to pursue another project to study writing education in China, I shifted my focus to the hybridization process, the rapid absorbing of Western ideas and technology in Chinese classrooms that has been underway for over a century and is more obvious now than ever. This process, which some call *Westernization*, was forced on China after the Opium War, but has accelerated with great gusto since Party boss Deng Xiao-ping declared "four modernizations" to be the Party and national goal. The study traces the gradual transformation of China's reading and writing-based humanist educational tradition to a career-oriented, compartmentalized, technology-centered education, and zeroes in on the college entrance exam, a relic of the centuries-old "Imperial Civil Service Exam," which many in the study perceive as blocking China's educational reform. Does this newer study, which focuses on change and hybridization, overwrite the findings of "*Good Writing*," which presents Chinese literary and educational tradition as more or less stable and self-contained, in many ways uniquely different from the West? I don't think so. I believe it is a matter of the analytical lens one chooses and the part of reality one wants to examine. Hatlen (1986) has made an enlightening observation of the effect of practicing seemingly competing theories. In discussing the dialectical encounter between the old rhetoric and the new, he says, "A theory is useful to the degree that it brings certain phenomena into focus, but in doing so any theory must inevitably leave other phenomena blurred, out of focus" (p. 74). A moving long zoom lens brings forth the evolving historical dimension of reality otherwise overlooked, but at the same time it renders unavailable what a stable lingering shot allows us: a closer and sustained look at a phenomenon at a given moment. To put it in linguistic terms, we need both diachronic and synchronic approaches. A new theory can be an addition to or a revision of the old, not necessarily a rejection.

Which brings me back to the two key terms in the debate about contrastive rhetoric: culture and essentialism. My new study, "Track (Dis)connecting: Chinese High School and University Writing in a Time of Change" (Li, 2002), instead of finding that Chinese writing classes are indistinguishable from their Western counterparts, shows that even a culture as receptive to changes as China's has not lost its distinctive cultural identity, not at this point in history. Writing a morality thesis is still the order of the day, and to be able to write arguments without an argumentative edge is still what gets a high school student into the door of a Chinese university. Yes, China is changing and changing rapidly, but fluidity is a valid concept only in relation to stability, just as permeability is a phenomenon that exists only when there are still borders. To play up one dimension of reality to eliminate the existence of another is "neither necessary nor accurate," to borrow another line from Hatlen (1986, p. 73).

Are those of us who see individuals as culturally constructed guilty of what Ruth Spack (1998) criticizes as portraying ESL students as "bound by their language and culture"? To borrow Wittgenstein's metaphor of culture as a "prison-house" (Eagleton, 2000, p. 96), are we representing them as helpless and powerless prisoners of culture? Terry Eagleton (2000) believes such criticism only indicates that "we are held captive here by an image of captivity" (p. 96). The charge that seeing writing as a cultural phenomenon as much as, say, a cognitive activity essentializes unique individuals implies there is an essential self insulated from its context. In his recent work on culture, Eagleton elucidates the relationship between self and culture. He writes:

> The "essential" self is not one beyond cultural shaping, but one which is culturally shaped in a specific, self-reflexive way . . . to belong to a culture is just to be part of a context which is inherently open-ended. . . . Like the rough ground of language itself, cultures work exactly because they are porous, fuzzy-edged, indeterminate, intrinsically inconsistent, never quite identical

with themselves, their boundaries continually modulating into horizons. (pp. 95–96)

Having said all that, I want to make it clear that I do not believe that we should simply ignore criticisms and go about our business as usual. On the contrary, I believe we need more self-reflection, more rigorous cross-examination, and more questioning of our individual and collective theoretical orientations to keep the field alive and to keep us edgy and fresh. This book, highlighting the constructed nature of our knowledge in its title, is very timely. It reflects the field's awareness that, as noted by Bissex (1987), "In traditional research the emphasis has been on the results; in observational research the process *is* part of the result" (p. 14).

The purpose of such discussions is not to find *the* mode of inquiry inherently suitable for ESL writing research or for contrastive rhetoric. I agree with Connor (1999) that we need multiple approaches: "hence historical, linguistic, philosophical, and rhetorical approaches are all prevalent" (p. 153). But I want to add that, as we welcome all guests, we should also at least try to understand what each of them brings to the table. That is, what does each approach avail us of or prevent us from seeing? Understanding the limitations and advantages of each approach and methodology could at least help us avoid making embarrassing claims such as my longitudinal study has uncovered the truth while your limited survey arrives at false conclusions. I agree with Polio (2001) that "researchers should be more explicit when reporting methodology" (p. 109). She suggests that such reports should include "printing any rating scales used, carefully defining terms, and providing readers with examples to supplement the definition" (p. 109). While Polio is concerned mostly with quantitative studies and requests methodological information for the purpose of replication, I am more interested in qualitative studies and desire more information to understand the constructing agents behind the scene.

Because most studies in contrastive rhetoric are based on written texts, I would like more of them to include the full text being analyzed whenever possible. I understand that logistics make it next to impossible to include all the texts when a study looks at large numbers of texts, but not anymore. With new technology, such large data can be easily scanned and stored on the homepage of the author or the publisher, which I hope will become a routine practice for all empirical studies. The same should apply to interview transcripts. This would allow readers to judge the judgment of the researcher hopefully from diverse vantage points where they are located. In addition, they can read the same body of data and offer a variety of interpretations, broadening and deepening our knowledge while bringing out the limitations and advantages of any particular position.

For case studies, whether the object of inquiry is written products or ESL students, I would like the researcher to reveal the criteria, if not the process, for selection: Why were certain texts or individuals chosen for close examination instead of others? Was it a matter of serendipity or a deliberate search for certain characteristics? If the latter, where did that grid come from? Why is a particular text, for example, considered worthy of our attention, how typical is it, and what other texts were rejected in the process? In other words, how was typicality construed and arrived at? Studies that fail to report the selection criteria often create the false impression that their findings are apples picked directly from *the* tree, as if there were only one tree or, even worse, that they were the only apples growing on that tree.

Even more important, we should make explicit our theoretical frameworks and subject them to scrutiny, discussion, and updating. This takes more than self-reflection on the part of researchers; our journal editors should also try to include more philosophical inquiries. Empirical research is the dominant mode of inquiry in ESL writing, and there is nothing wrong with that, but when one can peruse the entire archive of a journal and find precious few essays engaging in philosophical rumination, something is seriously missing. Philosophical inquiries can jolt us out of the comfortable theoretical rut to look at a familiar landscape with a fresh eye. The recent criticism of essentialism, when understood in proper perspective, can lead to more studies of the interface among cultures as Spack (1998) suggests, as well as of the interactions between the larger culture and more immediate and personalized context as Matsuda (1997/2001) suggests. It can also divert some of our exclusive focus from the typical to the atypical, from the norm to the disruptions of the norm, giving us a richer and more nuanced knowledge of reality. Philosophical inquiries can be pursued without engaging in the vain display of fancy jargon or chasing the newest theory for the sake of appearing trendy. Finally, the political implications of our work should not be ignored. We must ask ourselves, from time to time, exactly who or what group of students will benefit or lose when we put into practice a certain theory or publicize certain findings.

REFERENCES

Berlin, J. (1988). Rhetoric and ideology in the writing class. *College English, 50*, 477–494.

Bissex, G. L. (1987). Why case studies? In G. Bissex & R. H. Bullock (Eds.), *Seeing for ourselves: Case study research by teachers of writing* (pp. 7–19). Portsmouth, NH: Boynton/Cook Heinemann.

Connor, U. (1999). *Contrastive rhetoric: Cross-cultural aspects of second-language writing*. New York: Cambridge University Press.

Eagleton, T. (2000). *The idea of culture*. Malden, MA: Blackwell.

Faigley, L. (1992). *Fragments of rationality: Postmodernity and the subject of composition*. Pittsburgh: University of Pittsburgh Press.

Foucault, M. (1975). *Discipline and punish: The birth of the prison* (A. Sheridan, Trans.). Harmondsworth: Peregrine.

Hatlen, B. (1986). Old wine and new bottles: A dialectical encounter between the old rhetoric and the new. In T. Newkirk (Ed.), *Only connect: Uniting reading and writing* (pp. 59–86). Upper Montclair, NJ: Boynton/Cook.

Heath, S. B. (1983). *Ways with words: Language, life and work in communities and classrooms*. Cambridge, England: Cambridge University Press.

Li, X. (1996). *"Good writing" in cross-cultural context*. Albany, NY: State University of New York Press.

Li, X. (2002). "Track (dis)connecting": Chinese high school and university writing in a time of change. In D. Foster & D. R. Russell (Eds.), *Writing and learning in cross-national perspective* (pp. 49–87). Urbana, IL: NCTE; Mahwah, NJ: Lawrence Erlbaum Associates.

Lincoln, Y. S., & Guba, E. G. (1985). *Naturalistic inquiry*. Beverly Hills, CA: Sage.

Matsuda, P. K. (2001). Contrastive rhetoric in context: A dynamic model of L2 writing. In T. Silva & P. K. Matsuda (Eds.), *Landmark essays on ESL writing* (pp. 241–255). Mahwah, NJ: Lawrence Erlbaum Associates. (Reprinted from *Journal of Second Language Writing, 6*(1), pp. 45–60, 1997.)

North, S. M. (1987). *The making of knowledge in composition: Portrait of an emerging field*. Upper Montclair, NJ: Boyton/Cook.

Polio, C. (2001). Research methodology in second language writing research: The case of text-based studies. In T. Silva & P. K. Matsuda (Eds.), *On second language writing* (pp. 91–116). Mahwah, NJ: Lawrence Erlbaum Associates.

Said, E. (1993). *Culture and imperialism*. London: Chatto & Windus.

Spack, R. (1998). The rhetorical construction of multilingual students. *TESOL Quarterly, 31*(4), 765–774.

Therborn, G. (1980). *The ideology of power and the power of ideology*. London: Verso.

Tobin, J. J., Wu, D. Y. H., & Davidson, D. H. (1989). *Preschool in three cultures*. New Haven, CT: Yale University Press.

Tompkins, J. (1986). "Indians": Textualism, orality, and the problem of history. *Critical Inquiry, 13*(1), 101–119.

Watson, J. D. (1968). *The double helix*. New York: Penguin.

III

COLLECTING AND ANALYZING DATA

10

Qualitative Research as Heuristic: Investigating Documentation Practices in a Medical Setting

Susan Parks
Université Laval, Quebec City, Canada

Increasingly, researchers in Applied Linguistics are beginning to turn to ethnographic/qualitative approaches to research. Although there exists a large literature on the epistemological foundations and methodological practices typically associated with these approaches, discussions pertaining specifically to the field of Applied Linguistics are scant. Such discussions, however, can be useful as they enable those within the field to become more cognizant of how various constructs and research strategies may apply to particular research concerns (as well as foster critical reflection on the use of such tools more generally). As one contribution, I draw on an ethnographic study that I conducted involving the appropriation of genre-specific writing skills by francophone nurses in an English-medium hospital, and I discuss it in relation to three issues that all researchers involved in this paradigm must grapple with: (a) the emergent design of such studies, (b) the representativeness of data, and (c) the researcher stance and role of theory. Prior to engaging in this discussion, I briefly review the target study I refer to.

TARGET STUDY: APPROPRIATION OF PROFESSIONAL WRITING SKILLS IN A MEDICAL SETTING

Published articles drawn from this study may be found in *Language Learning* (Parks & Maguire, 1999), the *Journal of Second Language Writing* (Parks, 2000), and *Applied Linguistics* (Parks, 2001). In terms of background information, it should be noted that this study involved longitudinal research conducted over a 2-year period in an English-medium hospital in Montreal (Canada). Although both English- and French-medium hospitals can be found in Montreal, in the province of Quebec where this city is located, the official language is French. The nurses who participated in the study had done their schooling in French and obtained their nursing degrees from French institutions. All of the graduates, except one, had been hired at an English-medium hospital, which I refer to as Thomas Memorial Hospital, immediately upon graduation from a university nursing program. Their general level of spoken English ranged from low intermediate to low advanced.

At the time I became interested in doing this study, I was employed as an ESL Program Coordinator in a language institute affiliated with a local university. At one point, nurses from Thomas Memorial Hospital approached me about the possibility of setting up an English for Special Purposes (ESP) course to facilitate the integration of the new francophone nurses into the hospital. I was involved both in setting up this course and teaching it. Although the course, which was offered on hospital premises, did not deal with writing, through my discussions with nurses I became aware that the new francophone nurses had difficulty doing their documentation in English. During this time, I also became involved in doctoral studies and, because I had become interested in L1 research on situated writing in academic and workplace settings (Berkenkotter & Huckin, 1995; Ede & Lunsford, 1990; Forman, 1992; Freedman & Medway, 1994; Lay & Karis, 1991; Odell & Goswami, 1985; Raymond & Parks, 2001; Spilka, 1993; Swales, 1990), I decided to use this site for my research project. With respect to this domain of research, one might further retrospectively note that in the early 1990s, examining text production *in situ* had become a new burgeoning area of inquiry as scholars involved in first language (L1) literacy sought to move beyond the limitations of cognitive approaches to writing and a narrowly defined focus on composition and essay writing. During this same period, I had also become increasingly aware of and interested in research conducted within a qualitative research paradigm.

ISSUE 1: EMERGENT DESIGN: NAVIGATING THROUGH THE FUNNEL

Ethnography as practiced in anthropology frequently conjures up the image of researchers venturing out into distant cultures and spending long periods of time learning the local language and gradually familiarizing themselves with the ways of thinking and doing of the targeted community. In such conditions, the characterization of the ethnographer as a stranger in a strange land appears apt. However, as anthropologists point out, such feelings of estrangement are not the prerogative of exotic climes, but can also occur within subcultures or discourse communities with which one has little direct experience in one's own culture. The early phases of fieldwork can, in this regard, be particularly stressful. As Agar (1980) contends, it is precisely this initial period that is the "source of the mystique of fieldwork. You are adrift, trusted by none, and unsure of what is going on around you" (p. 83). To describe how ethnographic research typically evolves over time, from initial feelings of anxiety and confusion to a more thorough understanding of the targeted phenomenon within the particular social context being investigated, Agar evokes the metaphor of the *funnel*. With greater knowledge of the social context, the researcher's open-ended approach to questioning gradually yields to a more precise formulation of research questions—a design aspect that is frequently termed *emergent*.

Target Study: Appropriation of Professional Writing Skills

In terms of my own study, venturing into the world of medical practice at Thomas Memorial Hospital quickly made me feel like a stranger in a strange land. Like anthropologists in a foreign land, I frequently wondered, especially initially, whether I would ever be able to respond to that most basic of questions: What is going on here? In reflecting on the reasons that made navigating through the funnel, to use Agar's metaphor, so difficult, I note five in particular: (a) the novelty of the types of written genres used by the nurses, (b) the specialized medical terminology, (c) the process of text production in the hospital milieu, (d) the difficulty of gaining access to the site, and (e) technical constraints related to data collection.

Types of Written Genres. Prior to engaging in this study, my experiences with written genres as a student, teacher, and researcher had been largely confined to those associated with the domains of literature, composition writing, and Applied Linguistics. Initially, I grappled with basic questions concerning the type of writing nurses engaged in. Once aware that the two main genres were nursing notes (documents written to provide updates on patients' evolving status) and care plans (documents used to organize the care of patients through the identification of problems and interventions), I then queried whether these genres were substantive enough to merit investigation. In contrast to most of the L2 writing research (primarily involving essays and compositions), the two latter genres consisted of a few lines of text and were very formulaic. Although in my research I have since illuminated how even for such seemingly simple documents the process of appropriation can be quite complex, this fact was not obvious to me initially. More generally, my experience in this hospital milieu served over time to help me better appreciate the extent to which genres as forms of social action (Miller, 1984) are truly embedded in and sustained by their attendant discourse communities.

Specialized Terminology. The task of trying to understand what nurses were talking or writing about was made more difficult due to the use of medical terms and concepts.

Process of Text Production. Prior to accompanying nurses on the hospital units, their work-related routines and documentation practices were completely unknown to me. In regard to these practices, questions that I asked myself at various points included the following: What are charts? Who writes in them and when? Do nurses do their documentation throughout the shift or at specific times? Do nurses ask colleagues for help with their documentation? If so, what do they ask about? Which colleagues tend to give help? Is asking for help socially acceptable or perceived as a nuisance? Do new nurses refer to the documentation of colleagues when they have problems writing? Is such documentation readily available? Does talk with patients help nurses with their writing? If so, how might this be reflected in a piece of writing? Do nurses write multiple drafts? How much time do they spend writing?

Gaining Access. As with any ethnographic study, gaining access to a site is a fundamental condition for carrying out the targeted research. In my case, access to the hospital was facilitated by the fact that I had been involved with clinical educators in setting up language courses for the new francophone nurses. Although I had ready access to the room where the English classes were given at the hospital, access to other locales had to be progressively negotiated and renegotiated. Early on in the study, the clinical educator, a key informant, arranged for my first foray onto a nursing unit where I was able to see firsthand what a chart, a document about which until then I had but the vaguest of notions, actually looked like. Following the English courses, when nurses began work on the units during what was referred to as their *clinical orientation*, it was also the clinical educator who gave me permission to accompany her as she interacted with nurses and gave them feedback on drafts of their nursing documentation. During this time, I was, however, primarily confined to the receptionist area of the unit. To obtain permission to accompany nurses into patients' rooms required a formal request to the Nursing Research Committee, a lengthy process that made it necessary for me to return to the hospital the following year and pursue my research with a new group of recruits. Although this process prolonged my study by a year, it proved indispensable to a more thorough investigation of issues pertaining to my research questions (see in particular, Parks, 2000). Because the collaborative processes that facilitated nurses' appropriation of the targeted genres were more prevalent when they first began their work on the units, I not only realized the importance of gaining access to the right locales of a site, but also of being in these locales at the right time.

Technical Constraints. During the study, I had to come to terms with a number of constraints related to data collection in this particular milieu. One problem pertained to obtaining copies of the nurses' documentation during their shifts. Although the Nursing Research Committee had granted me permission to make copies of nurses' documentation insofar as patient confidentiality was ensured, the charts could not be taken off the units. To get copies of documentation, I used carbon paper—a strategy that had, in fact, been suggested to me by a head nurse. Another problem pertained to the recording of talk. Although I was able to use a hand-held battery-operated tape recorder to record exchanges between the clinical educator and nurses, at other times this strategy proved too intrusive; in such instances, I resorted to rapid note taking, using a clipboard as support. By the end of a shift, nurses could be stressed out and eager to leave, so I took maximum advantage of odd moments during a shift when they were less busy to informally probe for purposes of clarification. Due to the intense physical demands of shadowing nurses during an entire shift, comfortable shoes proved indispensable.

Although ethnographic research in general tends to be challenging, this is particularly the case for researchers who wish to explore text production processes in discourse communities of which they are not members. In such instances, as discussed earlier, patience and extensive on-site observation may be necessary to understand the nature of the targeted genres and how the text production practices may facilitate or hinder new members' efforts to appropriate these genres.

ISSUE 2: REPRESENTATIVENESS OF DATA

One aspect of qualitative research that has been a source of scrutiny and criticism pertains to the degree to which the particular cases or data showcased are representative of the phenomenon being investigated. As one means of determining the latter's typicality, Miles and Huberman (1984) recommend counting. As they point out, the importance of various categories and themes in qualitative data is often associated in the researcher's mind with frequency of occurrence:

> . . . there is a lot of counting going on when judgments of qualities are being made. When we identify a theme or pattern, we are isolating something (a) that happens a number of times and (b) that consistently happens in a specific way. The "number of times" and consistency judgments are based on counting. (p. 215)

As a further means of coming to terms with the representativeness of data, Agar (1980) suggests that both formal and informal data-collection procedures be used. Informal procedures refer to the fieldwork strategies generally associated with qualitative research, such as interviewing and observation. However, due to the constraints involved in carrying out fieldwork, at times it may be difficult to go beyond an initial understanding of a particular phenomenon to more carefully delineate how a pattern is distributed within a larger population. In such instances, formal tasks that simulate situations or serve to elicit information in response to cues may also be used. In designing such tasks, Agar emphasizes that fieldwork is an essential prerequisite to ensure that the latter are meaningful to participants.

Target Study: Appropriation of Professional Writing Skills

Within my own study, both the distribution of patterns and the use of formal tasks were issues with which I grappled. One specific instance in this regard involved the use of a formal care plan task. As previously mentioned, care plans are documents that nurses use to report patients' problems and identify a course of action. Within the context of this study, I was interested in understanding whether the way nurses would write care plans at the hospital was the same as how they had learned during their studies at university. In keeping with Pettinari's (1988) research, which had explored how medical interns developed skills in writing medical reports, I envisaged focusing on one particular type of care plan that I would collect from the nurses at different points in time and analyse for possible changes. However, as I eventually discovered, such a strategy was not feasible because the nurses were sent to work on different units at the hospital, and there was no guarantee that they would all be involved in reporting on one particular type of problem repeatedly. Without a common problem, I surmised that specific changes would be difficult to identify; what might appear as a change could simply be due to the nature of the problem reported on or other factors such as conventions particular to a given unit. Another potential problem pertained to the difficulty of obtaining copies of their care plans when I myself was not observing on a unit, as the nurses did not always feel they had time to attend to this.

In an attempt to overcome these problems, I resorted to a formal task in which nurses were asked to write a care plan on three different occasions in response to a case study prompt prepared by the clinical educator. Because such prompts were familiar to students both within their university nursing programs and as a strategy used by the clinical educator during the ESP course, the care plan activity thus conceived corresponded to Agar's (1980) recommendation that tasks be relevant to participants' experiences. To encourage the identification of differences over time, which nurses themselves considered significant, they were shown prior versions of their care plans and asked to comment on them. This privileging of the emic (or insider) perspective proved important because, due to my status as an outsider and lack of familiarity with this genre, differences as identified by the nurses were not always obvious to me and items that I had identified as possible differences at times were not necessarily considered as such by the nurses (e.g., changes related to differences in wording). To render changes in the underlying patterns more salient, descriptive statistics were used as suggested by Miles and Huberman (1984). In addition, the formal care plan task also proved useful in pinpointing differences between the clinical educator's conception of what constituted good care plan writing and the new nurses' (for a discussion, see Parks, 2001).

However, despite the usefulness of the care plan task as discussed earlier, a word of caution is in order. Although the care plan task conformed to Agar's recommendation that formal tasks be meaningful to participants, comments that emerged during the interviews with nurses served to remind me that paper-and-pencil care plan tasks off the units are not necessarily the same as those on the units. This context sensitivity surfaced in relation to: (a) the construal of the task, (b) the construal of audience, and (c) the understanding of the case.

Construal of Task. In setting up the care plan task, I instructed nurses to write their care plans as they would if they had been working on a unit at Thomas Memorial Hospital. However, in asking them to do so, I assumed that nurses would try to identify as many problems as they could (i.e., write "comprehensive" care plans as they had been encouraged to do during their university nursing program). Although most, in fact, appeared to do so, two nurses did not. Commenting on their decision to limit themselves to the identification of a single problem in care plans 2 and 3, these nurses explained that on the units more problems would typically be added at later points as the need arose. In transposing this procedural knowledge to the case study task, they decided to focus on one sole problem that they deemed of importance. Their comments in this regard made me aware of the danger of interpreting the number of problems identified in the formal paper-and-pencil care plan task as a reliable indicator of what their ability to do so might be on the units in a practical, real-world context.

Construal of Audience. On the units, the audience for the care plans is clear: Nurses write care plans for their nursing colleagues to coordinate the care of patients. However, during the formal care plan task, two instances came to light where nurses had written items with audiences in mind other than their nursing colleagues. The most striking instance of this emerged in the third interview with Bertrand, who confided that he had written three of the four interventions for a urinary tract infection to impress the researcher. Bertrand explained that he had felt a single intervention would reflect poorly on him: ". . . if I take one intervention, you (researcher) say what he do." In other words, Bertrand thought that if there had been only one intervention, the researcher might assume that he was not knowledgeable as a nurse.

Understanding of the Case. Although considerable effort was made to ensure that nurses had read the case study prompt carefully and understood it, evidence of a misreading or misunderstanding of information stated in the text nevertheless surfaced in relation to various versions of the care plan task. Instances of these types of problems included the assumption that the patient was post-op instead of pre-op (Bertrand); that the patient may have been a child, whereas in fact her age was stated as 34 (Julie); or that the patient needed to learn how to care for her colostomy, when in fact she had been doing this for 2 years (several nurses). Such errors, involving the misunderstanding of basic facts about the patient, would be unlikely on a unit due to the process of caring for patients, which includes observation of and discussion with the latter as well as consultation of colleagues or other resources should they lack knowledge of a particular medical problem.

Thus, although as discussed earlier, formal tasks can be useful, careful attention must be paid to the interpretation of the results, especially so as to ensure that distortions due to context sensitivity do not invalidate data relevant to the research questions under investigation. In regard to this issue, Coughlin and Duff's (1994) distinction between task as blueprint (the way in which a researcher or teacher might ideally view a task as being carried out) and task as activity (the way in which subjects might actually invest in a task) is instructive. Also certain studies that have drawn more specifically on activity theory demonstrate how participants differentially invest in tasks (Dias, Freedman, Medway, & Paré, 1999; Parks, 2000; Raymond & Parks, 2002; Roebuck, 1998). To enhance the validity of formal tasks, I would also recommend the following two measures. First, it is crucial to engage participants in a follow-up discussion of the tasks to better understand how they interpret them and why. In the present study, it was the follow-up discussion that enabled the issues related to task sensitivity to emerge. Indeed in this case, the discussion frequently served to confirm aspects related to text production processes observed on the units. Second, data from the formal tasks should be triangulated with other data sources to ensure the trustworthiness of the interpretations being advanced. In the case of the target study, the pattern of changes evidenced in data from the formal care plan task was further checked through discussion of nurses' actual research practices on the units and comparison with care plans produced there.

ISSUE 3: RESEARCHER STANCE AND THE ROLE OF THEORY

Another issue related to qualitative research pertains to the way researchers perceive their role in a study, particularly in regard to the use of theory. Several of the more influential theoreticians of qualitative research practices take different positions.

At one extreme, Lincoln and Guba (1985) refer to the researcher as the "primary data-gathering instrument." As such the researcher is exhorted to adopt a neutral stance and avoid any prior theorizing as to the possible interpretation of data. Theory is depicted as *emerging* from the data as "*no* a priori theory could possibly encompass the multiple realities that are likely to be encountered" (p. 41). Data collection and analysis are portrayed as having one main objective: the presentation of the emic (or insider) as opposed to the etic (or outsider) perspective. In reflecting on Lincoln and Guba's position, however, I would like to emphasize two points. First, although as a mediator of participants' perspectives researcher neutrality is advocated, I would question to what degree such a stance is indeed possible. Such a position tends to assume that the researcher's task of constructing/reconstructing the emic perspectives of participants in a given social context is a relatively transparent, unproblematic undertaking. Second, the emphasis on participants' perspectives suggests that the emic perspective is the only valid (or most valued) form of knowledge. Although I would not quarrel with the importance of illuminating the emic perspective, I would posit that the broader theoretical perspectives that a researcher might bring to the discussion of a particular phenomenon could shed light on it—add to its comprehension—at levels that participants might not be privy to.

Compared with Lincoln and Guba (1985), other theoreticians of qualitative research have at times acknowledged a more pervasive role of theory in regard to the actual design of projects (Goetz & LeCompte, 1984; Yin, 1994). Agar (1980), for example, maintains that, in discussions of methodological procedures used to conduct qualitative research, "(m)uch theory lurks below the surface" (p. 189). For his part, Agar rejects the notion of the anthropologist as a neutral entity, especially in regard to the role of theory and the emic–etic distinction. Reflecting on the emic–etic issue, he states: ". . . it is difficult to imagine any ethnographic statement that is not a blend of these. A statement would almost always contain some assumptions about perception or intention on the part of group members, but it would also be constructed by the ethnographer in terms of his own professional context and goals" (p. 191).

More recently, for Sullivan and Porter (1997), who characterize their approach as postmodern, the undertaking of research is viewed as a fully ideological enterprise. In contrast to Lincoln and Guba's (1985) vision of a researcher capable of mediating between participants and their context in a "neutral" manner, the researcher here is cast as an active player whose theoretical beliefs and positionings inevitably surface during the research process (whether overtly acknowledged and problematized or not). Far from proscribing the interpretation of data using different theoretical frameworks, as recommended by Lincoln and Guba (1985), such initiatives are encouraged as they may bring to light the sociohistorical positionings of various individuals within a particular social context. More generally, methodology is viewed as "local, contingent, malleable, and heuristic and (. . .) research (as) generating situated knowledge or rather a kind of pragmatic know how (vs. know-that) kind of knowledge" (p. 78). Such a stance emphasizes that there is no one truth and that the knowledge generated is always intrinsic to the tools used.

Target Study: Appropriation of Professional Writing Skills

Although Lincoln and Guba (1985) advocate a neutral researcher stance, I would argue that such a position is basically untenable. As suggested by a number of researchers, in particular, Sullivan and Porter (1997), the researcher's ideological positioning is fundamental to the shaping of the research project. In regard to my own study, the formulation of the research questions and decisions as to methodological procedures were bound up with my interest in views of rhetoric and writing practice related to the role of collaboration and genre theory. Had I at the time still been partial to cognitive perspectives on writing (a position that an increasing number of publications at the time had given me cause to rethink), I would have proceeded differently. For example, in lieu of an ethnographic study, I might have devised an experiment in which nurses, designated as expert and novice based on years of experience in the field, individually wrote care plans in a laboratory setting while verbalizing their thoughts. The use of such a methodological procedure, referred to as *oral protocol analysis*, would have been intended to highlight differences in task representation and strategy use between the two groups. Needless to say, such a study would have shed little or no light on how factors related to social context might have been implicated in any observed differences. The problematic issues related to the development and use of this genre, as I have discussed in published accounts of this research, would most likely not have emerged.

Beyond the choice of a research paradigm, however, the exposure to certain theoretical positions also influenced how I ultimately framed the questions of my inquiry into writing practices. Because the eye is not neutral, the significance that one might attach to certain observed behaviours may be mediated by one's conception of the particular phenomenon under study. Specifically in regard to the present target study, because I had been sensitized to the notion of collaboration and its various manifestations, an event such as a nurse observed asking a colleague for help on the spur of the moment was noteworthy. Such fleeting interactions, which a less informed observer could have ignored, became, for me, an important aspect of the data-collection process and my account of how participants in this particular milieu appropriated genre-specific writing skills. In view of this, "truth" did not, as Lincoln and Guba (1985) suggest simply "emerge"; my particular research objectives and attendant theoretical stance were necessarily bound up with decisions as to what to focus on and, ultimately, the nature of the outcomes and claims.

Another issue related to researcher stance with which I had to grapple pertained to the emic–etic distinction. Within my own study, eliciting emic perspectives was essential in terms of identifying what rhetorical features nurses attributed to good exemplars of care plan writing, why they wrote them the way they did, or how they changed their way of writing. However, these insights were not sufficient to explain certain aspects of the data—notably those related to institutional differences. First, although individuals were able to give their opinion about certain aspects of care plan writing as it pertained to them, they were not necessarily cognizant of how broader patterns of behaviour were playing out within the hospital or how institutional differences in care plan writing might be related to broader disciplinary/societal discourses. In this regard, it might be noted, for example, that the clinical educator had thought that the newly hired university graduates would espouse the more elaborate form of care plans she endorsed as they had been extensively trained in this particular style of writing. She had hypothesized that what she considered to be differences in the quality of care plan writing was due to education: Some nurses had never been trained to write care plans while at nursing school; indeed she expected the new recruits to be models for such nurses. She had further (erroneously) anticipated that, as the new recruits had been thoroughly trained, they would be able to resist what she characterized as the "bad habits" of many of the regular staff nurses in regard to the way they did their care plans. In advancing such hypotheses, she was in fact unaware of how differences in conceptions of the role of a nurse had influenced her own position.

As explained in a previous publication (Parks, 2001), to more fully explain why differences existed in the way care plans were written (or not written) in different institutional contexts (English-medium hospital vs. French-medium hospitals vs. Francophone universities), it was necessary to understand how the use of care plan writing was related to efforts within the profession to more clearly delineate nursing as a discipline distinct from that of medical doctors. Although this discourse was articulated and understood by leaders in the field (as exemplified in books written by such nurses on these changes and their relevance for the nursing profession), the rank and file endorsed or resisted the proposed changes to varying degrees. However, even at the end of the study when I had a good understanding of what was actually happening in this milieu (beyond the level of a single institution), I did not have a theoretical framework that could account for the global picture of the data; genre theory as I had understood it at the time tended to deal with writing issues within isolated institutions. Although insights gleaned from interviews with participants offered pieces to the puzzle and pointed to the problem, they did not provide me with the overall solution. Indeed it was only when I became aware of Russell's (1997) account of genre theory that he associated with Engeström's systems version of Vygotskian cultural-historical activity theory that I was able to explain the data in a more comprehensive manner (see Parks, 2001).

To sum up, although the emic perspective is undoubtedly important, to arrive at a more comprehensive understanding of a given phenomenon, it may be necessary, as suggested by theoreticians such as Agar (1980), to go beyond such perspectives and relate them to broader theoretical discourses. Although the theoretical distinction between emic and etic perspectives is deeply entrenched within the qualitative research paradigm, such a dualism may not always be conducive to the broader understanding of issues, especially if the emic is presented as the more valued form of knowledge. As suggested by Sullivan and Porter (1997) and others in this volume (e.g., Atkinson, Silva), research paradigms and specific methodological tools may be best viewed as heuristics, the choice of which depends to a large degree on the research questions and ideological positioning of the researcher.

CONCLUSION

Although there exist numerous publications that deal with issues related to the epistemological and methodological aspects of conducting qualitative research, the implications of such discussions may not always be clear as the cases dealt with rarely relate to the domain of rhetoric/writing practices. Drawing on a study involving the appropriation of genre-specific writing skills, I have discussed three key issues that all researchers in this paradigm need to grapple with: (a) the emergent design of the study, (b) the representativeness of data, and (c) the researcher stance and the role of theory. Although the exploration of writing practices in discourse communities other than those one is most familiar with merits further investigation, the challenges, as noted earlier, can be considerable. Because the focus of such studies involves language, obtaining recordings of oral discourse and copies of written documents can pose particular challenges. Also as suggested before, the examination of publications on qualitative research reveals that consensus on key issues is far from being the case. Two of these issues, which I had to grapple with in the context of my own research project, involved the use of formal tasks and the role of theory, especially in relation to the emic and etic perspectives. Although discussions of methodology at times tend to give the impression that the strategies advocated are cast in stone, researchers are increasingly coming to understand how the latter may be better viewed as heuristics, the choice of which depends on the nature of the research questions.

REFERENCES

Agar, M. (1980). *The professional stranger.* New York: Academic Press.

Berkenkotter, C., & Huckin, T. (1995). *Genre knowledge in disciplinary communication: Cognition/culture/power.* Hillsdale, NJ: Lawrence Erlbaum Associates.

Coughlin, P., & Duff, P. (1994). Same task, different activities: Analysis of SLA task from an activity theory perspective. In P. Lantolf & G. Appel (Eds.), *Vygotskian approaches to second language research* (pp. 173–191). Norwood, NJ: Ablex.

Dias, P., Freedman, A., Medway, P., & Paré, A. (1999). *Worlds apart: Acting and writing in academic and workplace contexts.* Mahwah, NJ: Lawrence Erlbaum Associates.

Ede, L., & Lunsford, A. (1990). *Singular texts/plural authors: Perspectives on collaborative writing.* Carbondale: Southern Illinois University Press.

Forman, J. (1992). *New visions of collaborative writing.* Portsmouth, NH: Heinemann.

Freedman, A., & Medway, P. (Eds.). (1994). *Genre and the new rhetoric.* London: Taylor & Francis.

Goetz, J., & LeCompte, M. (1984). *Ethnography and qualitative design in education research*. New York: Academic Press.

Lay, M., & Karis, W. (1991). *Collaborative writing in industry: Investigation in theory and practice*. Amityville, NY: Baywood.

Lincoln, Y. S., & Guba, E. G. (1985). *Naturalistic inquiry*. Beverly Hills, CA: Sage.

Miles, M. B., & Huberman, A. M. (1984). *Qualitative data analysis: Sourcebook of new methods*. Newbury Park, CA: Sage.

Miller, C. (1984). Genre as social action. *Quarterly Journal of Speech, 70*, 151–167.

Odell, L., & Goswami, D. (Eds.). (1985). *Writing in nonacademic settings*. New York: Guilford.

Parks, S. (2000). Professional writing and the role of incidental collaboration: Evidence from a medical setting. *Journal of Second Language Writing, 9*, 101–122.

Parks, S. (2001). Moving from school to the workplace: Disciplinary innovation, border crossings, and the reshaping of a written genre. *Applied Linguistics, 22*, 405–438.

Parks, S., & Maguire, M. (1999). Coping with on-the-job writing in ESL: A constructivist-semiotic perspective. *Language Learning, 49*, 143–175.

Pettinari, C. (1988). *Task, talk and text in the operating room: A study in medical discourse*. Norwood, NJ: Ablex.

Raymond, P., & Parks, A. (2001). Les genres textuels et leur pertinence dans l'apprentissage et l'enseignement d'une langue seconde. In C. Cornaire & P. Raymond (Eds.), *Regards sur la didactique des langues secondes* (pp. 45–69). Montréal: Les Éditions Logiques.

Raymond, P., & Parks, S. (2002). Transitions: Orienting to reading and writing assignments in EAP and MBA contexts. *Canadian Modern Language Review, 59*, 152–180.

Roebuck, R. (1998). *Reading and recall in L1 and L2: A sociocultural approach*. Stamford, CT: Ablex.

Russell, D. (1997). Rethinking genre in school and society: An activity theory analysis. *Written Communication, 14*, 504–554.

Spilka, R. (Ed.). (1993). *Writing in the workplace: New research perspectives*. Carbondale: Southern Illinois University Press.

Sullivan, P., & Porter, J. (1997). *Opening spaces: Writing technologies and critical research practices*. Greenwich, CT: Ablex.

Swales, J. (1990). *Genre analysis: English in academic and research settings*. Cambridge, England: Cambridge University Press.

Yin, R. (1994). *Case study research: Design & methods*. Thousand Oaks, CA: Sage.

11

Mucking Around in the Lives of Others: Reflections on Qualitative Research

Linda Lonon Blanton
University of New Orleans, USA

Hindsight is clearer than foresight. The adage, although trite, is still powerfully true, I realized recently when finishing up—and taking stock of—a research project. Although I would have preferred to bask in the glow of a positive experience brought successfully to a close, the work of taking stock is, I believe, of enormous value to a researcher. A researcher can learn a great deal through the process of reflection—even if it triggers feelings of regret and doubt, and especially when this is precisely the emotional outcome.

How to proceed, how not to proceed in future projects—these insights may come through reflection. Most of all, however, reflection behooves a researcher to establish or reestablish a touchstone for intellectual honesty and human decency. Here is the story.

CHOICES

At the outset of the process, I toyed with titles on my way toward composing an abstract of my research—this as a self-imposed strategy for organizing my thoughts and getting at answers to several questions. How had I gone about constructing knowledge for myself (or anyone else)? What understanding had I gained (about my subject matter or myself as researcher)? Something to do with qualitative research was a given (a point I explain later). That, I wouldn't take back, but what else loomed large about the research experience? If I had it to do over, would I do it again? The phrasing that came to mind first was, "How Do You Know When to Quit?" But no, that wouldn't do. As a point of focus, it sounded uncomfortably flip. (I visualize these things on billboards or at least in tables of contents.)

I then tried "Despair and Exhilaration: All in a Day's Work," but rejected it as too manic. My next candidate was "What *Was* I Thinking?" No, too self-deprecating. After discarding others too pitiful to mention, I finally settled on, as the least bad, the title "Mucking Around in the Lives of Others," while silently adding, ". . . where I had no business being."

But before I pursue this line, let me say that what I noticed above all was the tenor of my thinking. My extreme negativity was, I realized, indicative of the potential of qualitative research for upending the researcher. As Petty (1997) put it in a sort of guide for surviving ethnographic research, I was reacting to the not-so-pleasant feeling that "everything is different now" (p. 68). The particular nature of my dis-ease, I also realized, was reflected in every title.

MATCH BETWEEN RESEARCHER AND RESEARCH APPROACH

Yet on a good day, if you were to ask about qualitative research as a methodology, you would hear me saying things like, "I'm addicted to qualitative research. I just can't get enough" or "I was born to be a qualitative researcher," while quickly adding, ". . . if I was born to be a researcher at all." For anyone interested in this self-reflection, I think my adoration of qualitative research results in part from an insatiable curiosity about others. What they think. Why they make the choices they do. How they feel. In particular, I'm fascinated by the issue of identity in how people balance their public and private selves—a matter I recently explored in regard to how academics write for publication (Blanton, 2003a).

Although not exclusively so, people in academia are my primary interest. I guess it is because school is where I have spent so much of my life. (I count from Grade 1, age 6.) This curiosity most often leads me to wanting to know about aspects of academic life that are unspoken or largely invisible. For some strange reason, I am especially interested when the venue or context seems at odds with the content, as in recent articles in the *Chronicle for Higher Education* on alcoholism (Anonymous, 2002) or nakedness—albeit a metaphor for risk-filled teaching (Temes, 2002)—or, less shocking, an article on clothes (Parini, 2001). I'd call it "elucidation by juxtaposition." Dissonance can rattle intellectual complacency or so it seems to me.

More seriously, I also think I am suited to qualitative research because my birth culture *is* a storytelling culture, a matter related to issues I've raised in several recent essays (Blanton, 2002, 2003a). I grew up in the mountains of northern Arkansas, in a rural, predominately oral, culture, where public and private discourse is often framed as stories. In this culture, stories serve to relay and relate information, conduct business, pass the time of day, entertain listeners, admonish wrong do-ers, and create/maintain/and repair ties (both of diachronic history and current relationships).

Because qualitative researchers are, in the end, storytellers, for me it's a natural, a given, that values, concepts, information, and insights are communicated in this way. So unlike Leki (1999), who worries that qualitative research can "only tell a story, not the truth" (p. 17), I have no worry about the distinction between reality (i.e., truth) and interpretation. Given my cultural formation, truth is all (and only) interpretation—with the exception of certain verifiable aspects of the physical world—and truth can best be formulated and transmitted through narratives, through stories.

My point, and I do have one, is that in large part the role that researchers play in the enormous endeavor of constructing knowledge is shaped and molded by who they are in the world. But I have soft-pedaled this view. Before I send my graduate students out to do qualitative research, I tell them (along the lines of Glesne & Peshkin, 1992; Marshall & Rossman, 1995) that deciding to *do* qualitative research and then searching for a research project is not normal. I tell them that normally the choice of approach, whether qualitative or quantitative, follows from the nature of the question the researcher wants answered. Well, yes, but what I don't exactly tell them is that, in my opinion, a researcher may be more philosophically and culturally suited to one approach than another.

But because I don't want to bias my graduate students altogether, I don't exactly reveal that just about the only questions that interest me are ones that can be answered qualitatively. I'm not, mind you, bragging about that. While I'm glad that my medical doctor wants to know the experimental results of research on the West Nile virus—which treatments work, which don't—this is not an issue that intellectually intrigues me.

POSITIVES

I'm telling about my degree of comfort, even love, for qualitative research as a preamble to discussing the pit I've recently dug for myself. I should have seen the danger, but I didn't. Here is probably why. My major qualitative experience until recently had been with ESL children, in a K–12, English-language-medium school in Casablanca, Morocco. Some might be familiar with that research, which I published (Blanton, 1998) as *Varied Voices*. For those interested, an extension of that work is now out in a special issue of the *Journal of Second Language Writing* (Blanton, 2002).

More to the point, the whole of the Morocco experience has been a joy—a tremendous source of personal and professional satisfaction to me for over a decade now. Like the Energizer bunny, the work (and its effect on me) just keep on going. On some naïve level, I suppose, I thought that my Morocco work was the way it *is* with qualitative research. Well, yes, I had come across ethnographies conducted with prison populations (Tunnell, 1998), case studies of dying patients in hospice settings (Karim, 2000), and other difficult studies. But, hey, I'm in ESL, a fairly positive arena in which to work.

In relief, I can now see that I had determined for myself a positive intellectual framework in Morocco by deciding, among the myriad of possibilities, to investigate what was working right. There I spent time in classrooms—with creative teachers and irrepressible children—where literacy and language were developing fast and furiously, and my so-called job was to learn for myself how it was happening. What was there not to like? You can't hang out with bubbly 5-year-olds for very long and not catch their infectious joy.

NEGATIVES

Fast forward to my current study—and I need to tell about it to make sense of my dilemma. For a year, I met weekly with two immigrant ESL students, members of the population now known as *Generation 1.5* (i.e., U.S.-educated students, not home speakers of English), who come to college and end up spending time, and even floundering, in ESL programs after having received high school diplomas just like everyone else (see Harklau, Losey, & Siegal, 1999, for a thorough discussion).

Both of the students I studied were spinning their wheels in my department's ESL program. One, a young woman from Ethiopia, had spent six semesters to move *two* ESL levels—from a 12-hour reading-writing-listening-speaking course, to a 6-hour reading-writing course, to a 3-hour writing course. There she was stuck. The other, a young man from Vietnam, had progressed from the 12-hour advanced intensive course through each of two successive levels—one semester at a time—until he too got stuck. He had failed the last ESL composition course (the level just before the "regular" first-year composition sequence) three semesters in a row.

The Ethiopian student—I call her Meseret—had begun U.S. schooling in 10th grade in 1996, when she first arrived in New Orleans, her port of entry to the United States. There she graduated from high school in 3 years—with the help of individual tutoring, some content courses taught through ESL, a fairly strong background already in math, and a lot of school-sponsored prepping for the state-mandated exit exam. Thinking that she wasn't as strong as she wanted to be in reading and writing, she placed herself in ESL when she got to college, but was flabbergasted when told she had to take the 12-hour intensive program. Her surprise turned to despair when she realized that she was, as she put it, "never gonna get out of ESL."

The Vietnamese student, whom I call Tran, started school in New Orleans in eighth grade, in 1991, after a year in transit from his home village. By the 11th grade, he was fully mainstreamed. He found that by translating, filling in the blank, memorizing definitions, liking math, and getting help from Vietnamese kids who had been here longer, he could get by.

I learned all this and more from these students through the course of my research. But when I first started meeting with them, I had no specifics of their background or the scope and cause of their writing difficulty. Well, in truth, I was acquainted with Tran from having had him in an ESL reading course when he first arrived in college years ago, but I think I learned little about him then. (I'm not proud to say that.) I wasn't acquainted with Meseret at all, but knowing that I wanted to do case studies of some Generation 1.5 students, a colleague, in whose class Meseret was enrolled, sent her my way.

In short, I proceeded blindly to find out, in depth, why the two students were stuck in ESL—blind because of ignorance (which was okay because the research was designed to remedy that), but also blind, I now see, because of a certain arrogance on my part. I thought that with my help—and this was my reciprocity plan—suddenly, magically, the students' writing would turn around. Arrogant, also, because I must admit to a certain attitude on my part toward my department's ESL entry/exit procedure: an outmoded Michigan test and an in-house timed writing sample on an innocuous topic, graded in large part on grammar and syntax. With my help, these students would surely get over the hurdle my department had placed in their way.

Although over the years I have taught a fair share of ESL courses and read more compositions than I care to think about, I suppose I can say in retrospect that in the busy-ness of my teaching life, I never had or made the opportunity to really know my students' educational histories. All I knew, I knew by extrapolation from reading and responding to their daily school work and from classroom interaction. But now that I was taking the time to understand how two students' past histories help explain their present circumstances, what I discovered astounded me.

In the oddest of coincidences, it turns out that both Meseret's and Tran's literacy education—that is, reading and writing instruction in the medium of a language in which they were deeply fluent and were working at grade level—was profoundly interrupted at the end of their sixth-grade year of schooling. This was when Tran left Vietnam, and this was when Meseret, still in Ethiopia, matriculated to an English-language-medium curriculum (as opposed to a curriculum taught through Amharic, her home language), even though, as she says, she didn't really know or speak English.

From that point on through high school, Tran (in the United States) and Meseret (in both Ethiopia and the United States) translated, regurgitated answers to book questions, memorized, and got by, by hook or crook. All in all, it seems clear to me that after the students' switchover to English-language-medium schooling, their literacy never took off again, never really resumed—assuming, of course, that literacy development can "jump" languages.

COMPOSITION, NOT LITERACY

Now to the college classroom. To dramatize why these two students aren't passing their composition courses—and, ultimately, it *is* their writing that dooms them—imagine teaching a college ESL composition curriculum, no matter what the proficiency level, to students whose literacy development basically halted in sixth grade. Even if teaching remedial college composition to *native* speakers of English, where English language fluency is not at issue, would a teacher have any chance of success with students who basically read and write at the sixth-grade level?

Composition courses—by their nature, or at least as we know them—focus on rhetorical and syntactic form, *not* on literacy development. (There would be nothing intrinsically wrong with that if the instruction met students' needs.) First-year composition, in my experience, presumes previous composition instruction, even essay writing. And with ESL college composition curricula largely designed to ready students for the first-year composition class—through a series of "dummy run[s]" (Larson, 1992, p. 32)—traditional ESL writing courses don't serve students like Meseret and Tran either. In a Catch 22, these students can't profit from composition instruction—either in ESL or, if they could ever get there, in first-year composition. They're not literate enough.

LITERACY, NOT COMPOSITION

Meseret and Tran, as individuals who don't relate to the textual world as readers and writers, have little meaningful exposure to the look and feel of texts in English *or* in their home language. Not since sixth grade have they done much, if any, reading or writing in *any* language. Not in their home language, since they neither read nor write out of school, and not in English either, really. In English, their school reading and writing experiences have been reductive, minimalist, and artificial. All in all, the students have received little to no input on which to build literacy since about the sixth grade.

Not surprisingly, in attempting to meet the cognitive demands placed on them by their composition classes, Meseret and Tran end up disassociating themselves from their writing. In assignment after assignment, they fail to bring their own thoughts and experiences into their texts: I could see this from studying their class work. Instead they write in a vacuum, their content and form dictated by what they think "the teacher wants." Rather than write about what they know—with the chance that form would be shaped by thought—they fabricate content and shoehorn it into their narrow version of a rigid five-paragraph framework. The school writing I saw *was* a mess—grammatical errors, mangled syntax, and incoherent content. No wonder they, without a base of literacy on which to build increasing competence in composition, grasp at straws in the form of simplistic expository formulae.

Interestingly enough, in my year-long e-mail correspondence with them, Tran and Meseret composed "alternative" texts. Although far from perfect, their electronic messages were clearer, more grammatical, and more coherent than any of the school writing they showed me. Overall, though, even if some English has, for them, "seeped in," as evidenced in their e-mail messages, it is not enough—and it is not of the "right" kind. (It doesn't "fit" the kind of academic discourse expected in the English-school-essay genre.)

BAD NEWS

In the end, within the confines of institutional schooling and proficiency testing, I see no hope for Tran and Meseret. The ESL composition instruction they have received is designed for students successfully schooled through the secondary level—students who could, after high school, profit from exposure to and practice in writing school essays in English. Not surprisingly, these may turn out to be international (F-1 visa) students. (Immigrant ESL students with strong literacy grounding don't enroll in college ESL programs anyway.)

What is absent from Meseret's and Tran's English-language school experience is text-rich immersion of the sort that produces literacy. This experience might have, could have, and should have happened ages ago, and we have absolutely no knowledge if literacy development, interrupted in childhood, can resume in adulthood and to what degree. With certainty, we know that it will *not* happen, to any significant degree, within the confines of college composition instruction.

So what do I do with this "bad news" (Newkirk, 1996, p. 13)? Tell Meseret and Tran to forget about college? To drop out before they flunk out and go work at Burger King? Admit to them that, as much as I wish otherwise, I can do nothing for them? And what about my ESL colleagues? Tell them their instruction is a waste for students like Meseret and Tran—students whose prior literacy education, or lack thereof, left them unprepared for college composition instruction? Frankly, I cannot see my way clear to really honestly discuss my findings with either the students or my colleagues. Instead my cowardly choice is to warn others farther afield.

CONCLUSION

So, a word to the wise. When organizing a research project, choose your population very, very carefully. Know what you're getting into and what you may need to be prepared to do with your results. Of course if new to qualitative work, a researcher will find valuable and interesting "how-to" information in an array of useful books (e.g., Coffey & Atkinson, 1996; Creswell, 1994; Ely et al., 1991; Glesne & Peshkin, 1992; Marshall & Rossman, 1995; Nunan, 1992; Seidman, 1998; Weiss, 1994). And these books will stimulate a novice researcher to think about things like design techniques and the role of theory.

What the general literature does not warn about is the complication of transmitting negative findings. Of course a researcher can always write up the study for professional peers to read, as I have mine (Blanton, 2003b). But what about a researcher's obligation to the subjects of her research—in my case, to Tran and Meseret? Do I just abandon them and walk away?

In the end, I say to any researcher who wants to avoid the discomfort of this sort of ethical dilemma, you should set out to study success, not failure. If, however, you intend to muck around in the lives of others—particularly in the lives of the vulnerable—then my advice is to proceed with extreme caution. Devise an ingenious plan for rendering results, even results potentially damaging to your research subjects, in a way that brings about positive change. (I can figure out no such plan.)

My only consolation at this point is that I may be helping to "talk into being" (Fairclough & Chouliaraki, 1999, p. 4) an ethical matter that needs to be of professional concern to those conducting research in ESL. Small consolation, indeed.

REFERENCES

Anonymous. (2002, May 3). Addicted in academe. *The Chronicle of Higher Education*, p. B3.

Blanton, L. L. (1998). *Varied voices: On language and literacy learning*. Boston: Heinle & Heinle.

Blanton, L. L. (2002). Seeing the invisible: Situating L2 literacy acquisition in child-teacher interaction. *Journal of Second Language Writing, 11*(4), 295–310.

Blanton, L. L. (2003a). Narrating one's self: Public-private dichotomies and a (public) writing life. In C. P. Casanave & S. Vandrick (Eds.), *Writing for scholarly publication: Behind the scenes in language education* (pp. 147–157). Mahwah, NJ: Lawrence Erlbaum Associates.

Blanton, L. L. (2003b). *Student, interrupted: The case of two immigrant ESL writers*. Manuscript submitted for publication.

Coffey, A., & Atkinson, P. (1996). *Making sense of qualitative data: Complementary research strategies*. Thousand Oaks, CA: Sage.

Creswell, J. W. (1994). *Research design: Qualitative and quantitative approaches*. Thousand Oaks, CA: Sage.

Ely, M. (1991). *Doing qualitative research: Circles within circles*. London: The Falmer Press.

Fairclough, N., & Chouliaraki, L. (1999). *Discourse in late modernity*. Edinburgh: Edinburgh University Press.

Glesne, C., & Peshkin, A. (1992). *Becoming qualitative researchers*. White Plains, NY: Longman.

Harklau, L., Losey, K. M., & Siegal, M. (Eds.). (1999). *Generation 1.5 meets college composition: Issues in the teaching of writing to U.S.-educated learners of ESL*. Mahwah, NJ: Lawrence Erlbaum Associates.

Karim, K. (2000). Conducting research involving palliative patients. *Nursing Standard, 15*/2, 34–36.

Larson, R. L. (1992, December). Classes of discourse, acts of discourse, writers, and readers. *English Journal, 81*(8), 32–36.

Leki, I. (1999). "Pretty much I screwed up": Ill-served needs of a permanent resident. In L. Harklau, K. M. Losey, & M. Siegal (Eds.), *Generation 1.5 meets college composition: Issues in the teaching of writing to U.S.-educated learners of ESL* (pp. 17–43). Mahwah, NJ: Lawrence Erlbaum Associates.

Marshall, C., & Rossman, G. B. (1995). *Designing qualitative research* (2nd ed.). Thousand Oaks, CA: Sage.

Newkirk, T. (1996). Seduction and betrayal in qualitative research. In P. Mortensen & G. Kirsch (Eds.), *Ethics and representation in qualitative studies of literacy* (pp. 3–16). Urbana, IL: National Council of Teachers of English.

Nunan, D. (1992). *Research methods in language learning*. Cambridge, England: Cambridge University Press.

Parini, J. (2001, December 21). By their clothes ye shall know them. *The Chronicle of Higher Education*, p. B24.

Petty, R. (1997). Everything is different now: Surviving ethnographic research. In E. Stringer (Ed.), *Community-based ethnography: Breaking traditional boundaries of research, teaching, and learning* (pp. 68–84). Mahwah, NJ: Lawrence Erlbaum Associates.

Seidman, I. (1998). *Interviewing as qualitative research: A guide for researchers in education and the social sciences* (2nd ed.). New York: Teachers College Press, Columbia University.

Temes, P. S. (2002, August 9). The naked professor. *The Chronicle of Higher Education*, p. B5.

Tunnell, K. D. (1998). Interviewing the incarcerated: Personal notes on ethical and methodological issues. In K. B. de Marrais (Ed.), *Inside stories: Qualitative research reflections* (pp. 127–137). Mahwah, NJ: Lawrence Erlbaum Associates.

Weiss, R. S. (1994). *Learning from strangers: The art and method of qualitative interview studies*. New York: The Free Press.

12

Coding Data in Qualitative Research on L2 Writing: Issues and Implications

Colleen Brice
Grand Valley State University, USA

Analyzing case study evidence is especially difficult because the strategies and techniques have not been well defined in the past.
—Yin (1994, p. 102)

Qualitative research is endlessly creative and interpretive. The researcher does not just leave the field with mountains of empirical materials and then easily write up his or her findings. Qualitative interpretations are constructed.
—Denzin and Lincoln (1994, p. 15)

Analyzing data is undoubtedly one of the most difficult aspects of qualitative research. This is a result of both the nature of the research process and the lack of adequate discussion of data analysis procedures in the existing literature as the writers quoted earlier suggest. Although acknowledgment of these difficulties is growing in what Denzin and Lincoln (1994) have termed this *fifth moment* of qualitative research—a period defined by the dual crises of representation and legitimization, discussions of research methods in research reports continue to be brief—glossing over problems the researchers may have encountered in the research process and presenting relatively unproblematic accounts of data coding procedures. As Keith Grant-Davie (1992) points out, however, such accounts "invariably hide a trail of difficult and questionable decisions" (p. 270).

In this chapter, I reflect on one such hidden trail—specifically, the questions I faced and the difficulties I encountered in the process of coding data in a case study of students' reactions to teacher feedback. My goal in conducting this self-examination is twofold: (a) to share my coding process with other researchers pursuing similar lines of inquiry so that they may use it as a resource, and (b) to bring to light specific problems I experienced in establishing the reliability of my coding scheme—problems which, I argue, raise questions about the applicability of current goodness criteria for qualitative research within constructivist, interpretivist paradigms and suggest the need for revised criteria that are more suitable to the kind of scholarship generally done in L2 composition—that is, single-authored, small scale, non-funded studies.

THE STUDY AND ITS UNDERPINNINGS

The case study I reflect on in this paper was designed to investigate how ESL writers respond—cognitively and affectively—to teacher feedback on drafts of their writing. Participants included six undergraduate ESL students from one section of a required, first-year university composition course and their teacher. I was interested in an array of questions related to L2 writers' affective and cognitive reactions to teacher feedback, including:

- What kinds of emotions do various types of comments inspire in L2 writers?
- How do L2 writers understand the various comments they receive on their drafts?
- What do they do in response to confusing comments?
- What kinds of feedback do they find most and least helpful for revising?
- What kinds of feedback do they expect and prefer, and to what extent are their expectations and preferences being met?
- What kinds of feedback do they recall from draft to draft?
- What personal, educational, and cultural background factors seem to influence writers' expectations, preferences, and reactions?

I chose a descriptive case study approach to pursue my research questions, as this approach allows for an emergent, flexible research design and focuses attention on the role of context. This enabled me to readjust the focus of my inquiry as I interacted with participants and learned what issues were important, and to examine students' reactions to teacher feedback within the larger (natural) context of the student-teacher relationship. My understanding of case study design was informed by several scholars in the fields of applied linguistics, composition studies, and social science, including Erlandson, Harris, Skipper, and Allen (1993), Johnson (1992), Lauer and Asher (1988), Lincoln and Guba (1985), Merriam (1998), Nunan (1992), Stake (1988), and Yin (1994), as well as published reports of case studies in the fields of applied linguistics and first and second language composition, and collections that focus on issues of validity, reliability, and ethics in qualitative research (Denzin & Lincoln, 1994; Kirsch & Sullivan, 1992; Mortensen & Kirsch, 1996).

Lincoln and Guba's (1985) authoritative text on naturalistic inquiry provided me with a set of criteria (credibility, transferability, dependability, and confirmability) for establishing the trustworthiness (quality) of my research. I tried my best to make my work trustworthy by engaging in the activities that were feasible in my context. These included: prolonged and persistent observation, triangulation in data collection, the keeping of a research journal, some member checking, and providing detailed descriptions of context, methods, and results in my report.

My data included: (a) semistructured audiotaped interviews with participants on their reactions to the comments they received from their teacher on all interim and final drafts during one semester; (b) check lists that solicited participants' emotional reactions to teacher feedback immediately following their first reading of the feedback; (c) copies of all commented-on interim and final drafts; (d) observations of class and conference sessions; (e) semistructured audiotaped interviews with the teacher about his approach to response and his written feedback on specific students' drafts; (f) interviews with the participating students and teacher on their educational and professional backgrounds; and (g) a research journal in which I recorded my observations, insights, and procedures as the study progressed.

In the remainder of this chapter, I focus the first of these—audiotaped recordings of interviews with participants on their reactions to their teacher's feedback—describing the process by which I coded the interview transcripts and discussing a few of the difficulties I faced along the way.

THE CODING PROCESS

In qualitative research, data analysis is a complex, analytic, and creative process in which some form of classification—or coding—is inevitably involved. It is an active process in which researchers identify salient patterns or themes by reading through data reiteratively and then attempt to explain them by looking for connections among the patterns and the context

(Lincoln & Guba, 1985). Findings do not just "emerge," as is often claimed in research reports. Broadly speaking then, coding refers to the process of looking for meaning, and this process spans the length of the research process itself (Erlandson et al., 1993; Grant-Davie, 1992; Lincoln & Guba, 1985; Merriam, 1998).

In its more narrow sense, coding refers to the actual activity of breaking up and grouping data into categories that reflect major issues that have been identified in the data. Conventionally, this is a two-step process, with unitization preceding categorization (cf. Lincoln & Guba, 1985; Merriam, 1998; Nathan-Dryden, 1987; Perl, 1978).

CODING SCHEME 1: PARSE BEFORE YOU PIGEONHOLE

In my first attempt to code student interview transcripts, I was guided by this "unitize and then categorize" approach, working on the assumption that this was obligatory. The research I had read proposed a variety of criteria for unitizing data, noting that units could vary greatly in length depending on the purpose of the inquiry.

Given that I was working with spoken data, I could not use syntactic units, such as the sentence, or rhetorical units, such as the paragraph. I did not have formal sentences or paragraphs in the transcripts. I warily decided to use the T-unit—an independent clause and all of its non-clausal elements, excluding subordinators—as this unit had been used frequently in composition research when formal sentence boundaries could not be assumed, and because it would enable me to generate coding categories that were mutually exclusive, which is a criterion for good categories, according to qualitative research methodologists (Hunt, 1965).

I parsed 100 pages of transcripts into T-units, marking unit boundaries with parentheses. Following this, I read through the transcripts to get an overall impression of students' reactions and perceptions—to identify themes that could characterize students' responses to the commentary. Several readings of the data led to the generation of a detailed coding scheme that could be used to code individual T-units for the function of a student's response. This initial coding scheme drew on the coding schemes developed by other writing researchers, specifically Nathan Dryden (1987), whose categories were adapted from Perl (1978). Adapted extensively to suit the focus of this research project, the coding scheme contained 36 categories, including codes such as, "+/–U: expresses understanding/lack of understanding of teacher comment," "ET: explains teacher's expectations, policies, or requirements," "ExW: expresses preferences/wants," and "DC: describes comment/feedback received."

I applied the coding scheme to the parsed data, targeting the primary function of each T-unit and assigning it one code. The coding process was relatively unproblematic. T-unit boundaries were easy to identify, and because I had such a detailed coding scheme, it was possible to acknowledge subtle distinctions in the focus of various units. Unfortunately, this ease of application came at a great price: the loss of meaning. Individual T-units did not retain enough of the context, in many instances, to allow for meaningful interpretation. I abandoned this approach, realizing that I needed a coding scheme that was less fine-grained and less functional, that related to the major questions I was asking and divided data into larger, more meaningful chunks. I found myself at a loss, however, concerning the type of unit that I might use to parse the data before I categorized it.

CODING SCHEME 2: CATEGORIZE IN ORDER TO UNITIZE

The initial problems I experienced with coding led me back to the literature on qualitative research in search of more information on the coding of transcribed data. The discussions of data analysis tended to be brief and vague. For example: "Data analysis usually involves a continual process of looking for meaning by sorting reiteratively through the data" (Johnson, 1992, p. 90). I broadened the scope of my reading, which led me to the "episodic unit"—a unit that conflates the activities of parsing and classifying data. An episodic unit is based on the categories in a coding system, and it lasts for as long as a participant continues to make the same kind of comment. It was developed by Grant-Davie (1992) for use in the coding of oral reading protocol transcripts, within which the boundaries of various utterances are less clear than in written data. I saw obvious advantages to using the episodic unit to code my own transcripts. It would enable me to parse my data into units that retained enough context to be meaningful.

I read through several interview transcripts and developed new, broader categories that reflected the major issues students raised in their comments. I followed Lincoln and Guba's (1985) guidelines, trying to make my units heuristic (aimed at an understanding I needed to have) and independent (interpretable on their own; the smallest unit of meaning possible). The coding scheme that resulted from this revision is presented in Table 12.1. It contained 18 coding categories that were related to the major questions I was investigating—half the number of categories in the first coding scheme. Categories focused on students' preferences and expectations for teacher feedback, understanding and recall of teacher feedback, emotional reactions to teacher feedback, reported revision responses to teacher

TABLE 12.1
Coding Scheme for Student Interview Transcripts, Version 2

Coding Category	*Code*
Explains how comments made her/him feel; expresses emotion in response to feedback	F
Expresses positive/negative judgment of comment or response practice	+/–L
Discusses expectations concerning feedback or specific comments	+/–E
Describes the type of feedback desired/preferred and not desired/preferred on first, second, or final drafts	+/–W
Expresses understanding/lack of understanding of comment	+/–U
Describes what action she/he plans to take to find out what particular written comment(s) or grade means	P
Explains type of comments that will be most/least helpful for future writing	+/–HC
Accepts/agrees or rejects/disagrees with comment or advice offered in comment	+/–AC
Recalls/does not recall comments from previous draft	+/–RC
Explains whether and how comments on previous drafts were used to revise current draft	+/–RV
Describes oral feedback received from teacher (during conference, class, office hours) or relays teacher's explanation of particular comment(s)	DT
Explains the criteria she/he thinks the teacher used to evaluate a draft	TC
Explains her/his criteria for good writing/a good draft of a particular assignment	SC
Discusses/relays grade received; explains why she/he thinks she/he got grade	G
Expresses positive/negative feelings about grade	+/–G
Expresses positive/negative judgment about the teacher	+/–T
Expresses positive/negative judgment about the class	+/–Cl
Expresses positive/negative judgment about self, writing ability, draft	+/–S

feedback, and attitudes toward/assessment of themselves/their writing, their teacher, and the course.[1]

I applied this scheme to analyze about 50 pages of interview transcript to try it out, and it went fairly well. One problem I faced immediately, however, related to the mutual exclusivity of categories. In many cases, I found that participants' remarks reflected more than one category of response simultaneously. For example, in the excerpt of transcript below, the participant's remarks provide both an explanation of what she did in response to teacher feedback that she did not understand—in this case, the grade she received on her first paper—and an indication of what she wants in terms of feedback—in this case, comments explaining her grade.

[1]This scheme, after some revision based on interrater reliability coding, became the final coding scheme I applied to all of my data. The revised, final version is presented in Table 12.2.

TABLE 12.2
Coding Scheme for Student Interview Transcripts: Final Version

Comprehension (+/–U): Expresses understanding/lack of understanding of comment
Plans (P): Describes what action she/he plans to take to find out what particular written comments mean
Recall (+/–RC): Does/does not recall comments from previous draft/previous paper
Feeling (F): Expresses emotion in response to comment/feedback; talks about how feedback made her/him feel
Helpful (+/–HC): Identifies comment that is/is not helpful for writing/revising
Accepts/Rejects Comment for Revision (+/–RV): Explains whether and how she/he will or has utilized comments on current or previous draft to revise
Expectations (+/–E): Discusses her/his expectations concerning feedback (aspects of her/his writing that she/he expected the teacher to comment on which the teacher may not have commented on, expectations about feedback on first, second, final drafts); indicates she/he did/did not expect certain feedback
Wants (+/–W): Describes the type of feedback she/he does/does not want or appreciate (like) on first, second, or final drafts
Teacher Criteria (TC): Explains the criteria she/he thinks the teacher used to evaluate a draft
Student Criteria (SC): Explains her/his criteria for a particular assignment
Evaluates Self/Writing (+/–S): Expresses positive/negative judgment about self or writing ability
Evaluates Teacher (+/–T): Expresses positive/negative judgment about the teacher
Evaluates Class (+/–CL): Expresses positive/negative judgment about the class
Peer Review (PR): Describes peer review session
Evaluates Peer Review (+/–PR): Expresses positive/negative judgment about peer review

The codes P (describes what action writer *plans* to take to find out what particular written comments mean) and +W (describes the type of feedback writer *does/does not want* or appreciate (like) on first, second, or final drafts) both seem to apply to this episodic unit, the boundaries of which are indicated by parentheses:

> *Researcher*: Okay, so you saw that paper and you got your grade in class?
>
> *Participant*: (Yeah because I know the grade so I want to talk to him, and uh not only for this reason, because yesterday—today we were handing in the second [draft of our] summary. So, and um for my understanding he ask us to do something related to the first paper, and I did do some research on the library and I didn't find anything to support my point, so I found something else. So that's why I went to his office—to find out two things, and one is about grade. I mean I don't care too much about the grade, but I really do want to know what uh what what was wrong with my paper so I can improve myself. That that's what I want to know. And second is uh, second one is um I was hoping

that he can give me some direction about those I mean this [inaudible word] project. **[P/+W]**)[2]

The question for me, then, became, should I recognize this fact in my coding and apply a slash code (P/+W), or should I limit myself to one code per unit, assigning the code for whichever of the two categories I believed the unit best fit into?

After considerable reflection on the issue, I decided to indicate multiple category-ship where I felt it was applicable, using slash codes, such as P/+W for the excerpt above, to signal this because of the inherently interrelated nature of the issues I was studying. For example, it is generally the case that students do not prefer (–W) the types of feedback that they find unhelpful (–HC) or confusing (–U). So it is very plausible that in sections of transcript, a participant might intersperse remarks about their feedback preferences within a discussion of specific comments they find unhelpful or confusing. And it is also plausible that the remarks may be organized in such a way as to make it impossible to tease them apart without losing context necessary for interpretation of those belonging to either category.

ESTABLISHING THE RELIABILITY OF CODING SCHEME 2

Having developed a coding scheme that seemed appropriate to my study, the next step, according to my understanding of guidelines for quality in the application of coding instruments, was to test its reliability. It was my understanding that in order to ensure the reliability of my analysis, the tools I used to arrive at that analysis needed to be reliable themselves. Thus, I needed to determine whether my scheme could be applied consistently to the transcript data. In order to do this, I asked a peer to participate in an interrater-agreement coding session. The peer I chose had expertise in L2 composition and experience in qualitative research, was familiar with the project in general, and luckily for me, was a generous friend who was willing to code for meager recompense (pizza and a game of *Scrabble*).

At the coding session, I gave her copies of the coding scheme and a copy of the participant's commented-on second draft relevant to the tran-

[2]Note that the coding for this episodic unit appears in boldface type in brackets at the end of the unit. This procedure is used for all coded transcript excerpts throughout the article. In the actual transcripts, codes were marked in the right-hand margin alongside the episodic units to which they referred.

script to be coded. We began by reviewing the coding scheme to gain a common understanding of the categories. I explained the concept of the episodic unit and showed her examples of different categories in transcripts that I had already coded using the revised scheme. We also read the participant's draft and the teacher's written feedback on the draft, and we discussed the assignment for which the draft was written.

Following this training session, we began to code the data. We had two sessions. For the first session, I gave my peer a copy of the transcript on which I had already marked what I perceived the unit boundaries to be. Her task was to apply the coding scheme to categorize the various episodic units. For the second rating session, I asked her to do it all on her own: to unitize as she categorized.

In both sessions, we achieved fairly strong interrater agreement. In the first session, we applied the same code to 29 of the 40 episodic units in the segment of text (72.5% agreement). In the second session, we agreed on the boundaries and categories of 53 of 65 episodic units in the segment of text (81.5% agreement). However, we also had some problems that suggested that the interrater reliability coding process does not and cannot work to establish the reliability of a coding instrument or a researcher's application of that coding instrument, much less to demonstrate the dependability of their overall analysis in the research report in multi-method research that employs extensive interviewing and observation of participants. I discuss two problems my peer and I experienced to illustrate my point.

PROBLEM 1: I KNOW MORE THAN MY PEER RATER DOES

The first problem relates to the difference in our exposure to the participant (whom I will refer to as Amy from here forward) whose comments are recorded in the transcript that we coded during our interrater agreement coding sessions. I conducted the interview from which the transcript was derived. I was there. I saw Amy's reactions and heard her voice as she gave her answers. I worked with Amy for a long time in a variety of contexts. I knew things about her personal and educational background that informed all of the interpretations I made. My peer did not have any of this. The transcript did not and could not carry my history with Amy, the context, or the numerous important paralinguistic cues that help people interpret each other's behaviors and affective states, so there was a significant disparity in our ability to interpret Amy's responses. Consider the following excerpt of transcript:

Amy: (But I wish I said I wish you could told me, I mean after my first draft, you told you told me this kind of, you gave me instruction more directly. Maybe you can talk to me, you say, "Okay, I don't want you to," because he said he he didn't want me to [crying] to feel bad. What's the word he used? **[+W]**) (I mean it was good, he said he doesn't want to disappointed me, he he want to encourage me. **[+T]**) ('Cause I talked to him, I say, "listen, this my first paper, I have ever write any paper, I even never take an English or composition class." So, and uh, it was . . . he said because uh he didn't want to, I mean, to to let me feel bad, so that's how he still says the topic the topic is good, but I need to more detailed thing. I I said, "you should tell me how detailed it should be." And uh, today he told me, he said, "I wish you could write something about for example living New York City and one day you you you you maybe one day you went out took out something." And uh, and uh it it's really something I experiencing. And I said, "even even though the paper in the paper the the the example I gave to you is, it's, I mean that's that's the thing I really did in New York City, I just didn't say it, okay? Right?" So, he said. But anyway, I I just by now I say, "I really learned [inaudible word] I I just needed some directions or instructions from you, so, see, I I can learn better so I know where is my weak point so I can start it over from there." Yeah. **[+*Rv* versus +W/–T]**)

My peer and I coded the last episodic unit we identified in this segment differently. This unit begins at "'Cause" and ends with "Yeah." She categorized this unit as +Rv ("explains whether and how comments on previous drafts were used to revise current draft"). This is a logical coding. She noted that Amy was telling her teacher that the examples she had included in her paper *were* based on her own experiences in New York City, so she interpreted this as an example of the student explaining how she had used her teacher's feedback to revise her first draft.

I did not interpret this unit as an example of +Rv. Instead, I interpreted it as +W/–T—an example of Amy "describ[ing] the type of teacher feedback she desires/prefers/wants on first, second, and final drafts" and "express[ing] negative judgment about the teacher." In this segment (and in those preceding it in the transcript), Amy is reporting what happened when she went to talk to her teacher earlier that day about the grade she received on her first paper. The teacher had distributed students' grades that morning in class. Because he did not provide written comments on final drafts—which were the third drafts in a three-draft system in which first and second drafts were commented on but not evaluated—he did not return them. Students received their grades on separate sheets of paper. Amy had received a B minus, and she said wanted to know why. She said that she went to her teacher's office that morning to discuss two things:

her grade and the next assignment. She explained, "I mean, I don't care too much about the grade, but I really do want to know what uh what was wrong with my paper so I can improve myself. That's what I want to know" (Amy transcript, p. 17).

According to Amy's account, when she asked her teacher about her grade, he told her that she received the grade for two reasons: 1) her topic was not a good one for the writing project they were engaged in because it was not researchable (and the project required primary and secondary source research), and 2) she had written her paper too seriously. The class was completing the sequenced writing project, as outlined in Ilona Leki's (1991/1992) *TESOL Journal* article, which engages students in writing five papers on one topic of their own choosing. In the first paper, which is what Amy is referring to in this discussion, students are asked to tell readers what topic they have chosen for the project and explain what they know about it and what experience they have had with it. Amy felt that her teacher's explanation of her grade contradicted feedback he had given her when she went to talk to him about the first draft of her paper. She had gone to speak with her teacher after class on the day he returned first drafts with written feedback. She did not understand the first part of his end comment on the last page of her draft, which read: "Well, your draft is almost too neat. I was not expecting anything like this from you at this time. I like your example of the price of clothing you cited. You need to do much more of that." For her sequenced writing project, Amy had chosen to write about the advantages of living in a big city, specifically New York City, where she had resided for several years prior to coming to school in the Midwest. According to her account, when she met with her teacher to discuss his feedback, he told her that her topic was a good one but she needed to concentrate on something specific that she liked about living in New York (narrow her focus) and add more details from her personal experience.

In the excerpt of transcript earlier, then, Amy is complaining about the feedback she received—about the contradiction between what her teacher told her about the viability of her topic on her first draft (good/viable) and on her final draft (not good/not viable). The quick switches in the transcript—between Amy's remarks about her conference with the teacher on her *first* draft and her conference with him on her *final* draft (which took place earlier on the day the interview was recorded) are difficult to perceive when reading the transcript. More importantly, the transcript does not adequately reflect the participant's affective state. I indicate that Amy was crying, but this does not adequately convey her emotional condition. She was very upset during the session, and she broke into tears several times as she was explaining her feelings. These two factors seem to account for the differences in my peer's and my own coding of this unit.

PROBLEM 2: I AM MORE ATTUNED TO PARTICIPANTS' LANGUAGE USE THAN MY PEER CODER

A related problem my peer and I experienced in coding relates to the interpretation of the participant's speech. Amy's speech contains errors in pronunciation, vocabulary, and grammar. Because I had a great deal of experience working with Amy face to face, I could more easily interpret portions of transcript in which the vocabulary, grammar, and syntax were confusing. I was present when Amy made these comments to hear the intonation she used, which carries a great deal of the meaning in an utterance. The transcript does not reflect this. Consider the example below, in which I have highlighted phrases that Amy stressed and provided phonetic transcriptions (in brackets []) for words she mispronounced:

> *Amy*: (It's it's all right. I mean, he didn't do anything wrong to me. He he was good. And uh, I'm just I just I I don't know it's my failure or his failure that I didn't get his point. **[+T]**) (I mean if I was um so much away from the the direction whose us whose whose expected, *I think he he should have told me before the final draft. And at least make it clear* **[+W]**) (*—you you saw his um his uh comment on my paper was very*, I mean, I mean, my paper, the the final paper I wasn't satisfied because I think after something he said to me *even the style he asked me to change*. I think it's a little bit [wagd]. I mean not that clear. It's [wagd], [vagd], right. It's vague; it's not that clear. I mean the comment he gave it to me even vaguer than the one, I mean. **[*–U/–S* versus –U/–HC]**)

My peer coded the last unit in this segment –U/–S ("Expresses lack of understanding of comment"/"Expresses negative judgment about self or writing ability"). She thought Amy was saying that she did not understand the teacher's comments and that she was not satisfied with her final draft. We agreed on half of this coding. I too gave this segment a dual (slashed) code, with the first code being –U, but for the second code I did not assign –S; instead, I assigned –HC ("Identifies comment that is not helpful for writing/revising"). What the student was saying she was not satisfied with in this segment is not her final draft, but instead the written feedback she received. The difference in our coding of this segment is likely the result of Amy's syntax and vocabulary. The following segment is particularly troublesome with regard to these two features: "I mean, my paper, the the final paper I wasn't satisfied because I think after something he said to me even the style he asked me to change. I think it's a little bit [wagd]. I mean not that clear."

As I interpreted it, within the context of the surrounding statements, Amy was saying: I wasn't satisfied with *the teacher's written comments* on my first draft because they were vague, unclear comments—they did not indicate that I should change the style of my paper—but something my teacher said to me (today, when discussing the grade I received on my final draft) suggested that this was what he had wanted me to do. However, this segment could easily be interpreted as my peer interpreted it, to be saying: I wasn't satisfied with *my final draft* because my teacher asked me to change the style of the paper but my final draft was not that clear. In addition, the terms [wagd] and [vagd] are difficult to interpret. Amy uses [wagd], [vagd], and [veyg] (vague) interchangeably in the last statements in this segment as she struggles to say the word "vague." These mispronunciations are clearly something that would cause difficulty for independent readers of the transcript, and they seem to account for some of the disparities in coding that my peer and I experienced.

DISCUSSION: THE RELATIONSHIP BETWEEN CODING AND DEPENDABILITY, RECONFIGURED

What I think the examples I have discussed in this paper illustrate is that the interrater reliability coding process, as conceived within composition studies, is problematic, and that second language writing data raises additional, unique difficulties with the practice. The main problem is related to the expectations researchers have of the process, namely, that it can establish the dependability of a researcher's data analysis or even of their entire study. Grant-Davie (1992) has pointed out that reliability tests have been taken to establish not only a researcher's consistency in applying a coding scheme but also the objectivity of the coding itself. He explains:

> If proven reliable, a coding system acquires added authority, the implication being that it describes, rather than interprets, what is in the data. A high reliability rating thus suppresses the subjective, interpretive nature of coding and endows the system with the appearance of impartiality, making it seem a "truer," more "scientific" instrument of analysis. (pp. 282–283)

Of course a coding scheme neither describes nor interprets data. The task of interpretation resides with the person employing the coding scheme to help with the job of identifying patterns and understanding the issues under investigation. Given that there are dramatic differences in the knowledge bases of the people involved in employing a coding scheme during interrater reliability testing, it is unreasonable to expect them to code any given data set identically. The researcher has a bank of knowledge about and experiences with study participants that an independent coder does not have, and this knowledge and experience significantly shape their coding, as is evident in my earlier account.

In addition, second language data can pose interpretive challenges of their own, adding another layer of difficulty to the coding process. In the case of transcribed oral data, the presence of various performance features (e.g., hesitations, repetition) and production errors (syntactical, grammatical, lexical), together with the lack of suprasegmental information, can make it difficult for a reader to parse and interpret the utterances. Again researchers have a great advantage over independent coders in interpreting such data. They have worked with the participant over a period of time, and they were likely present when the data were recorded to hear and see how the participant said what they said, and this auditory and visual information carries a great deal of the meaning.

Given these problems with the interrater reliability process, qualitative researchers cannot expect to use it as a means to establish their dependability in analyzing data or the dependability of their studies. This raises two important questions: (a) what is the purpose of cross-coding in qualitative inquiry in L2 composition if any?; and (b) how can researchers ensure that their analyses and studies are dependable?

In response to the first question, I think it is important to recognize that, although cross-coding cannot establish the dependability of a coding scheme or a researcher's analysis of data, it can still be a worthwhile process to engage in. I found it beneficial to discuss my research with a peer and to get her perspective on the coding instrument I was developing. During the interrater reliability coding sessions, I thought of a number of questions that may not have occurred to me were I working on the data alone. In addition, my peer thought of questions for me while she was coding the data, and discussing these helped me to not only refine my coding scheme, but also to think about the project more generally.

In regard to the second question, I am not suggesting that qualitative researchers in L2 composition *not* consider dependability. Dependability certainly must be considered, but current guidelines for establishing dependability in qualitative research in general are not realistic or applicable to the type of research done in L2 writing, and this may account, in part, for L2 writing researchers' reliance on interrater reliability checking. I am referring to the types of quality criteria outlined in qualitative methodology texts (e.g., Erlandson, et al., 1993; Huberman & Miles, 1994; Lincoln & Guba, 1985; Merriam, 1988; Schwandt & Halpern, 1988; Yin, 1994), in which some type of external audit is recommended for establishing the dependability of a study.

Consider the complex process advocated by Lincoln and Guba (1985), who are looked to by many qualitative L2 composition researchers for guidance. The authors propose that qualitative researchers conduct what they term a *confirmability audit* to establish the dependability (reliability) and confirmability (neutrality) of their inquiry. Based on Halpern's (1983) model, this audit involves several steps. First, a researcher must develop an audit trail or formal, presentable documentation of the processes and products of their inquiry—referred to by Yin (1994) as case study protocols and case study databases. This trail includes the following six kinds of information: raw data, data reduction and analysis products, data reconstruction and synthesis products (e.g., coding schemes, draft of final report), process notes, materials relating to intentions and dispositions (e.g., research proposal, personal notes), and instrument development information. They must then get a disinterested peer, who has both expertise in research methodology and substantial knowledge of the topic under investigation, to agree to audit the processes and products of their study—a process that Lincoln and Guba (1985) estimate takes about 7 to 10 days, and which they contend is "not so difficult to carry out as might be imagined" (p. 325).

This does not seem viable to me. I had neither the means nor the time to engage in such an external inquiry audit, and I believe my situation is reflective of that of most independent researchers working on small-scale, nonfunded projects. I think those of us who do research in second language writing need to develop guidelines of our own—practical and realistic guidelines that apply to the kind of work generally done in L2 composition. I realize this will not be a simple task. Issues of dependability and credibility in qualitative research are complex, and the kinds of qualitative research being done in the field of second language composition are many and varied. It requires time and dialogue among members of the field.

In the interim, I would suggest the following two guidelines, neither of which is revolutionary, but both of which are feasible. First, I suggest that researchers' dependability in analyzing data be assessed—by editors, reviewers, publishers, and readers—based on the extent to which they ground their findings in data in their report. This suggestion has implications for expected manuscript length, which is the subject of my second suggestion. I suggest that we (writers, readers, reviewers, editors, and publishers in L2 composition) revise our expectations regarding length for qualitative research reports. Specifically, increased length limits would enable researchers to include more evidence to support their findings, and it would also allow them to more fully describe their data analysis procedures and any coding schemes they developed and/or employed. This would help other researchers seeking to conduct related inquiry, and it would better enable readers to assess for themselves whether the analysis, and the study itself, can be considered dependable and confirmable.

I realize that I have only touched on a few of the thorny issues that arise in data analysis in this chapter. However, I hope that my reflections help others who are engaged in similar research, and that this volume opens up the floor for further discussion of the difficulties of qualitative inquiry in second language composition.

REFERENCES

Brice, C. (1998). *ESL writers' reactions to teacher feedback: A multiple case study*. Unpublished doctoral dissertation, Purdue University, West Lafayette, IN.

Denzin, N. K., & Lincoln, Y. S. (Eds.). (1994). *Handbook of qualitative research*. Thousand Oaks, CA: Sage.

Denzin, N. K., & Lincoln, Y. S. (1994). Introduction: Entering the field of qualitative research. In N. K. Denzin & Y. S. Lincoln (Eds.), *Handbook of qualitative research* (pp. 1–17). Thousand Oaks, CA: Sage.

Erlandson, D. A., Harris, E. L., Skipper, B. L., & Allen, S. D. (1993). *Doing naturalistic inquiry: A guide to methods*. Newbury Park, CA: Sage.

Grant-Davie, K. (1992). Coding data: Issues of validity, reliability, and interpretation. In G. E. Kirsch & P. A. Sullivan (Eds.), *Methods and methodology in composition research* (pp. 270–286). Carbondale, IL: Southern Illinois University.

Guba, E. G., & Lincoln, Y. S. (1994). Competing paradigms in qualitative research. In N. K. Denzin & Y. S. Lincoln (Eds.), *Handbook of qualitative research* (pp. 105–117). Thousand Oaks, CA: Sage.

Halpern, E. S. (1983). *Auditing naturalistic inquiries: The development and application of a model*. Unpublished doctoral dissertation, Indiana University, Bloomington, IN.

Huberman, A. M., & Miles, M. B. (1994). Data management and analysis methods. In N. K. Denzin & Y. S. Lincoln (Eds.), *Handbook of qualitative research* (pp. 428–444). Thousand Oaks, CA: Sage.

Hunt, K. W. (1965). *Grammatical structures written at three grade levels*. Champaign, IL: National Council of Teachers of English.

Johnson, D. M. (1992). *Approaches to research in second language learning*. New York: Longman.

Kirsch, G. E., & Sullivan, P. A. (Eds.). (1992). *Methods and methodology in composition research*. Carbondale, IL: Southern Illinois University.

Lauer, J., & Asher, J. (1988). *Composition research: Empirical designs*. New York: Oxford University Press.

Leki, I. (1991–1992). Building experience through sequenced writing assignments. *TESOL Journal, 1*(2), 19–23.

Lincoln, Y. S., & Denzin, N. K. (1994). The fifth moment. In N. K. Denzin & Y. S. Lincoln (Eds.), *Handbook of qualitative research* (pp. 575–586). Thousand Oaks, CA: Sage.

Lincoln, Y. S., & Guba, E. G. (1985). *Naturalistic inquiry*. Beverly Hills, CA: Sage.

Merriam, S. B. (1988). *Case study research in education: A qualitative approach*. San Francisco: Jossey-Bass.

Mortensen, P., & Kirsch, G. E. (1996). *Ethics & representation in qualitative studies of literacy*. Urbana, IL: National Council of Teachers of English.

Nathan-Dryden, I. J. (1987). *The composing processes of five Malaysian ESL/EFL college writers: A multimethod approach*. Unpublished doctoral dissertation, State University of New York at Buffalo.

Nunan, D. (1992). *Research methods in second language learning*. Cambridge: Cambridge University Press.

Perl, S. A. (1978). *Five writers writing: Case studies of the composing processes of unskilled college writers*. Unpublished doctoral dissertation, New York University, New York.

Schwandt, T. A., & Halpern, E. S. (1988). *Linking auditing and metaevaluation*. Newbury Park, CA: Sage.

Seidman, I. E. (1991). *Interviewing as qualitative research: A guide for researchers in education and the social sciences*. New York: Teachers College Press.

Stake, R. K. (1995). *The art of case study research*. Thousand Oaks, CA: Sage.

Yin, R. K. (1994). *Case study research: Design and methods*. Thousand Oaks, CA: Sage.

13

Digging Up Texts and Transcripts: Confessions of a Discourse Analyst

Ken Hyland
University of London, UK

Like most people who study writing, I am interested in what people do when they write and why they do it. But the different ways that writing is perceived means that these questions are approached by researchers in an enormous variety of ways. For some, writing is a kind of cognitive performance that can be modeled by analogy with computer processing through observation and writers' on-task verbal reports. Others are interested in the impact of immediate local contexts of writing and observe the actions of individual writers. A third group looks to the cultural and institutional context in which communication occurs to explore the ideologies and power relations that writing expresses and maintains. In other words, all methods are inseparable from theories: We look for answers in the places that will best inform our views of what writing is.

As a fairly orthodox applied linguist, I prefer to start with texts. Influenced by Swales, Bazerman, Nystrand, and others interested in writing as interaction, I regard these as the concrete expressions of social purposes. Precisely because these purposes are social, and therefore intended for particular audiences, I believe we need to see writing as mediated by the institutions and cultures in which it occurs. Every act of writing is embedded in wider social and discursive practices that carry assumptions about participant relationships and how these should be structured and negotiated. Our experiences and perceptions of audience shape our communicative practices in significant ways, influencing the way we structure information, the relationships we establish with our readers, and the extent to which we personally appear in our texts. This chapter illustrates one way in which these thoughts work out in practice by reflecting on a recent study of Hong Kong undergraduates' writing (Hyland, 2002). I discuss the main issues under four headings: framing issues, selecting methods, collecting data, and analyzing data.

FRAMING THE ISSUE

The study partly emerged out of a sense that my undergraduate students had considerable problems constructing a credible representation of themselves and their work in their research writing. They seemed reluctant to claim an appropriate degree of authoritativeness in their texts or to personally get behind their statements, making their work seem anonymous and disembodied. When thinking about this, I was influenced by the work of Ivanič (1998), Kuo (1999), and others who pointed to the use of *I* as critical to meaning and credibility, helping to establish the commitment of writers to their words and setting up a relationship with their readers. I was also sensitized to notions of self-mention and academic assertion by a study I recently completed on expert writers that found academics made extensive use of exclusive first-person pronouns to strengthen their arguments and gain personal recognition for their claims. However, my students were not explicitly affirming their role in the discourse in this way.

I decided to pursue these impressions by investigating how these students used authorial pronouns. I was also interested in going beyond this descriptive dimension to examine how these students perceived self-reference and to explore possible explanations for their communicative practices. It seemed that a useful way of framing the issue might be to relate the use of first person to the work on rhetorical identity. The notion of identity is relatively new in writing research, but I was attracted by a conception that saw identity as less a phenomenon of private experience than a desire for affiliation and recognition in particular social networks (Shotter & Gergen, 1989). The notion that identities are constructed from culturally available discourses appealed to me as a socially oriented discourse analyst because it firmly located identity in the practices and structures of social communities.

When we employ the discourses of a community, there is strong pressure to take on the identity of a member of that community—to represent ourselves in a way valued by it. The term *positioning* has been used to describe the process by which identities are produced by socially available discourses (Davies & Harre, 1990). This does not suggest that people simply slot into pre-ordained social identities with ready-made sets of expected behaviours. But while there is always room for individual negotiation and maneuvering, in adopting the practices and discourses of a community, over time writers come to adopt its perspectives and interpretations, seeing the world in the same ways and taking on an identity as a member of that community. Newcomers, however, are likely to find that the discourses and practices of their disciplines support identities very different from those they bring with them from their home cultures. These problems often prevent students from communicating appropriate integrity and commitments, and they undermine their relationship to readers. For me these seemed to be issues worth exploring and provided a context for the research.

SELECTING METHODS

Although research manuals imply that research design largely involves fitting suitable methods to particular questions, research methodologies are never simply an objective response to an atheoretical problem. Every orientation toward data, analysis, and interpretation carries implicit assumptions about appropriate research criteria and the nature of evidence. The questions we ask and the ways we pursue them are always informed by our theories and beliefs about writing. For those like me who see writing as situated rhetorical action, writing doesn't stand alone as the work of an isolated and creative individual, but is constructed on the basis of the writer's familiarity with certain texts and contexts in which he or she has participated. In other words, I consider all texts to be constructed with a particular purpose and audience in mind and influenced by a background of community practices and expectations, awareness of other texts, pursuit of personal goals, and so on.

Framing pronoun use in terms of the cultural constraints on rhetorical conventions of personality suggested two possible lines of inquiry. Crudely, social approaches boil down to a choice between materializing texts as a feature of a concrete communicative engagement and examining interaction as a series of real, situated encounters, or dematerializing texts and approaching it as a package of specific linguistic features (Myers, 1999). The first involves an ethnographic approach focusing on particular writers, exploring what Nystrand (1987) calls the *situation of expression*, to investigate the personal and social histories of individual writers as they interact in specific contexts. The second involves removing texts from their actual circumstances of construction to make assumptions about the relationships between linguistic forms and rhetorical effects within particular communities.

Clearly the first line of inquiry portrays the richness of composing as writers negotiate their immediate writing circumstances. But I don't believe that concentrating on the local setting captures the culture and event within which the action is embedded and which the discourse invokes. Texts do not function communicatively at the time they are composed, but when they are read as they anticipate particular readers and the responses of those readers to what is written. Texts evoke the institutional frame within which the text is created—a social milieu that intrudes on the writer and activates specific responses to recurring tasks. By examining the genres and meanings that writers adopt, I believe we gain a great deal because we can explore the ways writers see their audience and how they seek to construct and engage in academic realities.

For these reasons, I followed the "dematerialising" route. I decided to look for preferred choices of pronoun use in a representative collection of student writing rather than single texts. As Sinclair (1991), Stubbs (1996), and others have shown, corpus studies demonstrate that writing is characterised by impressive regularities of pattern with endless variation. In what they include or omit, all texts make assumptions about their readers, shaped by prior texts, repetitions, and orientations to certain routines or conventions. A corpus approach brings a distributional perspective to linguistic analysis by providing quantitative information about the relative frequency of use of particular elements in different contexts, pointing to systematic tendencies in the selection of meanings. Therefore, corpora reduce the burden that is often placed on individual texts (or on intuitions) and dramatically show how particular grammatical and lexical choices are regularly made. In the research I conducted here, I explored the frequencies and patterns of co-occurrence in students' use of authorial pronouns to provide evidence for typical practices and perceptions.

Thus, this quantitative work seeks to identify significant patterns of meaning invisible to ethnographic approaches, but text analyses must be balanced with an understanding of the production and reception of those texts. We need deeper understandings of how and why writers make the choices they do by learning what text users think they are doing when they write and read. I therefore decided to support and explore the text analytic data with interviews. Although I had never used these methods before with L2 writers, I had previously found them invaluable when studying expert practices (e.g., Hyland, 2000). I was comfortable with them and confident in their usefulness in offering insights into writing.

THE TEXT DATA

To ensure that the text samples were representative of undergraduate research writing, I compiled a corpus of 64 final year project reports. This genre seemed to offer the best access to Hong Kong students' academic writing because it is required in virtually all programmes and is by far the most substantial and sustained piece of writing they do in their undergraduate careers. The reports are based on year-long research projects and are used to assess students' ability to apply theories and methods learned in their courses and to demonstrate the skills of reviewing literature, conducting research, analysing results, and presenting findings. Students are assisted by regular individual consultations with a supervisor and produce reports between 8,000 and 13,000 words long designed to reflect the research article formats of their discipline.

One question that occurs early in compiling a corpus is, "How big?" This is the issue of representativeness, and there is little agreement on it. No corpus can ever be more than a small sample of the writing that people do in a particular genre, yet developing a massive corpus may be counterproductive. Not only does it require additional time and resources to gain access to texts, but ever larger corpora can make it impossible to deal with the output. Moreover, a large corpus does not necessarily represent a genre better than a smaller one, particularly if it is used to study high-frequency items. More important is that the sample is carefully collected to include a cross-section of the focus texts and that it provides an adequate quantity of target tokens for the researcher to work with. I wanted a corpus that would represent a broad cross-section of academic practice, including hard sciences, engineering, applied social sciences, technology, and business, and collected eight reports from each of eight different degree programs to do this.

Collecting a corpus requires persistence and patience. Some reports were easier to get than others, and in many cases I had to harass the departments with several e-mails and visits. It was then necessary to track down the writers and get their informed consent to use their reports, and often I had to take the course leader to lunch. Even when I eventually got the reports, many were supplied in hard copy, which meant that they had to be scanned and cleaned to be computer readable.

I computer searched the corpus for the first-person uses *I, me, my, we, us, our, mine*, and *ours* using *WordPilot 2000*, a commercially available concordance programme, and I checked all cases to ensure they were exclusive first-person uses. The frequency counts showed 637 occurrences of self-referential pronouns and determiners, roughly 10 in every 10,000 words. In making several sweeps of the data to compile a count of the different forms, I also noted down what seemed to be recurring pragmatic functions. Unlike some corpus analysts, I use a corpus to assist rather than drive my research, and there is nothing I use a corpus to do that could not feasibly, if more tediously, be done on paper. Concordance lines are an important tool, however, as they display all occurrences of a particular feature in its immediate co-text environment, allowing the researcher to get an idea of the meanings conveyed by the form. Generally a single line of text was sufficient to identify a pronoun function, but *WordPilot* provides instant access to the wider co-text, and often this helped me clarify ambiguities.

Checking concordance lines is a recursive procedure that involves trying to narrow down, expand, and combine initial general categories. This is a way of coding data that, although influenced by the researcher's theoretical knowledge and experience, ensures that the categories are relevant to the research questions and are constructed from the data. The approach produces categories that satisfy qualitative criteria in that they are:

- Conceptually useful: help to answer research questions
- Empirically valid: created from the data itself
- Analytically practical: easy to identify, specific, nonoverlapping

This recursion allowed me to classify each instance as associated with the performance of one of five functions, either stating a goal, explaining a procedure, stating results or claims, expressing self-benefits, or elaborating an argument. This kind of coding needs to be carefully validated to avoid simply reflecting the researcher's subjective perceptions. Swales (1981) recognised the danger of this 20 years ago when he cautioned that "the discourse analyst labels something as x and then begins to see x occurring all over the place" (p. 13). Interrater agreement is crucial, and in this case I asked a colleague to independently code a sample of the corpus. As one might expect, there were disagreements, but discussions and reanalysis of problematic cases reduced these to satisfactory levels. More important, specialist informants—specifically, some writers and readers of these texts—were brought in later to help confirm findings, validate insights, and add psychological reality to the categories, authenticating what users saw as plausible interpretations.

Texts are most usefully studied comparatively across corpora to better understand the background of expectations highlighted by different patterns of use. The frequency of particular forms and the functions they express can be identified and then studied in more detail. I used an existing corpus of 240 published research articles closely related to the student fields to explore expert uses. These papers were selected from journals familiar to students from their reading lists and recommended by subject specialists. This corpus totaled 1.3 million words, deliberately twice as large as the student database to strengthen observations about general expert academic practices, as opposed to those about a specific student population.

Another decision to be made was whether to apply statistical analyses to the frequency and collocation data. Some researchers use Mutual Information scores or t-scores—statistical procedures that show the significance of a particular word co-occurring with another word (e.g., Hunston, 2002). In this case, I was not interested in lexical collocations, but the frequency with which authorial pronouns were used to express particular functions. My intention was not to establish detailed nonparametric comparisons, but to discover broad distributional differences of items between the two groups. I saw the frequencies as a springboard to more qualitative study—a basis for characterising broad similarities and differences in the two genres to develop possible explanations of underlying communicative purposes and interactional practices.

Nor were the comparisons made to evaluate learner performance or suggest a deficit orientation to what L2 writers can achieve. Novice and professional writers are likely to differ considerably in their knowledge and understandings of appropriate academic conventions and practices, making direct comparisons unhelpful. The study of parallel corpora, however, can provide information about what different groups of language users actually *do*. They are useful because of what they tell us about different writers' linguistic and interactive schemata, and in my case they helped to throw light on student perceptions of academic conventions and on how student writers sought to accommodate their own cultural practices to the demands of the new community. Analysis of the two corpora showed that first-person pronouns were substantially more frequent in the published corpus and that the students generally sought to downplay their authorial identity by consciously avoiding its most authoritative functions, such as making a commitment to an interpretation or claim. In other words, they sought to deny ownership and responsibility for their views, and I set out to investigate this further.

THE INTERVIEW DATA

Frequency and collocational data provide descriptions of existing practice, but are not ends in themselves. Although corpus analyses are excellent for raising awareness of uses, for telling us what writers do, to stop here runs the danger of reifying conventions rather than explaining them. What we can't do with corpora we must do in other ways, and interviewing is perhaps the most productive. Asking questions and getting answers, however, is not as easy as it seems. Not only is there the problem of finding willing respondents with the time and interest to participate, but second language students may find it difficult to consciously formulate their thoughts on their writing practices, let alone verbalise them.

Finding a supervisor from each field was not difficult; academics generally need little encouragement to talk about their work or their students.

The informants, generally experienced and published researchers, were asked to provide information about their own writing, that of their students, and their impressions of disciplinary practices. In contrast, finding students was more difficult. Students often felt threatened by requests for an interview and had to be coaxed by the offer of a voucher from the university bookshop.

Student interviews also involved a different strategy, requiring more scaffolding and a more supportive environment. They typically see communication as less interesting than their supervisors and generally have less metadiscursive awareness. Thus, I conducted the sessions as focus groups with four or five students to stimulate participation and provided more input and encouragement. Myers (1998) points out that "the effectiveness of focus groups depends on a tension between the moderator's constraints and participants' interactions" (p. 85), and I found that these interactions were most productive when groups were relatively heterogeneous. I tried, as far as it was practical, to mix students by gender, discipline, age, and so on to encourage participants to compare their practices and bounce opinions off each other. All interviews were taped and written up as a summary immediately after the session and subsequently returned to several times, often with the assistance of the subjects.

Both the focus groups and interviews began with detailed examinations of text extracts from student dissertations, using what Odell, Goswami, and Herrington (1983) call a *discourse-based interview*. This format requires participants to respond to features in selected texts as either writers or members of the readership for whom the texts were composed. Odell et al. point out that discourse-based interviews help us test discourse theorists' claims about the ways considerations of audience and purpose are important for writers. The method seeks to make explicit the tacit knowledge or strategies that writers and readers bring to acts of composing or assessing writing, allowing them to interpret meanings, reconstruct writer motivations, and evaluate rhetorical effectiveness. The supervisors were also given published examples of their own work and asked to consider the reasons for their choices at specific points in them. The interviews included questions such as, "Why do you think the writer uses *I* here?", "What alternatives could she have used?", "What impression do you get of the writer?", and so on. The aim was to explore what participants believed writers had tried to achieve with specific choices, obtaining the perspectives of insiders acting in their authentic roles as consumers or creators of texts.

The discourse-based sessions then moved to more general observations of pronoun use: "Do you use *I* in your writing?", "Why/Why not?", "Do you notice it in your reading?", "Is it common in Chinese academic texts?", and so on. The purpose here was to learn how respondents perceived the literacy practices of the cultures and communities that influenced their writing. I sought to avoid making judgments or imposing any kind of hypotheses on participants. I simply told them I was interested in how students wrote their dissertations and how this related to their disciplines. These discussions generated a lot of material about beliefs and practices and raised issues concerning intentions, previous encounters with the feature in textbooks, teaching and manuals, their experiences of institutional conventions, and the pressures to conform to them. Here then the focus was on the informants' views of the social and ideological perspectives of their disciplines.

The supervisor interviews were exploratory and heuristic, seeking to develop explanations rather than test hypotheses, and they followed a semistructured, open-ended format. Cohen, Manion, and Morrison (2000) refer to this as an "interview guide approach" (p. 271), where the topics and issues are specified in advance as an outline and the interviewer decides the sequence and the emphasis of the questions. The method offers a systematic way to cover salient issues, yet is flexible enough to allow for follow-up of interesting possibilities when participants introduce their own ideas and connections. I also prefer the more conversational and egalitarian style of interaction that this approach allows, and I find that it reduces the potential awkwardness that can arise from the stuffy formality of the interview context and from casting colleagues into the role of interview subject. The focus groups, in contrast, were more structured and directive to help students overcome their reluctance to volunteer their views.

To consider these methods for a moment, I think it must be recognised that participants' perspectives are not fixed objects, but are socially constructed in the interview situation, negotiated through interaction with the researcher and the researcher's interests. An orientation to the activity as an interview is likely to have an influence on the ideas expressed, and we can only guess at the ways cross-cultural factors might influence the meaning-constructing effects of the interaction. There is, however, no direct access to writers' perceptions of their cultural practices, and we have to rely, at least partly, on what respondents tell us. Participant accounts are suggestive of their experiences of the situated activities they routinely engage in and are essential for an interpretive and explanatory analysis of texts, allowing us to see the factors that might contribute to disciplinary coherence and meanings. Interviewing, for all its shortcomings, seems to be the most effective way to bring the insider's understandings of what it is they do when they read and write in their disciplines to the analysis.

SOME THOUGHTS ON ANALYSIS

Few studies are reflective about interpreting interview data, but clearly no data speak for themselves and no method allows the researcher to be neutral and invisible. All methods force us to rely on indirect evidence to (re)construct informants' implicit knowledge and, irrespective of whether the researcher counts occurrences of themes, observes gestalts, factors variables, or constructs metaphors from the data, inference will always be involved.

Drawing on methods employed by other researchers, I approached the transcription data recursively using a form of *content analysis*, identifying the meanings of expressions by categorising phrases and utterances, beginning with obvious or recurring topics and looking for themes. Subsequent passes through the data helped generate and refine categories, identify core ideas, find links, and gradually build a picture of the data. I attended to the frequency that particular ideas occurred, the strength of their expression, their distribution across the informants, and the rationale for the study. What is important in this process is seeing plausibility, using an intuition informed by the literature, the frequencies and relationships suggested by the text analyses, and the perspectives of different participants to make sense of the data.

Similarly, the analysis of text data is never totally open ended, but always, at the very least, guided by an intention to understand the workings of some aspect of writing. Analysis can never be exhaustive and comprehensive, but is always focused and selective. The role of subjectivity in this process should not be underemphasized. All data analysis involves making connections and developing categories, and this is not and cannot be some kind of objective, pretheoretical exercise. The ways that we generate constructs by identifying specific phenomena as instances of larger patterns in data involve a degree of intuition, inspiration, and luck. But, essentially and inevitably, they rely most heavily on the emergence of what we see as a result of our training and experience. Contrary to any kind of naïve inductivism, all explanations are underdetermined by evidence because observation statements are always made in the language of some theory. Ultimately, our explanations are only as reliable as the theories they presuppose.

My research began with a curiosity about pronoun use, but this was a curiosity informed by assumptions about writing and an idea of the methods best suited to explore it. Although I hope I was open to the unanticipated, my basic analytical framework meant I focused on some features more than others and I looked at them in a certain way. I saw writing as situated interaction and followed the idea that traces of writers' backgrounds, understandings, and cultures can be found by matching repeated forms to writer purposes.

These methods and presuppositions led me to the view that the authorial pronoun is a significant means to promote a competent scholarly identity; a demonstration of the writer's position and rights to ownership of his or her perspectives and text. Authorship in academic writing in English both carries a culturally constructed individualistic ideology and places the burden of responsibility for the truth of an assertion heavily on the writer's shoulders. Yet the texts and interviews showed that this notion of a rational, uniquely individual writer is a product of a culturally specific ideology. Although the students in my study were sensitive to the effects of author pronouns, they were reluctant to accept its clear connotations of authority and commitment. Such an identity both exposes the writer and reduces group solidarity; as a result, L2 students often view the use of *I* with misgivings.

I believe that a process of inquiry that approaches texts as the products of socially and culturally situated writers can help illuminate how cultural differences can lead writers to employ different rhetorical and pragmatic discourse practices. Culture shapes our communicative practices in significant ways, influencing our preferences for structuring information, the relationships we establish with our readers, and how far we want to personally appear in our texts. Students from Western backgrounds may have a similar sense of being manipulated by the particular pragmatic conventions inscribed in academic discourses in English, but cultural norms are an additional complicating factor pressuring learners to abandon their familiar, everyday conventions.

Methods of inquiry, therefore, draw heavily on theoretical presuppositions about what people are trying to achieve in the choices they make when they write. Explanation involves selecting texts and features through the filter of our theories and research interests and sifting out the ways that writers' interests, beliefs, affiliations, experiences, values, and practices appear to influence their writing. From a social perspective, we must also make decisions about how these perceptions and beliefs carry traces of wider participation frameworks not immediately accessible in the composing context. Because these are not things that can be directly observed, the researcher must select from a repertoire of interpretations rather than hit on the truth. By grounding these interpretations in written and oral data, we help ensure that they are not pure speculation either.

CONCLUSIONS

Nothing here is particularly new. I did not set out to create a new methodology, but to inquire into *discourse*, a process of social interaction, rather than just *texts*, and to do this by giving explicit attention to written products and the perspectives of insiders. My main argument has been that, by abstracting away from any specific writer to examine recurring features in a large number of texts, we can infer more subtle relations between writers and readers and between linguistic choices and contexts than would be possible through the intensive studies of a few texts or of writers in the act of writing. I selected the methods because I was familiar with them, believed in them, and felt they reflected the ways I understood writing, seeing writers' expressions of academic identity as constructed through repetition in writing, rather than in the beliefs of individual writers.

It seems to me that I might have handled these methods more expertly and I may have inadvertently missed important nuances and meanings. Interviewing and text analytic skills improve with practice and involve considerable trial and error. It is also true that this approach fails to offer insights into the local, contingent factors that might influence particular cases of writing and as a result loses something in human richness. But it does offer a powerful description of community practices, suggesting something of the extent of variation and similarity in texts and the complex interactions that occur in writing. For me, understanding writing involves both looking at what people write and how they comprehend what they write to see it as a socially situated practice. All I claim for my findings is that they are a plausible interpretation of the use of first-person pronouns by a particular group of students working in this genre.

REFERENCES

Cohen, M., Manion, L., & Morrison, K. (2000). *Research methods in education* (5th ed.). London: Routledge.

Davies, B., & Harre, R. (1990). Positioning: The discursive production of selves. *Journal for the Theory of Social Behaviour, 20*(1), 43–63.

Hunston, S. (2002). *Corpora in applied linguistics*. Cambridge, England: Cambridge University Press.

Hyland, K. (2000). *Disciplinary discourses: Social interactions in academic writing*. London: Longman.

Hyland, K. (2002). Authority and invisibility: Authorial identity in academic writing. *Journal of Pragmatics, 34*(8), 1091–1112.

Ivanič, R. (1998). *Writing and identity: The discoursal construction of identity in academic writing*. Amsterdam: Benjamins.

Kuo, C.-H. (1999). The use of personal pronouns: Role relationships in scientific journal articles. *English for Specific Purposes, 18*(2), 121–138.

Myers, G. (1998). Displaying opinions: Topics and disagreement in focus groups. *Language in Society, 27*, 85–111.

Myers, G. (1999). Interaction in writing: Principles and problems. In C. N. Candlin & K. Hyland (Eds.), *Writing: Texts, processes and practices* (pp. 40–61). London: Longman.

Nystrand, M. (1987). The role of context in written communication. In R. Horowitz & S. J. Samuels (Eds.), *Comprehending oral and written language* (pp. 197–214). San Diego, CA: Academic Press.

Odell, L., Goswami, D., & Herrington, A. (1983). The discourse-based interview: A procedure for exploring the tacit knowledge of writers in non-academic settings. In P. Mosenthal, L. Tamor, & S. A. Walmsley (Eds.), *Research on writing: Principles and methods* (pp. 221–236). New York: Longman.

Shotter, J., & Gergen, K. (1989). *Texts of identity*. Newbury Park, CA: Sage.

Sinclair, J. (1991). *Corpus, concordance, collocation*. Oxford: Oxford University Press.

Stubbs, M. (1996). *Text and corpus analysis*. Oxford: Blackwell.

Swales, J. (1981). *Aspects of article introductions* (Aston ESP Research Report #1). Birmingham: University of Aston.

14

Using Concurrent Protocols to Explore L2 Writing Processes: Methodological Issues in the Collection and Analysis of Data

Rosa M. Manchón
Liz Murphy
Julio Roca de Larios
Universidad de Murcia, Spain

In this chapter, we reflect on the inquiry process in a research project in which concurrent protocols were used to explore L2 writing processes. The original drive behind this project was to contribute to current theorizing on second language writing, and to do so with data from a study conducted in a foreign language context. This aim was narrowed down further to the investigation of whether and how cognitive activity while writing might be influenced by three independent variables: (a) the writer's command of the L2, (b) the cognitive demand of the task to be performed, and (c) the language of composition (i.e., whether writers composed in their native language [L1] or foreign language [L2]). The research was thus purely cognitive in orientation and did not claim to have any important contribution to make to a more social or sociocognitive writing theory.

To investigate whether and how composing processes were influenced by the three independent variables of our work, it was necessary to engage in the following activities:

1. To collect data from L2 writers at different proficiency levels while writing more and less cognitively demanding tasks in their L1 and L2. We therefore collected think-aloud data provided by three groups of Spanish EFL learners at three different levels of proficiency (each made up of seven participants) while writing a narrative and

an argumentative time-compressed task (1 hour) in their L1 (Spanish) and L2 (English). In addition, participants completed two follow-up questionnaires.

2. To prepare our data for coding and analysis.
3. To set up a valid, reliable, and theoretically grounded coding scheme to make sense of the think-aloud data (one of the most time-consuming, challenging, and crucial tasks faced by researchers working with protocol data).
4. To decide on criteria that would guide our application of the coding scheme to the data analysis in a principled manner—another question of prime importance when working with concurrent protocols.

In the ensuing discussion, we reflect on some of the methodological problems we experienced in the first three areas mentioned, focusing mainly on our efforts to reduce the threats to validity associated with this methodology. At this point, it is important to remember that an instrument is valid if it measures what it purports to measure. To be more precise, validity is not a property of the instrument (i.e., an instrument is not valid or invalid per se), but as Leong and Austin (1996) pointed out, *validity* refers to "the appropriateness and usefulness of interpretations and inferences made from the instrument" (p. 76). In this respect and despite the criticisms leveled against the use of concurrent protocols (for a review of the controversy, see Bracewell, 1994; Bracewell & Breuleux, 1994; Cooper & Holzman, 1983; Dobrin, 1986; Ericsson & Simon, 1984, 1993; Faigley & Witte, 1981; Flower & Hayes, 1985; Jourdenais, 2001; Nisbett & Wilson, 1977; Smagorinsky, 1994a, 1994b; Steinberg, 1986; Stratman & Hamp-Lyons, 1994; Witte & Cherry, 1994), it is important to note that concurrent protocols are no different from any other methodology in that all methods involve potential threats to validity. In the case of concurrent protocols, the challenge faced by researchers is "to identify and reduce causes of their invalidity" (Russo, Johnson, & Stephens, 1989, p. 767). Our own attempts in this direction are discussed in the following sections.

DATA-COLLECTION PROCEDURES

The Rationale Behind the Choice of Concurrent Protocols

We opted for a form of direct observation and, among the possibilities within these, for concurrent protocols for both practical and theoretical reasons (for a description of different observation methods and protocol reports, see Janssen, van Waes, & van den Bergh, 1996; Jourdenais, 2001).

From the practical angle, we did not think that our human and material resources would allow us to use a methodology that required recording 21 participants individually completing four different tasks. In addition, more theoretical considerations meant that, to achieve our research aims, we needed a methodology that would tap directly into working memory, thus giving us a more "accurate" picture of our participants' online processing. Introspective and think-aloud protocol reports were the options available, but we finally decided on the latter for the practical reasons mentioned earlier.

The Writing Tasks

Tasks, Prompts and Topics. The main data source for our studies consisted of the participants' think-aloud verbalizations while performing four writing tasks using the following prompts:

> ARGUMENTATIVE L2 TASK: Success in education is influenced more by the student's home life and training as a child than by the quality and effectiveness of the educational program. Do you agree or disagree? (taken from Raimes, 1987).
>
> ARGUMENTATIVE L1 TASK: *El fracaso escolar se debe más a la falta de responsabilidad del profesor en el cumplimiento de sus deberes como enseñante que a la actitud, esfuerzo, aptitudes, motivación por parte de los alumnos. ¿Estás de acuerdo o en desacuerdo?* [School failure is more a result of teachers' lack of responsibility in carrying out their teaching than of the attitude, effort, aptitude, and motivation of the pupils. Do you agree or disagree?]
>
> NARRATIVE L2 TASK: Write about something that went wrong in your life. Write what happened, when, where, how you felt then, and how you feel about it now.
>
> NARRATIVE L1 TASK: *Escribe sobre algo que te haya ido muy bien en la vida. Escribe qué sucedió, cuándo, dónde, cómo te sentiste entonces y cómo te sientes sobre ello ahora.* [Write about something that went right in your life. Write what happened, when, where, how you felt then, and how you feel about it now.]

We chose argumentative and narrative tasks on account of their different cognitive demands (cf. Cumming, 1998; Grabe & Kaplan, 1996). In our view, the chosen tasks entailed differences in rhetorical form, appropriate register, sources of information, and relation to personal experience.

To control for confounding variables, we took two decisions regarding the choice of topics. First, we chose similar topics in the L1 and L2 writing tasks, basing our decision on the research evidence that different topics might affect the quality and quantity of writing (Hamp-Lyons, 1990; Reid, 1990; Sasaki & Hirose, 1996; but see Whalen & Ménard, 1995, for arguments against this procedure). Second, for both the argumentative and narrative tasks, we chose topics with which all participants were familiar ("education" in the case of the argumentative assignments and "a personal experience" for the narrative tasks) in the belief that topic familiarity would enhance the participants' degree of involvement—an expectation confirmed in previous studies (Friedlander, 1990; Gaskill, 1986). However, we were also aware that this decision was not without problems given that access to readily available information in one's memory may diminish the need for heuristics and self-regulatory procedures (Roca de Larios & Murphy, 2001). To minimize this risk and prevent a further confound due to task differences, we decided on prompts (for both the narrative and argumentative tasks) that, in principle, would lead to knowledge transforming (Scardamalia & Bereiter, 1987).

However, the choice of knowledge transforming tasks entailed a disadvantage related to reactivity, which is one possible serious cause of invalidity of thinking aloud and protocol analysis. In this context, reactivity refers to the fact that having to write and verbalize thoughts at the same time may disrupt the writer's cognitive processes in comparison with what she or he would do when writing in a different condition (see Janssen et al., 1996; Stratman & Hamp-Lyons, 1994). Janssen et al. (1996) posited that reactivity effects may be task dependent and knowledge-transforming tasks may produce more reactive effects. Put briefly, knowledge-telling and knowledge-transforming tasks entail different degrees of problem solving. The more problem solving (i.e., the more knowledge transforming a writing task involves), the more likely it is for the writer to be affected by having to write and verbalize at the same time due to working memory limitations and allocation of attentional resources. Therefore, seen from this perspective, our choice of knowledge-transforming tasks was questionable. Seen from a different angle, however, there were benefits to be gained. In our view, having our participants engage in more problem solving (which was precisely the phenomenon we wanted to investigate) would, in theory, guarantee more conscious attention on the part of the writer to his or her cognitive activity. Given that such activity would be in focal attention, and that, according to Ericsson and Simon (1993), it is precisely information in focal attention that is available for verbal report, we were likely to obtain more useful and informative protocols with this kind of task (see Janssen et al., 1996).

The Recordings. The next stage was the recording of the verbalizations. One needs to avoid two main problems associated with the method: the first is reactivity, and the second is the possible effects of the interaction between writer and researcher.

Reactivity effects are counteracted by means of the instructions given to participants and also by carefully designing the practice stage or trial run. The wording of the instructions must incorporate safeguards against the participants' forming expectations and interpretations about what is required of them and the type of information they should report (see Jourdenais, 2001). Similarly, measures have to be taken during the practice stage to ensure that writers are simply trained in performing "the unusual task of talking aloud and reporting task activities" (Jourdenais, 2001, p. 359). To fulfill these requirements, before the first session our participants were instructed in Spanish to verbalize all thinking while composing in the following terms (translated):

> I'd like you to write a composition on a topic that we are going to give you now. While you write your composition, I would like you to say aloud anything and everything that goes through your mind. You have to do everything that you would normally do when writing a composition, the only difference being that today you are going to do it talking aloud. You may use any language that you normally use when writing. You will have a maximum of 1 hour to complete the task.

Informants were then given the opportunity to practice the think-aloud method with a mock composition ("Advantages and disadvantages of . . ."). Regarding this trial run, we decided not to provide modeling so as to avoid the potential danger of the writers restricting their "thoughts" to the type they had seen modeled (Smith, 1994). We also felt that any modeling of the think-aloud technique might have influenced the participants' choice of language, something to be avoided because one of the problems associated with concurrent protocols is the difficulty that some writers might experience in providing their verbalizations in the L2.

Regarding the possible interaction between researcher and writer (see Smagorinsky, 1994a), our research team decided to record all the informants at the same proficiency level concurrently. This decision, although originally based on practical reasons, had the added bonus of neutralizing any variation in data due to interaction between researcher and participant. A situation where informants are sitting in language laboratory booths, where they all receive instructions at the same time from the research team, and where there is little or no interaction between researcher and informant once the task has started might be less conducive to bias arising from differential interaction between subject and researcher than a setting where one writer is alone in an office with one or more researchers.

In addition to recording participants concurrently, it was also decided that two people would be present during the recording sessions: the students' English teacher (or ex-teacher in the case of the most proficient group) and a member of the research team. It was hoped that this common pattern would neutralize differences between the different recording sessions and would help to create a nonthreatening environment.

Order of Tasks and Practice Effect

Although the ideal procedure would have been to control for task order by administering the assignments alternately, it was not feasible because the informants belonged to the same year groups, were in constant contact, and could therefore disclose the tasks to one another after each session. The order of the assignments was thus held constant across the three groups: the L2 tasks before the L1 tasks. This lack of counterbalancing could have produced some task effect.

An additional methodological problem, which may not have received sufficient attention in research to date, is practice effect. Recall that our design included four different tasks, and having to perform these different tasks could result in accumulated practice in the use of the think-aloud procedure. This means that in a comprehensive piece of research like ours, one may end up with more informative and accurate protocols as the research project progresses because of the accumulated practice with the method (or indeed, alternatively, some writers may become weary of the tasks and their performance may deteriorate as a result). We must admit that there are indications both in the protocols and in the follow-up questionnaires that some participants did experience this practice effect—some participants gradually became more confident with the method, and thus experienced less difficulty in writing and thinking aloud at the same time. This practice effect is a drawback of research like ours, which involves various consecutive tasks, as well as a crucial methodological aspect of working with concurrent protocols. Researchers should therefore bear this in mind at the stage of research design and seriously take it into account when analyzing and interpreting the content of the protocols.

THE RETROSPECTIVE QUESTIONNAIRES

A frequently heard criticism of concurrent protocols is that cognitive processes are not directly manifest in protocols, but have to be inferred and interpreted (Kasper, 1998; Smagorinsky, 1994a). Therefore, "by incorporating multiple sources of information regarding learners' behavior, researchers can be more confident in the analysis" (Jourdenais, 2001, p. 360). Acknowledgment of this issue, the results of the pilot study, and an assessment of material and human resources prompted us to use general follow-up questionnaires that could be administered to a whole group at a time after the completion of each task. We designed two questionnaires that asked general questions regarding the participants' attitudes about the topics of the compositions, the rhetorical situation, the writing environment, and their perceptions of their own composing processes. However, when analyzing the data, we felt that more detailed questionnaires would have helped us in our analysis and interpretation of the data. This issue is a good example of some of the problems that arise when working with protocol data. Thus, in contrast to what one may infer from published empirical research, working with protocol data entails finding a compromise between, on the one hand, researchers' original objectives, hypotheses, and/or research questions and, on the other, the systematic investigation of what they gradually discover they need to look at in the data. This is, in Smagorinsky's terms, the paradox faced by researchers using concurrent protocols as their data source: "while their hypotheses determine the coding system, often their hypotheses emerge from or are shaped by the application of the coding scheme" (Smagorinsky, 1994a, p. 11). In our case, coming to terms with this paradox has led to the production of a number of studies, some of which were not part of our original research plan. Thus, our questionnaires included nothing about backtracking, a phenomenon that we later studied in depth (see Manchón, Murphy, & Roca de Larios, 2000; Manchón, Roca de Larios, & Murphy, 1998, 2000). They included only general questions about formulation processes, which later became a key research area (Roca de Larios, Manchón, & Murphy, 2003; Roca de Larios, Marín, & Murphy, 2001) and about the use of the L1 in L2 writing, the third important line of research within the project (Murphy, Manchón, & Roca de Larios, 2002). In short, we are tempted to think that this is a methodological issue faced (although not always voiced) by researchers working with protocol data and one that, we must admit, is generally solved ad hoc in terms of the validity and reliability of the data analysis.

PREPARING THE DATA FOR CODING/ANALYSIS: THE TRANSCRIPTIONS OF PROTOCOLS

When preparing the data for coding and analysis, researchers must find satisfactory solutions to the problem that, although concurrent protocols tell a story (Smagorinsky, 1994b, p. xiii), protocols do not afford direct access to cognitive processes. As suggested in the literature, in verbal data we are only dealing with the traces of the writing process. To deal with these issues, researchers make decisions regarding the criteria to be used in the transcription of the protocols, on the one hand, and in setting up and applying the coding scheme to the data, on the other hand.

Following Ericsson and Simon (1984), the standard procedure to be followed in the transcription of the protocols is "to make careful verbatim transcripts of the recorded tapes" (p. 4). They also recommend: (a) carrying out this task in such a way as to end up with manageable transcriptions, and (b) doing the transcription in a way that allows "reliable coding and captures relevant information for subsequent coding operations" (Ericsson & Simon, 1984, p. 279).

Bearing these ideas in mind and after reviewing previous empirical studies, we decided on the following procedure. First, the cassettes were transcribed using the ordinary writing system. Second, as suggested in the literature, our transcriptions included features of spoken discourse, the elimination of which would mean that the coder missed crucial interpretive resources (Ericsson & Simon, 1984; Kasper, 1998). In our case, all utterances were transcribed, including false starts, hesitations, repetitions, pauses (which appear in Excerpt [1] as numbers of seconds in parentheses), and paralinguistic features (laughter, coughing, etc.). Third, apart from the actual transcriptions of the protocols, a number of further steps were taken to prepare the transcriptions for coding (see Excerpt [1]). The first was to distinguish the written text (underlined) from the processes that generated it. The second step was to isolate rereadings/repetitions (in italics in [1]). The last stage involved signaling in the protocols any revisions made to the written text. Annotations were made to the underlined text in the protocol (a word was crossed out, a phrase was added, etc.), and at the point of verbalization a coding of revision or repair was registered.

> [1] let's see *the issue under consideration in this piece of writing* let's see if it works (3) so *the issue under consideration in this piece of writing* . . . is that students . . . is that students no . . . that students no . . . [CROSSES OUT "that students"] (3) *is* one of educational principle . . . *is* one of educational principle . . . *educational principle* . . . yes . . . that's better. (4)

DATA ANALYSIS: SETTING UP THE CODING SCHEME

We already mentioned that analyzing protocols means interpreting protocols. However, we would agree with Witte and Cherry (1994) that in this respect concurrent protocol data are no different from any other type of data given that data always have to be interpreted: they "never mean in and of themselves" (p. 23). Bracewell (1994) neatly summarized the challenge researchers face when he states that, "we all realize that it is important to listen carefully to what one's writers say and to try to look into the heart of the matter. The real issue is *how* to listen carefully and *how* to look into the heart of the matter" (p. 294).

We would say that these "hows" entail four tasks to be accomplished by the research team (all of them deserving equal theoretical and methodological attention):

- Deciding what part of the protocol is to be considered for analysis.
- Establishing the categories in the coding scheme.
- Establishing segmentation criteria.
- Applying the categories to the data for data analysis.

In the following section, we focus on the first two issues.

Deciding What Part of the Protocols Is Going to Be Subjected to Analysis

Although obvious, the first decision researchers must make (and one that is not always made explicit or sufficiently justified in published research) is whether to answer their research questions they need to look at the whole protocol or at one part only. The stance taken depends on the theoretical framework guiding the study as well as on the research questions. Let us illustrate this issue with two examples from our own research.

In our research on backtracking[1] (BAKT), we tried to answer questions on the forms BAKT takes in L2 composing (i.e., rereadings, backtranslations, etc.) and the strategic purposes BAKT serves. Accordingly, we were only interested in those segments in which writers rescanned the prompt, their notes, and their previously written text in whatever way and for whatever purpose. However, further decisions as to which BAKT segments were to be subjected to analysis were taken once we operationalized BAKT as a strategy. In the problem-solving literature (Hayes, 1989; Newell, 1980; Newell & Simon, 1972), a problem exists when: (a) there is a gap between a self-imposed or other-imposed initial state and an intended goal state, and (b) the gap cannot be bridged without a search process. The problem-solving process is the thinking process one uses to get from the initial to the goal state and is defined by Anderson (1980) as a

[1]*Backtracking* has been defined as those actions performed by the writer to take stock of the ideas and constraints of the text produced so far to bring them to bear on current needs (Manchón et al., 2000, p. 14).

"goal directed sequence of cognitive operations" (p. 258). This sequence of operations (known as strategies) constitutes a solution to a problem.

Following this characterization, a distinction was established between *Mechanical BAKT* and *Purposeful BAKT*, our focus obviously being only the latter. *Mechanical BAKT* was operationalized as a behavioral action in which writers say aloud whatever they are actually writing down (i.e., the physical actions of writing and uttering are almost simultaneous). In contrast, *Purposeful BAKT* is never simultaneous to the actual writing down of words, and the writer's action involves an attempt to "do something" with the segment rescanned. The application of this operational distinction meant that we did not consider for analysis those backtracking operations immediately following the written text (WT), except when the BAKT segment and WT were different (i.e., when BAKT entailed a manipulation of the rescanned segment through, for instance, a paraphrase or translation) or when pauses longer than 3 seconds indicated some unspoken struggle with a problem. Thus, in Extract [2], "specialized" would not be counted for analysis, whereas the other BAKT segments would.

> [2] I think that education is important (4) *is important is important I think that education is important* and (4) education (3) should . . . depender depend *should* depend of specialized *specialized* people (5) *specialized people it should depend of specialized people* . . . aunque *pienso que la educación es importante y la educación debe depender de gente especializada* and and (Level 1).

There are cases, however, that are not so straightforward. A good example would be our research on the use of the native language in L2 composing. Expressed in simple terms, we intended to extract patterns of use of this strategic resource. We started by analyzing only the L1 verbalizations contained in the protocols, and a coding scheme was developed to account for the data. However, we soon realized that this restriction would not lead to a valid analysis of the phenomenon under investigation because, by not counting L2 verbalizations, we would get only a limited picture of the writers' composing behavior. Our reasoning was that the analysis of the L1 utterances alone could give us a clear enough idea of the uses the writers make of their mother tongue, for what purposes (planning, generating text, backtracking, evaluating, etc.), and how this resource is shared across those purposes. We could also see the effect of increasing levels of L2 proficiency on total L1 use as well as on these different purposes so we could get some sort of developmental picture. However, analysis of utterances in both languages meant that much more could be revealed—namely, a student's strategic behavior with respect to language choice, the balance between the two languages for each purpose, and whether and how this balance shifted in relation to developing proficiency.

Establishing the Categories and Setting up the Coding Scheme

The coding scheme is the filter through which one looks at one's data to report, in a valid and reliable way, the story told in the protocols. In setting up our coding schemes, we basically followed guiding principles for the analysis of protocol data suggested in the literature on the topic. First, a critical reading of the relevant literature (including the empirical studies available at the time) made us realize that, as Kasper (1998) contended, the analysis of think-aloud data requires equal theoretical and methodological attention. Second, encoding must have a theoretical basis (Ericsson & Simon, 1984; Kasper, 1998). Manchón stated that "establishing categories and ensuring reliability in the data analysis is necessary but not sufficient," adding that "a whole array of strict methodological decisions (ideally framed in a given theoretical paradigm) must guide both the drawing up of the coding scheme and its actual application in the data analysis" (Manchón, 2001, p. 53).

Our approach to protocol analysis has always been informed by cognitive, problem-solving theories of writing. One example has already been presented of how the problem-solving paradigm informed our operationalization of what were to be considered writing strategies when dealing with the phenomenon of BAKT. In drawing up the actual coding scheme, we attempted to devise a theoretically grounded categorization of this important strategic writing behavior. We came up with a categorization of purposes that distinguished between the use of BAKT for retrospective and prospective purposes—a distinction informed by de Beaugrande's (1984) look-ahead and look-back principles of text production. Within each of these macrogroups, further distinctions were introduced to account for the data in a principled manner.

Our research on formulation provides another example. When setting up the coding scheme for the study of formulation, we had to deal with two types of problems: first, establishing criteria that would allow us to distinguish formulation from the other macro writing processes postulated in cognitive models of writing (i.e., planning and revision), and, second, analyzing the different manifestations of formulation in the protocols so as to develop coding categories that would pin down the different behaviors involved in this process as precisely as possible. This was needed because our approach to the data was a conceptualization of formulation that differed somewhat from previous research. Thus, instead of considering formulation as mere transcription of plans and ideas analyzable from the perspective of fluency, we were interested in the kinds of operations that make possible sentence production and their integration into a text. The first analysis of the protocols showed that, by and large, the participants used two main types of behavior when formulating: at times the process went more or less fluently, whereas at others the writers clearly stopped to tackle particular problems. Therefore, our coding scheme had to distinguish between these two types of behavior. So we established a preliminary distinction between *fluent formulation* and *problem-solving formulation*. We decided to consider as "fluent" formulation those segments that, although not completely automatic, nevertheless show that the writer progresses through the text without having to tackle problems, at least explicitly.

In line with the conceptualization of problem solving mentioned earlier, we considered that there was a *formulation problem* when the protocols indicated the existence of a gap (of various types and at a variety of levels) between an intended meaning (already constructed or in the process of construction) and the lexical units and syntactic structures needed to express it. The application of different theoretical and methodological criteria (specified in Roca de Larios et al., 2001) allowed us to identify two main types of problem space (the segmentation unit used) in the formulation process: lexical searches and restructuring. The category of *lexical searches* included all those searches for words and expressions needed to express the message clearly and appropriately. *Restructuring*, in contrast, was defined as the search for an alternative syntactic plan once the writer predicts or anticipates that the original plan is not going to be satisfactory for a variety of linguistic, ideational, or textual reasons (Roca de Larios et al., 1999).

A third principle—essential in our view for the development of research in the field (see Manchón, 2001), although often absent in published research—must be applied to the coding of the data: A coding scheme should ideally be "a theoretically grounded model of the cognitive processes and types of information involved in the activity under study, *not a mere list of strategies*" or observed behavior (Kasper, 1998, p. 359; italics added). We feel that if the previous requirement is met—that is, if the coding scheme is guided by a theoretical approach to the data—one is more likely to end up with a model rather than a mere list of observed phenomena. This theoretical approach forces the researcher to look for levels of analysis and levels of generalization, so the resulting coding scheme offers a more valid and complete account of the data.

Fulfilling all these requirements entails "passing through your data more times than you want to count" (Smagorinsky, 1994b, p. xi). Judging by our own experience, one has to engage in a recursive process because the shaping of the coding scheme always involves a number of passes through the protocols with a series of tests and reviews of the data until no more changes are required (Kasper, 1998; Smagorinsky, 1994b). If this is a collaborative research process, as in our case, there are obvious benefits. One is that the discussion with others helps improve the quality of the category system (Kasper, 1998). Another is that when beginning the necessary task of checking interrater reliability, the corater is already trained. Moreover, from the affective point of view, it helps to be able to share with others the frustration experienced when the data do not fit neatly into the categories drawn up to deal with them (as inevitably happens). Teamwork also helps to deal more effectively with the problem mentioned earlier, which is that working with protocol data involves a compromise between your original aims and your gradual construction of a model from the data.

CONCLUSION

In light of the lessons learned from our experience, we should like to make the following points. First, there is no doubt that there are benefits associated with the use of concurrent protocols for the study of cognitive processes. However, the possible contribution of these types of studies is limited when researchers, as in our case, approach the data analysis from a strict cognitive perspective. This is so because, although writing involves cognition, cognitive processes are constructed in particular social and historical circumstances (see Roca de Larios & Murphy, 2001). Second, this methodology is neither more nor less valid than any other, and the problems involved in interpreting protocol data have much in common with any other research endeavor. Part of the researcher's task is to take steps to identify and reduce causes of invalidity. As we have tried to illustrate, this entails taking principled measures regarding the design of the study, and the collection, coding, and analysis of the data.

How researchers go about their attempts to minimize potential problems is not always fully discussed in published research, certainly not in the L2 writing literature; this may constitute one more example of what we see as a general lack of attention to methodological issues in the writing literature as a whole. In this respect, it must be said that this book is a laudable attempt to begin to fill this gap. Therefore, we should like to take this opportunity to congratulate the editors of the present publication, and we hope to see more discussion of methodological issues in the future as a result of their initiative.

REFERENCES

Anderson, J. R. (1980). *Cognitive psychology and its implications*. San Francisco: Freeman.

Bracewell, R. J. (1994). Withered wisdom: A reply to Dobrin. In P. Smagorinsky (Ed.), *Speaking about writing: Reflections on research methodology* (pp. 290–294). Thousand Oaks, CA: Sage.

Bracewell, R. J., & Breuleux, A. (1994). Substance and romance in analyzing think-aloud protocols. In P. Smagorinsky (Ed.), *Speaking about writing: Reflections on research methodology* (pp. 55–88). Thousand Oaks, CA: Sage.

Cooper, M., & Holzman, M. (1983). Talking about protocols. *College Composition and Communication, 34*, 284–293.

Cumming, A. (1998). Theoretical perspectives on writing. *Annual Review of Applied Linguistics, 18*, 61–78.

de Beaugrande, R. A. (1984). *Text production: Toward a science of composition*. Norwood, NJ: Ablex.

Dobrin, D. (1986). Protocols once more. *College English, 48*, 713–726.

Ericsson, K. A., & Simon, H. A. (1984). *Protocol analysis: Verbal reports as data*. Cambridge, MA: MIT Press.

Ericsson, K. A., & Simon, H. A. (1993). *Protocol analysis: Verbal reports as data* (rev. ed.). Cambridge, MA: MIT Press.

Faigley, L., & Witte, S. (1981). Analyzing revision. *College Composition and Communication, 32*, 400–414.

Flower, L., & Hayes, J. R. (1985). Response to Marilyn Cooper and Michael Holzman, "Talking about protocols." *College Composition and Communication, 36*, 94–97.

Friedlander, A. (1990). Composing in English: Effects of a first language on writing in English as a second language. In B. Kroll (Ed.), *Second language writing. Research insights for the classroom* (pp. 109–125). Cambridge, England: Cambridge University Press.

Gaskill, W. (1986). *Revising in Spanish and English as a second language: A process oriented study of composition*. Unpublished doctoral dissertation, University of California, Los Angeles.

Grabe, W., & Kaplan, R. B. (1996). *Theory and practice of writing*. London: Longman.

Hamp-Lyons, L. (1990). Second language writing: Assessment issues. In B. Kroll (Ed.), *Second language writing research: Insights for the classroom* (pp. 69–87). Cambridge, England: Cambridge University Press.

Hayes, J. R. (1989). *The complete problem solver* (2nd ed.). Hillsdale, NJ: Lawrence Erlbaum Associates.

Janssen, D., van Waes, L., & van den Bergh, H. (1996). Effects of thinking aloud on writing processes. In C. M. Levy & S. Ransdell (Eds.), *The science of writing* (pp. 223–250). Mahwah, NJ: Lawrence Erlbaum Associates.

Jourdenais, R. (2001). Cognition, instruction and protocol analysis. In P. Robinson (Ed.), *Cognition and second language instruction* (pp. 354–375). Cambridge, England: Cambridge University Press.

Kasper, G. (1998). Analysing verbal protocols. *TESOL Quarterly, 32*(2), 358–363.

Leong, F. T. L., & Austin, J. T. (Eds.). (1996). *The psychology research handbook*. Thousand Oaks, CA: Sage.

Manchón, R. M. (2001). Trends in the conceptualizations of second language composition strategies: A critical analysis. *International Journal of English Studies, 1*, 47–70.

Manchón, R. M., Murphy, L., & Roca de Larios, J. (2000). *The strategic value of backtracking in L2 writing*. Paper given at the American Association for Applied Linguistics Conference, Vancouver, Canada.

Manchón, R. M., Roca de Larios, J., & Murphy, L. (1998). *Language ability, writing behaviors and the use of backward operations in L2 writing*. Paper given at the American Association for Applied Linguistics Conference, Seattle, WA.

Manchón, R. M., Roca de Larios, J., & Murphy, L. (2000). An approximation to the study of backtracking in L2 writing. *Learning and Instruction, 10*, 13–35.

Murphy, L., Manchón, R. M., & Roca de Larios, J. (2002). *Recourse to the native language in L2 composing*. Paper given at the Conference of the Spanish Association of Applied Linguistics, Jaén, Spain.

Newell, A. (1980). Reasoning, problem solving and decision processes: The problem space as a fundamental category. In R. S. Nickerson (Ed.), *Attention and performance* (Vol. 8, pp. 693–719). Hillsdale, NJ: Lawrence Erlbaum Associates.

Newell, A., & Simon, H. A. (1972). *Human problem solving*. Englewood Cliffs, NJ: Prentice-Hall.

Nisbett, R. E., & Wilson, W. T. D. (1977). Telling more than we can know: Verbal reports on mental processes. *Psychological Review, 84*, 231–259.

Raimes, A. (1987). Language proficiency, writing ability, and composing strategies: A study of ESL college student writers. *Language Learning, 37*, 439–468.

Reid, J. (1990). Responding to different topic types: A quantitative analysis from a contrastive rhetoric perspective. In B. Kroll (Ed.), *Second language writing* (pp. 191–210). Cambridge, England: Cambridge University Press.

Roca de Larios, J., Manchón, R. M., & Murphy, L. (2003). *Generating text in L1 and L2 writing: A temporal analysis of problem-solving formulation processes*. Paper submitted for publication.

Roca de Larios, J., Marín, J., & Murphy, L. (2001). A temporal analysis of formulation processes in L1 and L2 writing. *Language Learning, 51*, 497–538.

Roca de Larios, J., & Murphy, L. (2001). Some steps towards a socio-cognitive interpretation of second language composition processes. *International Journal of English Studies, 1*, 25–45.

Roca de Larios, J., Murphy, L., & Manchón, R. M. (1999). The use of restructuring strategies in EFL writing: A study of Spanish learners of English as a foreign language. *Journal of Second Language Writing, 8*, 13–44.

Russo, J. E., Johnson, E. J., & Stephens, D. L. (1989). The validity of verbal protocols. *Memory and Cognition, 17*, 759–769.

Sasaki, M., & Hirose, K. (1996). Explanatory variables for EFL students' expository writing. *Language Learning, 46*, 137–174.

Scardamalia, M., & Bereiter, C. (1987). Knowledge telling and knowledge transforming in written composition. In S. Rosenberg (Ed.), *Advances in applied psycholinguistics* (pp. 143–175). Cambridge, England: Cambridge University Press.

Smagorinsky, P. (1994a). Think-aloud protocol analysis: Beyond the black box. In P. Smagorinsky (Ed.), *Speaking about writing: Reflections on research methodology* (pp. 3–19). Thousand Oaks, CA: Sage.

Smagorinsky, P. (1994b). Introduction: Potential problems and problematic potentials of using talk about writing as data about writing process. In P. Smagorinsky (Ed.), *Speaking about writing: Reflections on research methodology* (pp. ix–xix). Thousand Oaks, CA: Sage.

Smith, V. (1994). *Thinking in a foreign language: An investigation into essay writing and translation by L2 learners*. Tübingen: Verlag.

Steinberg, E. (1986). Protocols, retrospective reports, and the stream of consciousness. *College English, 48*, 697–704.

Stratman, J. F., & Hamp-Lyons, L. (1994). Reactivity in concurrent think-aloud protocols. Issues for research. In P. Smagorinsky (Ed.), *Speaking about writing: Reflections on research methodology* (pp. 89–112). Thousand Oaks, CA: Sage.

Whalen, K., & Ménard, N. (1995). L1 and L2 writers' strategic and linguistic knowledge: A model of multiple-level discourse processing. *Language Learning, 45*, 381–418.

Witte, S. P., & Cherry, R. D. (1994). Think-aloud protocols, protocol analysis, and research design: An exploration of the influence of writing tasks on writing processes. In P. Smagorinsky (Ed.), *Speaking about writing: Reflections on research methodology* (pp. 20–54). Thousand Oaks, CA: Sage.

15

Taking on English Writing in a Bilingual Program: Revisiting, Reexamining, Reconceptualizing the Data

Sarah Hudelson
Arizona State University, USA

In this chapter, I revisit a study conducted a decade ago. I reexamine and critique the theoretical framework used, the research questions asked, and the data-collection techniques used. I also consider how my interpretations might have been different if I had used a different or an additional theoretical framework from the one employed, and if I had taken a more critical perspective with regard to the findings.

THE ORIGINAL STUDY

In the early 1990s, a colleague of mine, Irene Serna, and I (along with some doctoral students) investigated the native language literacy development of a group of Spanish speaking children enrolled in a transitional whole language bilingual education program. The transitional designation signified that the Spanish speakers began their formal literacy instruction in Spanish with the expectation that by the fourth grade they would have transitioned into all English literacy at school. The whole language designation meant that the school's principal and many of the teachers operated from a theoretical framework that children learn to read and write by engaging in reading and writing, and that children learn how written language works by using that written language for multiple purposes, in the investigation of interesting content.

In terms of a writing curriculum and writing instruction for young children, learners engaged in a significant amount of writing daily, although they had not previously studied the conventions of written language in discrete lessons. Perhaps the most significant convention not studied in isolation prior to engaging in writing was the alphabetic nature of Spanish. The writing curriculum being enacted, coming out of a perspective termed *emergent literacy* (Teale & Sulzby, 1986), was grounded in earlier work with native English-speaking preschool and primary age children, and it was one that many primary teachers at the school had studied. Several researchers (Edelsky, 1986; Ferreiro & Teberosky, 1982) examined how the emergent literacy perspective applied to young writers in languages other than English, while others were beginning to investigate emergent literacy in young second language learners (Hudelson, 1984).

Emergent literacy research has a significant part of its base in a constructivist view of learning—a view which asserts that learning involves learners creating or constructing their own understandings of the world (Piaget & Inhelder, 1969), including the natural world (Chaille, 1997), the mathematical world (Fosnot, 1989; Kamii, 2000), and the literate world (Ferreiro & Teberosky, 1982; Goodman, 1990). In terms of literacy and, more specifically writing, the constructivist perspective maintains that children need to experiment with written language to learn how written language works. This experimentation plays itself out in children's creation of hypotheses about how written language works and in their producing unconventional written language that demonstrates what their working hypotheses are at any point in time. As children create written text, as they experience more written language in the world around them including the world of school, and as others interact with them about what they are writing, their invented writing, through a series of approximations, gradually becomes more conventional. The constructivist perspective thus foregrounds children's cognitive work—children's figuring out the systems of written language and solving their writing problems using their developing knowledge of form and function.

Given our professional knowledge as bilingual educators, Irene and I wanted to document young children's Spanish language writing (and reading) development over time. Given our operating frameworks of constructivism, whole language and emergent literacy, we wanted to do this in classrooms where children were experiencing writing from the beginning of their schooling and where the children were engaging in writing for a variety of purposes through a variety of classroom literacy practices (e.g., journal writing, writers workshop, writing to learn in science, etc.). Focusing especially on writing, we were interested in documenting how children's Spanish writing developed over time. We wanted to know what strategies the children used to create written texts. We wanted to see how their writing moved from less to more conventional, especially in terms of orthography and segmentation. We wanted to see how the children responded to different kinds of writing, how writing functioned for them in the classrooms, and how they became engaged as writers.

To begin our study, we targeted eight children in each of two team-taught kindergarten and first-grade classrooms in an elementary school in Phoenix. We had plans to follow the children for 3 years, so we tried to target children we thought most likely to stay at the school. We also asked the teachers to identify children along a continuum of literacy behaviors at the beginning of the study—from those whose behaviors were most conventional to those whose behaviors were least conventional. We began visiting the classrooms 1 day a week, spending at least half a day in Spanish language arts time, but often remaining for entire days so we could see the children across the school day, including ESL time, which often occurred in the context of hands-on science activities.

On the days that we were there, we took the roles of participant observers, sometimes observing more and sometimes participating more. We sat with one or more of the target children during reading and writing time. We interacted with the child and the others around the target child. Sometimes we assisted the children with what they were doing or responded to their queries. We took field notes, focusing on the children's activity, but also on the teachers' actions. At the end of our time at the school on a particular day, we made copies of the children's work. Our data collection continued in much the same way for the second and third years of the study. We envisioned a series of longitudinal studies in which we would highlight each child individually and also consider likenesses and differences across the children. Some of that reporting has taken place in conferences, papers, and publications. I do not go into any of that work here because I want to focus on an unexpected occurrence that forms the basis for the rest of this chapter in a volume on second language writing.

FORAYS INTO ENGLISH AND ADDITIONAL QUESTIONS

Within the first year of the study, something happened that we had not anticipated and that resulted not in a change of plans, but in a revision of them. We discovered that, although all of their formal literacy instruction was in Spanish, some of the children began to make what I termed *forays* into English literacy—they began to write (and, to a lesser extent, read) in English. The teachers were focusing on the children understanding and using English orally, but some of the children, on a variety of occasions, were choosing to use written English. When we recognized this, we began to keep track of these forays. We added two questions to our study: What strategies are the children using to write in English—that is, how are they getting down what they want to express? Why are they choosing to write in English?

To answer these questions, we put all our notes on English writing and the children's English language work samples together to see whether we saw patterns in what the children were doing. What we discovered (Hudelson, 1993, 1994; Hudelson & Serna, 1992, 1994) was the following.

In terms of strategies, the children clearly used what they already knew about writing alphabetically in Spanish, Spanish orthography and Spanish phonics, and about word boundaries and orientation to assist them in writing English. But the children also used their growing knowledge of English print, English print available to them in their classrooms and communities, and they used their friends, the children with whom they sat and engaged during writing time, to assist them in writing English. Thus, the children drew on their well-developed linguistic resources from their native language, their developing linguistic resources from their second language, and human resources.

In terms of the question about *why* the children were choosing sometimes to write in English, we identified four patterns. (a) The children sometimes chose to write in English because there was a need to communicate with an individual interlocutor or a broader audience that was English speaking. Demonstrating sensitivity to audience, they used the language of the person or people they were writing to. (b) The children sometimes chose to write in English because the topic they were writing about was connected to English. Although they came from Spanish-speaking homes, the children interacted with English in the environment. They had engaged in particular experiences, both academic and nonacademic, in English, and it was natural to use English to write about these experiences. Particularly striking was what we called the *phenomenon of kid culture*, in which realities such as comic books and cartoons influenced children to represent and indeed create these heroes and monsters—and to use English to do this. (c) As they were writing in English, the children sometimes engaged in lexical-level code switching for particular effect or emphasis. (d) A fourth reason for making forays into English was the sense of accomplishment it gave the children. Those children who wrote in English felt confident that they could do so. They felt good about writing and reading in two languages. They stated that it was important to be able to use English and Spanish. These patterns led us to assert that the children who made forays into English did so because they were in control of their literacy; they were already literate in one language and they could choose to write in English.

In interpreting our findings, we connected our work to earlier studies of bilingual individuals, their language choices, and their code-switching abilities (Grosjean, 1982). We noted that the literature has demonstrated that young bilingual children are sensitive to the language abilities of their interlocutors and will switch based on their judgments of the other's language proficiency (Genishi, 1976; McClure, 1977; Valdes-Fallis, 1978). We also used Fishman's (1976) notion of marked and unmarked languages, acknowledging the taken-for-granted unmarked status of English as well as the marked, unusual in the school status, of Spanish, and suggesting the possibility that the unmarked nature of English could be an influence in children's choosing to use the language.

Even with our use of the literature on bilingualism, language maintenance, language shift, and marked versus unmarked languages (Hudelson, 1993), the underlying framework for our interpretations was constructivism. The focus was on the children and their decisions to use English and on the strategies the children used to construct written English. We interpreted what the children were doing as individual decisions based on individual interests and individual language proficiencies. We foregrounded the children as unique individuals, some of whom chose to make forays into English and some of whom did not, some of whom chose to use more English more than others. Even when we used the concept of marked/unmarked languages, we did not frame this construct in terms of political realities or the hegemony of English (Shannon, 1995). Rather we used the construct in a neutral way: The objective reality is that English is the unmarked, taken-for-granted language, and Spanish is the marked language.

TEN YEARS LATER: REVISIONING THE STUDY THROUGH NEW PERSPECTIVES

It is now 10 years later, and my own understandings and perspectives have changed and grown due, in part, to the influence of scholars whose works I have read. For this chapter, I want to highlight influences from three areas of scholarship. First, in the last 10 years, I have read a lot more in the area of sociocultural perspectives on language and literacy learning, including studies that use a sociocultural perspective as the guiding framework (e.g., Dyson, 1989, 1993; Toohey, 2000). A major sociocultural voice is Lev Vygotsky. Reading some of Vygotsky (1962, 1978) and various interpretations of his work (Toohey, 2000; Wertsch, 1985, 1991), some of what I understand the Vygotskian sociocultural perspective to be about is the social construction of learning—the perspective that social relations are central to human development, including intellectual development. Sociocultural theorists assert that children's mental processes are constructed through their relationships with others, including others who know more than they do. Thus, knowledge, including knowledge of how to utilize the symbolic system of writing and the multiple functions of that symbolic team, is formed socially as children work with often more knowledgeable others in their zones of proximal development. I also now understand better that, for Vygotsky, classrooms are situated in larger, concentric circles of context, so that children's participation in classroom practices must also be situated in multiple, nested circles of context beyond the classroom (Toohey, 2000).

Second, in the last 10 years, I have read work by scholars who use critical theory as a lens through which to examine schooling and literacy learning. These scholars have helped me understand that U.S. bilingual and ESL classrooms are sites of struggle (Auerbach, 1993). Schools are not neutral places where neutral bodies of curricular knowledge are passed on to students. In U.S. classrooms and society, English so dominates that it influences speakers of other languages to reject their own languages in favor of English. Hence, the price of learning English may be losing one's heritage language (Shannon, 1995; Tse, 2001). The teaching of English cannot be viewed as neutral. It is not possible to teach English without considering its cultural, social, and political contexts (Pennycook, 1994).

Third, in the last 10 years, I have also read more about what has been called the *ethnographic case study* (Merriam, 1988), which moves case study research from strictly intensive, holistic description to sociocultural interpretation of whatever the unit of study is. Thus, ethnographic case studies of children in a school setting would need to include a consideration of neighborhoods, socioeconomic factors, a community's racial and ethnic makeup, as well as views and understandings of parents, residents, and school officials in any description and interpretation of children.

This reading and thinking, and the invitation to write a chapter for this collection, have led me to reconsider the work I have just reported in terms of the constructivist framework we used, the ways we chose to collect and analyze the data, and our interpretation of our findings. Thus, the rest of this chapter is devoted to this reconsideration—to the presentation of an alternative way or ways to think about what we did and what we found. I have chosen to rethink the study under three headings: the questions we asked, the data-collection methods used, and the interpretations we developed.

Research Questions

As I hope I have made clear, our original questions came both from our reading of the research in emergent writing and from the constructivist perspective at the base of much of that research. Our interest was in documenting and analyzing what the children did, what their strategies were, how they responded to what their classrooms were offering, how they developed as writers over time, and how they saw themselves as writers. We had a hunch that there would be patterns of development across the children, but we also thought we would see individual differences in them, both as people and learners. We focused on the children's individual work in Spanish. Then when we discovered that children were writing in English as well as in Spanish, we added some questions about English literacy. But we still foregrounded the children's individual efforts. Given my growing understanding of a sociocultural framework for literacy learning, I would now choose not to do away with a constructivist framework and our interest in individuals, but to combine it with a sociocultural perspective and to add on some research questions that I see as more sociocultural in nature. Specifically, to be able to document more fully how children's development as writers, in both Spanish and English, was socially constructed in collaboration with others, I would add these kinds of questions:

- How do the case study children collaborate with teachers and peers as they become writers in Spanish and English?
- How do the children's teachers influence their writing development, both in Spanish and English?
- How do the children's peers influence their writing development, both in Spanish and English?
- What classroom practices and resources influence children's writing development in Spanish and English?

In addition, to take seriously Merriam's (1988) assertion that case study research has the potential to be ethnographic if it utilizes a sociocultural interpretation and Vygotsky's position that classrooms are situated in larger, concentric circles of context (Toohey, 2000), I would propose this kind of question: What are the multiple linguistic, social, cultural, and political contexts outside the classroom (school, family, local community, state) that may influence children's literacy practices in Spanish and English?

As I struggle to understand more fully a sociocultural framework for research, I am aware that in the analyses we presented, we did *hint* at the social nature of writing, the talk that accompanied writing, and the collaborative efforts some of the children engaged in. We shared examples of Benjamín, for example, who often asked peers and adults around him for help in spelling English words and who surreptitiously acted out Superhero exploits with his friend, Mario, as they drew pictures and labeled their characters Spiderman, Robin, Batman, and Superman. We noted that Juanita told us that she became a confident writer of English in the summer between second and third grade when her older brother and sister worked with her on English spelling. We discovered that Susana began to believe she could write in English when the resource ESL teacher began to visit her classroom and provide English "lessons" to the children. But we used examples such as these essentially to set the contexts for the children's individual efforts and intentions. We were not viewing the children through a sociocultural lens.

Data-Collection Methods

Adding on a sociocultural lens also means that the data collection in this study needs to be reexamined. The major way that we collected data was by placing ourselves as participant observers in the classrooms of our case study children. We sat near, and sometimes with, the children we had targeted during the writing times in the day. We took notes on their processes. If there was talk and activity as our target children composed, we took notes on what was happening. I know that I was better at capturing the activity than the talk. I tried to capture the essence of conversations, but this was not always easy and accurate because of the softness of the children's voices and the speed of their talk. We also collected copies of the work that the children produced the days that we were in their classrooms, and we were careful to describe the context for each sample. In addition, we talked informally with the teachers during lunch breaks and after school, and we spent time mapping out the classrooms and examining the resources available to children.

From time to time, we chatted with the children informally about what they were doing as writers. For those children who took on some English writing, I asked them about why they chose to write in English and how they figured out how to do it. From my perspective, these interactions did not always result in substantive information, and I know that this meant that I often made inferences about children's writing strategies in English on the basis of document collection and observations.

As I struggle now with considering a sociocultural framework for studying children's literacy learning, I realize that my data-collection techniques have been insufficient. If I want to understand better how learners collaborate to create knowledge and how more knowledgeable others may influence the learning of others, I need to have access to children's language in a more complete form than is available in my notes. Thus, if I were carrying out this study now, I would audiotape or videotape groups of children, including the focal case study children. I would work to do this unobtrusively so that I would record children interacting naturally with their peers around texts they were creating. The work of Anne Haas Dyson (1989, 1993, 1997) exemplifies how the use and analysis of audiotapes may be used in sociocultural analyses of children's talk around writing.

I would also use the technique of interviewing, thinking in advance about the general structure of the interviews, so that I could probe for more information than I gleaned from more informal interactions with children and teachers. I would ask children to reflect on some of their written work, especially their work in English (e.g., reasons that they wrote a particular piece in English, what their process was in the writing, what it was like writing in English, what they might tell other children about writing in English). I think that if I thought ahead about how to approach the interviews, what I hoped to glean from them, I would achieve more substantive results. I would also want to interview teachers about their classroom practices—about the environments they established for Spanish and English. And I would like to interview them about the focal case study children.

To attend to the multiple contexts in which the case study children live and learn, I would spend more time observing in the school at large and interacting with and perhaps interviewing staff. I would also propose to visit the homes of the case study children, interview parents, interact with siblings, and observe the children at home and in their neighborhoods. With these additional kinds of data collection, I would hope to present more fully developed, socioculturally grounded portraits of the children—portraits that would reveal what Dyson (1993) refers to as the multiple social worlds of child writers.

Our Interpretations

In her book *Social Worlds of Children Learning to Write in an Urban Primary School*, Dyson (1993) proposes that children are simultaneously members of several different social groups—what she terms *social spheres*. She analyzes primary children's writing processes and products from this sociocultural construct of spheres, developing three spheres of the official classroom, the unofficial peer culture in the classroom, and the home sphere. As I rethink my data, I am intrigued by the possibility of using Dyson's idea—of going back and considering the case study children as participants in multiple in and out of school social networks and the possible influences of these networks on their writing.

I also feel compelled to reexamine our almost uniformly positive view of the children's early writing in English. Ten years ago, we asserted that the children who added on English writing saw English as interesting and purposeful for themselves. We viewed the children as confident in themselves as writers in Spanish and willing to experiment in their new language. We viewed them as resourceful users of their native language. We saw them as in control of their learning of English because they chose to write in English. We characterized them as individuals with varying needs, interests, and rates of language and literacy development, including the development of English literacy. Although we acknowledged English as the unmarked language of school and community, we viewed this unmarkedness as politically neutral, and we framed the children's use of English in positive terms (Hudelson & Serna, 1994).

Ten years later, influenced by scholars who relate critical theory to English language learning, I think I must at least consider a less benign interpretation of the data. I must recognize that politics plays an important part in all education and particularly in bilingual education. If I use Vygotsky's notion of concentric circles of context, political realities that could, directly or indirectly, influence language choice and a shift to English from Spanish were evident, but unacknowledged, in each concentric circle.

Beginning with the circle of the school, the bilingual program was a fairly new phenomenon at the school, having been created because the school population had, in recent years, changed from almost entirely English speaking to majority Spanish speaking. At the school, bilingual education was controversial, and numbers of experienced teachers who had been at the school for many years were not in favor of using Spanish as a language of instruction. Newer teachers who believed in bilingual education made up the bilingual staff. When our study began, the school was carrying out a transitional model of bilingual education, meaning that there were bilingual classes only in Kindergarten through Grade 3. In addition, even in the primary grades, some classes in the school were designated as bilingual and others not. There was a lack of unity among the teaching staff with regard to native language instruction. There was also a lack of unity among school staff about the utilization of less traditional, more progressive methods to develop children's literacy (e.g., journal writing, writers' workshop, use of children's books that are especially predictable because of their repetition of language and incident or because of rhythm and rhyme elements, and children's literature, literature study groups, thematic cycles in science and social studies) instead of textbook learning. Expenditures of funds for literature, especially children's literature in Spanish, created consternation among some of the staff.

At the school district level, in the early 1990s this particular school was the one with the greatest socioeconomic, cultural, and linguistic diversity. It was also the school with the lowest standardized test scores. The attitude of many educators in the district was that the school was a lost cause—there was no way children were going to learn. More than once I heard the school described as "the armpit of the district." Negative attitudes at the district level were exacerbated when the principal decided to initiate a bilingual program and when she advocated for and hired teachers who shared a whole language philosophy of education. The fact that the local university was beginning to notice the school and place interns and student teachers at the site precisely because of its bilingual program and its progressive stance contributed to heightened tensions within the district and increased pressures on the school to use more traditional methods and to use less Spanish.

Within the community surrounding the school as well, the fairly rapid transformation of the neighborhood from English-speaking working and lower middle class to immigrant Spanish speaking, and the construction of new apartment buildings (inhabited mostly by Spanish-speaking families) where previously there had been mostly single-family dwellings, resulted in significant neighborhood tensions. Many residents who had lived in the neighborhood for many years made clear their displeasure at the different kinds of children who now walked back and forth daily in front of their homes. The school received complaints about bilingual signs. Protests became loud and prolonged when the school's principal sought to locate a health clinic and a Department of Economic Security office on the campus. And the power structure of Phoenix—even with its current 20% Latino population—clearly goes to the English speakers.

Finally, bilingual education has long been a contested policy at the state level. When I first moved to Arizona in 1975, the few school districts with bilingual programs established them using the authority of the *Lau vs. Nichols* Supreme Court decision, which mandated that non-English-speaking students not receive the same education as English speakers, and Title VII of the Elementary and Secondary Education Act, which allowed transitional bilingual education. There was no state legislation with regard to bilingual education. After a long struggle, bilingual education proponents passed legislation that allowed, but did not mandate, bilingual education as a way of serving the needs of non-English-speaking children. This meant that individual school districts, and even schools within districts, could make their own decisions with regard to native language instruction. In the early 1990s, an Official English proposition received voter approval at the state level (although it was later declared unconstitutional). On a regular basis, bilingual education detractors wrote pieces condemning bilingual education for the newspapers. And in 2000, Proposition 203, making bilingual education programs extremely difficult to sustain, was approved by 66% of Arizona voters.

All of these contexts should make it clear that bilingual education has been and is contested on many levels. While I am not making the claim that primary grade children are conscious of all of these contexts, the contexts are a reality. Certainly bilingual teachers at the school were aware of them. So were the parents. Those whom I met during this study expressed their desires that their children learn English. Spanish was all well and good, but they understood that their children needed to learn English. Although any single context probably did not influence a particular child to write in English on a particular day, taken together they need to be acknowledged as contributing to what Shannon (1995) has referred to as the "hegemony" of English; these contexts need to receive more attention in interpretations of findings than they did receive. In 2003, I would write more at length and more directly about the devaluing of native languages and the language shift that occurs in so many bilingual programs. I would also acknowledge the likelihood of the reality of subtractive bilingualism (Lambert, 1980), which would mean that numbers of the case study children would become less proficient in Spanish as they continued in school. I would discuss the broader political contexts that may have direct or indirect influences on children's language choices.

CONCLUSIONS

Writing this chapter has given me the opportunity to revisit work carried out a decade ago and to reconsider that work in light of my own change and development in the last 10 years. Although in this chapter I critique the constructivist framework used in the research reported, this critique does not mean that I reject constructivism. Rather, I assert that taking into consideration additional perspectives has provided me the opportunity to balance the constructivist focus on individual agency with social, cultural, and political complexities and realities. In a recently published chapter on research in writing, Sperling and Freedman (2001) make a similar argument as they assert, ". . . theories about writing and learning to write have evolved as social and cultural perspectives on teaching, learning, and language have achieved prominence and become integrated with the cognitive perspective that dominated writing research in the 1970s and the early 1980s" (p. 370). I hope this chapter makes a small contribution to conversations among educators involved with second language writers as our understandings continue to evolve and we work to understand, appreciate, and provide quality writing instruction for the linguistically and culturally diverse learners who enrich our classrooms.

REFERENCES

Auerbach, E. (1993). Reexamining English only in the English classroom. *TESOL Quarterly*, *27*(1), 9–32.

Chaille, C. (1997). *The young child as scientist: A constructivist approach to early childhood science education*. New York: Longman.

Dyson, A. H. (1989). *Multiple worlds of child writers: Friends learning to write*. New York: Teachers College Press.

Dyson, A. H. (1993). *Social worlds of children learning to write in an urban primary school*. New York: Teachers College Press.

Dyson, A. H. (1997). *Writing superheroes: Contemporary childhood, pop culture and classroom literacies*. New York: Teachers College Press.

Edelsky, C. (1986). *Writing in a bilingual program: Habia una vez*. Mahwah, NJ: Lawrence Erlbaum Associates.

Ferreiro, E., & Teberosky, A. (1982). *Literacy before schooling*. Portsmouth, NH: Heinemann.

Fishman, J. (1976). *Bilingual education: An international sociological perspective*. Rowley, MA: Newbury House.

Fosnot, C. (1989). *Enquiring teachers, enquiring learners: A constructivist approach for teaching*. New York: Teachers College Press.

Genishi, C. (1976). *Rules for code-switching in young Spanish-English speakers: An exploratory study of language socialization*. Unpublished doctoral dissertation, University of California at Berkeley.

Goodman, Y. (1990). *How children construct literacy: A Piagetian perspective*. Newark, DE: International Reading Association.

Grosjean, F. (1982). *Life with two languages: An introduction to bilingualism*. Cambridge, MA: Harvard University Press.

Hudelson, S. (1984). Kan yu ret an rayt en ingles: Children become literate in English as a second language. *TESOL Quarterly*, *18*(2), 221–238.

Hudelson, S. (1993, March). *Language maintenance and language shift in a bilingual program: Issues in adding on English literacy*. Paper presented at the annual convention of TESOL, Atlanta.

Hudelson, S. (1994, March). *Learners add on ESL literacy: Taking risks, taking charge*. Keynote Speech to Illinois Bilingual Education Association, Chicago.

Hudelson, S., & Serna, I. (1992, November). *Choosing to add on English literacy in primary bilingual classrooms*. Paper presented at the annual convention of the National Council of Teachers of English, Louisville.

Hudelson, S., & Serna, I. (1994). Beginning literacy in English in a whole language bilingual program. In A. Flurkey & R. Meyer (Eds.), *Under the whole language umbrella: Many cultures, many voices* (pp. 278–294). Urbana, IL: National Council of Teachers of English.

Kamii, C. (2000). *Young children reinventing arithmetic: Implications of Piaget's theory*. New York: Teachers College Press.

Lambert, W. E. (1980). The social psychology of language: A perspective for the 1980s. In H. Giles, W. P. Robinson, & P. M. Smith (Eds.), *Language: Social psychological perspectives* (pp. 415–424). Oxford: Pergamon.

McClure, E. (1977). *Aspects of code-switching in the discourse of bilingual Mexican-American children*. Urbana, IL: University of Illinois, Center for the Study of Reading.

Merriam, S. (1988). *Case study research in education: A qualitative approach*. San Francisco: Jossey-Bass.

Pennycook, A. (1994). *The cultural politics of English as an international language*. London: Longman.

Piaget, J., & Inhelder, B. (1969). *The psychology of the child*. New York: Basic Books.

Shannon, S. (1995). The hegemony of English: A case study of a bilingual classroom. *Linguistics and Education*, *7*, 175–200.

Sperling, M., & Freedman, S. (2001). Research on writing. In V. Richardson (Ed.), *Handbook on teaching* (4th ed., pp. 370–389). Washington, DC: American Educational Research Association.

Teale, W. H., & Sulzby, E. (Eds.). (1986). *Emergent literacy: Writing and reading*. Norwood, NJ: Ablex.

Toohey, K. (2000). *Learning English in school: Identity, social relations and classroom practice*. Clevedon, England: Multilingual Matters.

Tse, L. (2001). *"Why don't they learn English?": Separating fact from fallacy in the U.S. language debate*. New York: Teachers College Press.

Valdes-Fallis, G. (1978). *Code switching and the classroom teacher*. Arlington, VA: Center for Applied Linguistics.

Vygotsky, L. (1962). *Thought and language*. Cambridge, MA: MIT Press.

Vygotsky, L. (1978). *Mind in society: The development of higher psychological processes*. Cambridge, MA: Harvard University Press.

Wertsch, J. (1985). *Vygotsky and the social formation of the mind*. Cambridge, MA: Harvard University Press.

Wertsch, J. (1991). *Voices of the mind: A sociocultural approach to mediated action*. Cambridge, MA: Harvard University Press.

IV

CODA

16

Tricks of the Trade: The Nuts and Bolts of L2 Writing Research

Dana Ferris
California State University, Sacramento, USA

For this chapter, I was asked to discuss the practical aspects—the "nuts and bolts"—of L2 writing research—"from identifying a research topic to getting published in a refereed journal" (T. Silva, personal communication, September 23, 2001). This assignment has offered me the opportunity to make explicit processes and values of which I was not consciously aware—a journey that has been enlightening, humbling, and occasionally amusing. In this chapter, I discuss five specific nuts and bolts subtopics related to the process of L2 writing research, weaving my own experiences and evolution as a researcher into the discussion as well.

BACKGROUND: MY OWN RESEARCH EXPERIENCE

Like many others, I began my own career as an L2 writing researcher in graduate school at the University of Southern California (USC) under the expert guidance of Professor Robert Kaplan. My former classmate, Dwight Atkinson, and I have reminisced more than once about the class we took together in 1988 with Bob, entitled "Analysis of Written Discourse"—how this class captured our interest and fired our imagination about the kinds of questions and inquiries we might pursue. For my course paper, I completed my first major L2 writing research project, a replication of a study by Ulla Connor (1987) on the characteristics of persuasive writing. By the fall of 1988, I had "signed on" with Bob Kaplan to complete my Ph.D. qualifying paper and dissertation under his supervision. Over the next 3 years, with Bob's help, I completed two major research projects on L2 writing, both of which were later published in refereed journals (Ferris, 1993, 1994a, 1994b), finishing my doctorate in 1991.

After leaving USC to begin working at Sacramento State, I had a couple of very unproductive years, research-wise. Like most junior faculty, I was overwhelmed with the demands of teaching new courses and serving on committees, not to mention juggling the needs of a young child and a husband in law school. In 1992, however, I got back in the game. There were two factors that spurred me into action. One—and I'm rather ashamed to admit this!—was the California state budget crisis in the summer of 1992, which caused doom and gloom at the California State University (CSU) and rumors of widespread faculty layoffs—and there I was, at the bottom of the seniority ladder in my department, the sole support of my family at the moment, so I panicked. Aware that I might at any moment be back on the job market and that many institutions would require more scholarly productivity than I had been displaying, I lit a fire under myself and got four manuscripts (based on the aforementioned graduate school projects) out to journals during that summer of unease. To my astonishment, three of the four were eventually published.

The other factor that inspired me to do research again was attending the 1992 TESOL Convention in Vancouver. I was preparing for a new graduate course on "Teaching ESL Writing," so I systematically attended every presentation related to L2 writing research, teaching, and teacher preparation that I could cram into my schedule. Two talks at that convention proved to be tremendously significant and formative to my subsequent development as a researcher. The first was a paper by Ilona Leki at a colloquium on research in L2 writing, where she urged the audience to seriously consider replication of previous research as a means to extend the scientific discourse of our emerging discipline. Her argument made sense to me, and I left the colloquium with a resolve to find a good study to replicate—to do my own little part in advancing our research agenda. I found it that same afternoon at a paper presented by Pamela McCurdy (1992), a survey research study on student reactions to teacher feedback on their compositions, a paper that was also a replication of previous work published by Cohen (1987) and Cohen and Cavalcanti (1990). I was impressed by the clean, straightforward design of the study and the interesting, practical implications of her findings. It occurred to me that the inquiry could be extended by asking similar questions of ESL students in multiple-draft contexts.

I spoke to Pam right after her presentation and asked whether I could adapt her instrument for this purpose. She graciously agreed, sent me a copy of her paper, and gave me feedback later on my own findings. Before the 1992 spring semester was over, I had designed, piloted, and conducted the survey with 155 ESL students at Sacramento State. I presented the results of this project at the 1993 CATESOL and TESOL conferences and later published the study in the *TESOL Quarterly* (Ferris, 1995).

So the combination of pressing practical concerns and inspiration from other L2 writing researchers propelled me into a new era of enthusiasm and productivity. Since that point, I have completed seven major research projects on L2 writing, the findings of which have been presented at major conferences and/or published in journal articles, book chapters, and my own books. In addition, I have advised numerous M.A. TESOL students at Sacramento State (and others from a distance) on their L2 writing research projects. From working on these various projects, I have learned a number of valuable lessons about designing, completing, and disseminating L2 writing research.

WHAT I HAVE LEARNED: NUTS AND BOLTS

Identifying a Focus for Research

Inexperienced researchers, or those at a crossroads looking for a new line of inquiry, may wonder how to find a focus for their research program. For myself, I found my niche in a very natural way: by being challenged by real-life problems or questions in my own ESL writing classes and by the need to have answers (or at least advice) for the future L2 writing teachers in my graduate courses. Specifically, as I taught these teacher preparation courses, I kept reading L1 and L2 research reviews which argued that teacher feedback and error correction were largely ineffective (and possibly even harmful or abusive) for L2 writers. What I was reading did not resonate with my own experience as a teacher of ESL composition. So I was motivated toward this line of research by the conviction, based on my own teaching experience and instincts, that feedback was critically important to the development of student writing, but that we as a scholarly community had not yet succeeded in finding the right ways to construct feedback and evaluate its effects. Further, it is most valuable, in my opinion, to find a specific area or line of research and stick with it or pursue it for awhile, rather than jumping around from one unrelated area to another. In my own case, I have pursued two related lines of investigation—the nature and effects of feedback on student writing, especially teacher commentary, and the effects of error correction on the accuracy of L2 student writing—for the past 10 years.

There are two benefits of a narrower focus—one for the researcher her or himself, and the other for the field at large. For the individual researcher, pursuing a line of research in depth builds schema, expertise, and experience—what you have read and learned along the way continues to inform your thinking, the questions you ask, and the ways you pursue the answers. Scholars can gain confidence that they actually know what they are talking about, and they can find satisfaction that they are really contributing to the knowledge base of the discipline, rather than simply going "a mile wide and an inch deep." The psychic benefits of confidence and satisfaction should not be underestimated because they can provide internal motivation and energy when the external rewards seem few and far between.

A particular discipline also benefits from the expertise gained by an individual researcher as she or he builds a track record of projects completed and findings reported. The field of TESOL/Applied Linguistics has been weakened by an overabundance of research projects, which were poorly done, which raised important questions that no one ever pursued again, or which were never replicated in other contexts or with other student populations. By contrast, the narrower focus of people like Michael Long in second language acquisition, Bob Kaplan and Ulla Connor in contrastive rhetoric, Vivian Zamel and Ann Raimes in looking at the writing processes of ESL students, and Joan Carson, Gayle Nelson, John Murphy, and Jun Liu in peer response has provided the field not only with replicable research models and paradigms (an important contribution in its own right), but also sets of findings, insights, and generalizations that can be argued about, further investigated, and refined by future generations of researchers.

To summarize, my advice on the issue of identifying a research focus is threefold: (a) pursue questions that interest, puzzle, or trouble you; (b) once you have identified a focus, commit to sticking with it for awhile; and (c) let the questions raised at the end of one research project guide you toward your next steps or stages of inquiry.

Selecting Research Paradigms

The most important initial step in designing a research project is a well-articulated set of research questions or hypotheses. The nature of the research question should lead you naturally toward selection of the appropriate research methodology to investigate it. This may seem self-evident, but researchers in our field get tied up in knots over quantitative versus qualitative paradigms (and the discourse can get rather ugly on this issue). In my view, either—or better, a combination of both—quantitative and qualitative methodologies may be appropriate depending on what is being looked at.

My own thinking about research paradigms has evolved over the years, thanks largely to the thoughtful work and feedback of other L2 writing researchers. Although my earlier projects tended to focus on a specific research paradigm—*only* survey or *only* text analysis—my most recent projects have combined text analysis, surveys, case studies, pre- and posttest designs, interviews, transcripts, and so forth. It is only fair and forthright to say that combining approaches takes longer and is messier throughout the process of data collection, analysis, and reporting results. However, the more work I do, the less able I find myself to separate or decontextualize parts of the analyses.

The other important step in research design is to carefully review the previous research on the questions or topics you are investigating. I am embarrassed to admit this, but I have not always followed this advice. Perhaps as a leftover from my graduate student days, I saw "reviewing the literature" as a tedious, jump-through-the-hoops exercise that I had to do to demonstrate to editors, reviewers, and readers that I had done my homework, eaten my vegetables, or whatever. I would postpone it to the end of the process, *after* I had designed the study, conducted the research, analyzed the data, and, in some cases, even presented the findings at a conference and was finally getting down to submitting the report to a journal for publication.

A funny thing happened as I did this a few times. I discovered that, in most cases, other researchers actually had done some work on the questions I was investigating. Imagine this! They had designed sound studies, developed useful analytic models, and made interesting discoveries that would have sharpened my focus, improved the effectiveness of my own research, *and* (heavy sigh) would have saved me time. Humbled by this realization, I am now a repentant, transformed former sinner. Having identified, at least in broad strokes, a focus for investigation, the library or the Internet is now the *first* place I go, not the last. Even with topics on which I have done previous primary and secondary research, I check to see whether something new has been published since the last time I looked. (I must add here that I am extremely grateful for the annotated bibliographies provided by the *Journal of Second Language Writing* and *Research in the Teaching of English*, which keep me up to date and streamline this process considerably.)

In L2 writing research, there are a couple of research paradigms that need to be carefully considered. Most research on L2 writing involves text analysis at some stage—how can you evaluate students' processes or teachers' interventions without at some point looking at student texts and/or teacher feedback? But text analysis is complex and challenging, and it becomes even more so when looking at texts composed by L2 writers, whose "nontarget" constructions can make it challenging to ascertain their intentions and categorize them in some way. To do text analysis successfully, two elements are crucial: (a) carefully designed analytic models, and (b) rigorously implemented processes that apply the models consistently across the texts being studied.

Text analysis models for a particular study can be selected in one of three ways: (a) By finding a useful model and applying it to a new text sample (see e.g., Faigley & Witte, 1981, which has been variously applied in different L2 studies of student revision); (b) by adapting a good model so that it more precisely fits the focus of a particular study; or (c) by creating a completely new model. Once an analysis scheme has been identified, adapted, or created, it is equally important that it be utilized systematically across the sample (see Polio, 1997, for an excellent discussion of methodological issues related to text analysis).

Besides text analysis, a range of other research methodologies may be utilized to investigate L2 writing. In my own work, I have analyzed surveys, conference transcripts, teacher and student interviews, student error logs, teachers' journal entries, classroom observation notes, and pre- and posttest data. Again as with any other type of research, it is important that such instruments and data-collection processes be designed carefully and analyzed systematically. In the case of more qualitative paradigms, it is especially important that researchers calculate and report categories and percentages, rather than simply provide "observations" or "trends" (such as quotations from student interviews), which may be subject to researchers' selection biases. Readers need to know how and why the researcher has concluded that such evidence is representative rather than merely anecdotal.

In summary, once a research focus has been identified, three considerations should guide the design of an L2 writing study: (a) selecting analytic paradigms that flow logically from your research questions, (b) carefully reviewing previous L1 and L2 composition research related to your topic, and (c) adapting or designing analysis models and processes carefully.

Disseminating Research

I have to admit that this is not my favorite part of the process. I am now a tenured full professor at an institution that prioritizes teaching and service, not research and publication. In other words, it is not at all necessary to my academic survival that I stay productive as a scholar. I am truly internally motivated to do research by real-life questions that trouble me. For me the true satisfaction comes when I crunch numbers or otherwise complete my analysis and get the answers to my immediate research questions. The "finding out" is what motivates me. Once I have found out, I basically lose interest in the project. What pushes me to get things out to conferences and journals is the conviction that if the research is worth doing in the first place, it is also worth other people knowing about—presuming, of course, that the questions are interesting and the research was well executed!

I was not taught in graduate school how to present conference papers or how to write journal articles for publication. My earliest attempts at sending papers out led to astute reviewer comments such as, "This reads like a chapter of a dissertation (!). It needs to stand on its own as a piece of research and writing." As I worked at my academic writing skills and gained experience, my technique and success rate improved dramatically. Several specific strategies helped me become "self-taught" in writing for publication.

The first strategy was to study models. This process began for me in graduate school when I had to write a dissertation proposal for my committee. I had never written a dissertation proposal, nor had I ever taken a course in how to write one. So what did I do? I borrowed my friend's recently accepted dissertation proposal and carefully studied her style, her format, the depth of content and degree of explanation she used, and so forth. When it came time to write an article for publication, I gathered a few representative samples of studies along similar lines as the one I was writing and examined how the papers were set up, what kind of background information and research questions were presented, how the results were reported, and how the analysis, discussion, and conclusions proceeded. This process enabled me to construct schemata for various types of research reports. As I have gained experience, I have found that I need to do this less because I can pattern myself after my own "models."

My second strategy is to identify a target audience for my paper—namely, a specific journal to which I plan to submit it—before I begin writing. I have a couple of different principles for doing this. First, I always aim high: I figure I will send the manuscript to the most prestigious, competitive journal that seems appropriate given the content and scope of the research and let them reject me first before sending it to a smaller, regional, or more specialized journal. Second, I often aim for journals that have published prior studies along the lines of the one I am submitting for consideration. I have often already identified these during my preliminary review of the literature. This strategy can be beneficial, but it can also backfire depending on the practices of the journal and the biases of the editor.

Finally, the vast majority of the journal articles I have published were not accepted on the first submission. Rather, I typically receive extensive (sometimes contradictory) comments from reviewers and an encouragement in a cover letter from the editor to "revise and resubmit." My advice to prospective authors is: *Always* revise and resubmit when invited to do so! Several friends who are journal editors have noted with some surprise how relatively few authors actually do resubmit a paper.

Obtaining Research Support

Although I have not been successful in obtaining external support for my research, I have had better luck getting funded through CSU-internal grants programs over the years. These are highly competitive because funding is scarce. I have received nine different grants over the past 9 years and have been turned down only once in that period. These grants have included money for summer work (freeing me from the need to teach summer school), course release, and funds for graduate student support. In addition, I received a semester sabbatical leave to write a book several years ago.

I attribute my success rate in this latter arena to some careful investigation. I have volunteered for many years to be on the review panels for these programs. This has enabled me to understand the judging criteria and to assess the nature and quality of the competition in my area (arts and humanities). When writing proposals myself, I keep two important points in mind: (a) the stated objectives of the grant program—I explicitly explain how my proposal meets each objective; and (b) the fact that the audience (the reviewers) is interdisciplinary and that I therefore need to avoid insider field-specific jargon and write a clear, accessible explanation of my project for intelligent but nonspecialist readers.

Working Collaboratively

Over the years, I have done research projects completely on my own as well as with a number of graduate students and other professional colleagues (at Sacramento State and elsewhere). I was never a student who enjoyed assigned group projects in school, and it has surprised me a bit to discover how much I enjoy and benefit from doing collaborative research and writing projects. Most of my collaborations have been initiated by me, and a few have resulted from others coming to me to ask whether we could work together. I focus in this section on collaborations that I instigated.

Peers in the field have expressed surprise and some envy that I have found so many talented graduate students over the years to work with, especially given that I work in a terminal-M.A. (not doctoral) program that until fairly recently did not even include a thesis option. Although this circumstance is indeed a rather formidable obstacle—meaning that most of the students I teach are not especially motivated toward conducting research—I have been successful over the years in recruiting graduate student coworkers by pursuing two major avenues. First, I teach a graduate course once a year entitled "Teaching ESL Composition." I created this course and co-authored the textbook used in it (Ferris & Hedgcock, 1998), so I am both enthusiastic about the class and able to display a high level of knowledge and expertise. I am also able to share some of my own classroom research in this area, which at least some students find stimulating. It is not unusual for a couple of students in this class each year to approach me either to be their thesis supervisor or simply to ask whether they can assist me on my next research project either for independent study credit or simply for the experience. Second, if I have a particular project planned, I sometimes circulate a flyer in the M.A. TESOL graduate courses announcing that I need a couple of research assistants for the following semester and that I can offer them elective independent study credit if they so desire (and occasionally funding if I have obtained a grant with a budget for student assistants).

Using one or both of these avenues, I have recruited 12 outstanding graduate students over the past 7 years who have worked with me on various research projects. All of them have ultimately been co-authors on conference papers or journal articles (or both). For the most part, these have been extremely pleasant and successful collaborations for all concerned. They benefit me by forcing me to articulate the goals, methods, and timelines for the project so that less experienced researchers can participate. This has helped me to do my "homework" (the lit review!—although I often get the student researchers to help with this); to design the project thoughtfully, carefully, and perhaps with more clarity and precision than I might have done if I were working alone; to keep organized; and to stay on a schedule. The collaborations benefit the students by allowing them to participate and have input in a research project literally from start to finish. It is both a learning opportunity and an enjoyable interpersonal team-building experience for them.

There are also two lessons that I have learned from experience in working with graduate students on my research projects (as opposed to theirs). First, in the early days, I "protected" the students from the "grunt work" of research—photocopying, mailing, filing, and so on—thinking that they needed experience with data analysis instead. But I realized that they also needed a dose of reality about how much tedious, time-consuming detail research projects really can consume. Further, I was actually being unfair to myself, doing far too much of the work while my student co-authors got too much of the credit. In my more recent projects, the work—both the tedious stuff and the cognitively demanding stages—has been more evenly divided between me and the students. Second, I have learned from experience to spell out issues of authorship quite explicitly in advance.

I have also collaborated with colleagues at Sacramento State and elsewhere on various projects. Again for the most part this has been successful and pleasant. The benefit of working with peers is that their knowledge and experience are greater than that of graduate students. The potential downside is that there may be more jockeying for position, more professional egos involved, and more ambiguity about who is "in charge" and how disagreements get resolved. If such issues are not handled carefully, one could lose a friendship or create some awkwardness or hard feelings.

Another valuable type of collaboration is asking peers and colleagues to read drafts of a manuscript before submitting it for publication or to listen to a practice run of a conference presentation. These are wonderful things to do if one can manage it. I have done both at points, but not as much as I probably should or would like to. Time is the issue. Once I get a paper written, I want to send it out for review, and the delay involved in sending my paper to an equally busy peer and waiting weeks or even months for feedback sometimes is not workable for me. I also feel hesitant to burden colleagues with requests for assistance, again being well aware that their time constraints are likely at least as great as mine. That said, on the occasions I have "piloted" a paper for peers, it has always been an extremely valuable exercise for me and has nearly always resulted in a greatly improved product.

SUMMARY: IF I CAN DO IT, ANYONE CAN

A confession here: I was never on anyone's "Most Likely to Succeed" list. As far as my academic career goes, I pretty much did everything wrong. I had a baby right in the middle of my Ph.D. program. I changed research directions not once, but twice, at key points in my doctoral program, requiring me to start over from scratch. I left USC before I had even begun my dissertation to take a full-time teaching job at Sacramento State. Then I went to work at a university—Sacramento State—which had (and has) a heavy teaching load, major service and advising requirements, and little or no moral or practical support for research. In my department, although it is never said, it is understood that scholarship is something we do in our "spare time," and that we shouldn't expect to teach less or serve on fewer committees even if we are highly productive researchers and writers.

Despite my inauspicious beginnings and less than ideal scholarly environment, I have nonetheless been able to become and remain productive as a researcher and writer. As I reflect on this, I can identify several principles that have kept me moving ahead and that may be helpful to others who consider themselves "unlikely to succeed."

First, I have only researched questions that interested and motivated me. In one of my earliest Ph.D. courses, Professor Stephen Krashen offered this advice to budding researchers: "Pursue the questions that are burning inside you." Given the other demands on my time and attention and the lack of external rewards, I could never do any research at all if I did not focus exclusively on questions that truly interest me. I have found research to be too much work and too much of a grind to spend hours, days, and weeks of effort on things I really don't care about.

The second principle is not to give up too easily. Veteran researchers know the pain of being midway through a research project and realizing all the things we should have thought of and accounted for before beginning data collection. Most of us know the frustration of submitting a conference proposal or a journal article that we think is really good and having it received with indifference or even scorn or hostility. Over time I have learned to develop a thicker skin and a higher level of persistence.

Third, I have learned that if research is important to me, I will have to make it a priority, even sacrificing some personal time and more leisurely pursuits to make scholarly work possible. If I wait for "more time," "more money," or "more help" to do research—well, that day is probably never going to come.

The last thing I have learned is the importance of pacing myself wisely. One final confession: I have pushed myself too hard over the past 10 years and come close to the edge of burnout. One summer a few years ago, I wrote six articles and a book proposal. I mentioned this with some pride to my good friend and coauthor, John Hedgcock. He is a much saner, more balanced individual than I am. His response was, "So when are you going to take a break? It's August now, and a new year is starting. You're going to make yourself sick!"

I do not recommend that pace to anyone. I have intentionally slowed down a great deal over the past few years and said "no" far more often than I have said "yes." I now take vacations and days off. I have even taken entire semesters or years off—a semester off from teaching, a year off from conferences, a year off from new writing projects.

Despite my awareness that I have pushed too hard and moved too fast, I have no regrets (although I am glad that I have slowed myself down before becoming a premature academic statistic). Doing research in L2 writing over the past 15 years has been exciting, stimulating, and internally and externally rewarding. Most of all, it has enriched me in my primary area of passion—teaching. I cannot imagine my professional life without my scholarly pursuits. I humbly hope that some of my reflections will help other aspiring or struggling scholars to get in the game—or to stay in it!

REFERENCES

Cohen, A. (1987). Student processing of feedback on their compositions. In A. L. Wenden & J. Rubin (Eds.), *Learner strategies in language learning* (pp. 57–69). Englewood Cliffs, NJ: Prentice-Hall.

Cohen, A., & Cavalcanti, M. (1990). Feedback on written compositions: Teacher and student verbal reports. In B. Kroll (Ed.), *Second language writing: Research insights for the classroom* (pp. 155–177). Cambridge, England: Cambridge University Press.

Connor, U. (1987). Argumentative patterns in student essays: Cross-cultural differences. In U. Connor & R. B. Kaplan (Eds.), *Writing across languages: Analysis of L2 text* (pp. 57–71). Reading, MA: Addison-Wesley.

Faigley, L., & Witte, S. (1981). Analyzing revision. *College Composition and Communication, 32*, 400–414.

Ferris, D. R. (1993). The design and implementation of an automatic analysis program for L2 text research: Necessity and feasibility. *Journal of Second Language Writing, 2*, 119–129.

Ferris, D. R. (1994a). Lexical and syntactic features of ESL writing by students at different levels of L2 proficiency. *TESOL Quarterly, 28*, 414–420.

Ferris, D. R. (1994b). Rhetorical strategies in student persuasive writing: Differences between native and non-native speakers. *Research in the Teaching of English, 28*, 45–65.

Ferris, D. R. (1995). Student reactions to teacher response in multiple-draft composition classrooms. *TESOL Quarterly, 29*, 33–53.

Ferris, D., & Hedgcock, J. S. (1998). *Teaching ESL composition: Purpose, process, & practice*. Mahwah, NJ: Lawrence Erlbaum Associates.

McCurdy, P. (1992, March). *What students do with composition feedback*. Paper presented at the 27th annual TESOL Convention, Vancouver.

Polio, C. (1997). Measures of linguistic accuracy in second language writing research. *Language Learning, 47*, 101–143.

Contributors

Dwight Atkinson teaches in the Graduate College of Education at Temple University Japan. His research interests include literacy (both L1 and L2), qualitative research, culture, and sociocognitive approaches to learning and teaching. Recent publications include: "L2 Writing in the Post-Process Era" and "Writing and Culture in the Post-Process Era," both in the *Journal of Second Language Writing* (2003); "Writing for Publication/Writing for Public Execution: On the (Personally) Vexing Notion of (Personal) Voice" in *Writing for Scholarly Publication*, edited by Christine Pearson Casanave and Stephanie Vandrick (Erlbaum, 2003); "Language Socialization and Dys-socialization in a South Indian College" in *Language Socialization in Bilingual and Multilingual Societies*, edited by Robert Bayley and Sandra R. Schecter (Multilingual Matters, 2003); and "Toward a Sociocognitive Approach to Second Language Acquisition" in *Modern Language Journal* (2002).

Linda Lonon Blanton is director of the University Honors Program and professor of English at the University of New Orleans, where she has taught everything from soup to nuts—intensive ESL; teacher training courses in ESL methods and in composition; introduction to linguistics, language, and gender; and qualitative research in linguistics. Her academic interests have also taken her afield—to Morocco, Senegal, Spain, Tunisia, and Greece. She holds a master's degree in applied linguistics from New York University and a doctorate in linguistics from the Illinois

Institute of Technology. She has authored or co-authored 10 textbooks, one volume on ESL children's literacy development, and numerous book chapters and journal articles. One of her most recent projects, a cooperative venture with other veteran teachers, resulted in *ESL Composition Tales: Reflections on Teaching* (Michigan, 2002).

Colleen Brice is assistant professor of linguistics and TESOL in the Department of English at Grand Valley State University, where she teaches courses in linguistics and TESOL for undergraduate and graduate students. Her research interests include issues in L2 writing, teacher education, response to student writing, and sociolinguistics. With Tony Silva and Melinda Reichelt, she coedited *Annotated bibliography of scholarship on second language writing, 1993–1997* (Ablex, 1999). Her work has appeared in *Annual Review of Applied Linguistics*, *International Journal of English Studies*, *Language*, and *TESOL Journal*.

Christine Pearson Casanave taught at Keio University in Japan from 1990 to 2003. She then returned to her home base in California, where she now ekes out a living as an itinerant second language educator and works on various writing projects in her specialties of academic literacy and professional development. She maintains ties with Japan through adjunct work done for the graduate TESOL programs run by the Tokyo branches of Teachers College, Columbia University, and Temple University. She is the author of *Writing Games* (Erlbaum, 2002) and *Controversies in Second Language Writing* (Michigan, 2004), and co-editor of *Writing for Scholarly Publication* (Erlbaum, 2003).

Dana Ferris is professor of English at California State University, Sacramento, where she teaches courses in linguistics and TESOL and coordinates the ESL writing program. She is the co-author, with John Hedgcock, of *Teaching ESL Composition: Purpose, Process, & Practice* (Erlbaum, 1998), and author of *Treatment of Error in Second Language Writing* (Michigan, 2001) and *Response to Student Writing* (Erlbaum, 2003). She has also authored a number of journal articles and book chapters on various topics related to L2 writing. Her main research interests have been in teacher commentary on student writing and issues related to written error.

John Flowerdew is professor in the English Department, City University of Hong Kong, where he is currently coordinator of the research degrees program. His research interests include various approaches to discourse analysis, ESP/EAP, and the use of English in Hong Kong. For several years, he has been investigating the writing processes of Hong Kong Cantonese L1 academics writing for publication in English. He is co-editor of *Re-*

search Perspectives on English for Academic Purposes (Cambridge, 2001).

Richard Haswell is Haas Professor of English at Texas A&M University, Corpus Christi, where he teaches—in ascending order of importance—seminars in composition theory and practice; upper division courses in contemporary American poetry, language and society, and adolescent literature; and freshman composition. He has published *Gaining Ground in College Composition: Tales of Development and Interpretation* (Southern Methodist University Press, 1991), *Comp Tales: An Introduction to College Composition through its Stories* (with Min-Zhan Lu, Longman, 2000), and *Beyond Outcomes: Assessment and Instruction within a University Writing Program* (with nine co-authors, Ablex, 2001). His CompPile, an online, searchable bibliography of publications in rhetoric and composition (including ESL), now totals 70,000+ items. "Searching for Kiyoko: Bettering Mandatory ESL Writing Placement" was judged best article for 1998 by the editors of the *Journal of Second Language Writing*.

Sarah Hudelson is professor in the Division of Curriculum and Instruction, College of Education, Arizona State University, Tempe. She teaches literacy methods in an undergraduate elementary education teacher education program that focuses on preparing English as a second language and bilingual classroom teachers. She also teaches graduate students in language and literacy and advises doctoral students. A former elementary school teacher, she earned her Ph.D. from the University of Texas at Austin in Curriculum and Instruction. She has a long-standing interest in elementary school children's native and second language literacy development, particularly the development of writing in progressive classrooms where composition is a central part of a language arts curriculum. She has published in such journals as *NABE Journal*, *TESOL Quarterly*, *TESOL Journal*, and *Language Arts*, as well as in a variety of academic texts.

Ken Hyland is a Reader in Education and Head of the Centre for Professional and Academic Literacies at the Institute of Education, University of London. He has a Ph.D. from the University of Queensland and has taught in Britain, Sudan, Saudi Arabia, Malaysia, Papua New Guinea, New Zealand, and Hong Kong. He has published over 90 articles and book chapters on language teaching and academic writing. Recent publications include *Hedging in Scientific Research Articles* (Benjamin's, 1998), *Writing: Texts, Processes and Practices* (edited with Chris Candlin, Longman, 1999), *Disciplinary Discourses* (Longman, 2000), *Teaching and Researching Writing* (Longman, 2002), and *Second Language Writing* (Cambridge, 2003). He is co-editor of the *Journal of English for Academic Pur-*

poses (with Liz Hamp-Lyons) and is reviews editor of *English for Specific Purposes*.

Xiaoming Li, associate professor of English at the Long Island University, Brooklyn Campus, teaches ESL writing, Asian literature, and Asian-American literature. In her research, she draws on her training in linguistics, rhetoric, and literature as well as her bicultural educational experience to understand the assumptions, values, and traditions underlying the praxis of teaching writing. Her major publication is *"Good Writing" in Cross-Cultural Context* (SUNY Press, 1996). She has contributed chapters to a number of anthologies on teaching writing and has also published in newspapers and local literary magazines.

Rosa M. Manchón is senior lecturer in Applied Linguistics at the University of Murcia, Spain, where she teaches undergraduate courses in second language acquisition as well as postgraduate courses in research methodology in applied linguistics. Her research interests and publications focus on cognitive aspects of second language acquisition and use. She currently serves on the editorial board of the *Journal of Second Language Writing*.

Paul Kei Matsuda is assistant professor of English and associate director of Composition at the University of New Hampshire, where he works closely with doctoral students in Composition Studies and master's students in English Language and Linguistics. At the Conference on College Composition and Communication, he chairs the Committee on Second Language Writing. With Tony Silva, he founded and chairs the Symposium on Second Language Writing, and edited *On Second Language Writing* (Erlbaum, 2001) and *Landmark Essays on ESL Writing* (Erlbaum, 2001). With Kevin Eric De Pew, he edited the special issue of the *Journal of Second Language Writing* on early L2 writing (2002). Paul has published widely in journals and edited collections in both Composition Studies and Applied Linguistics. He serves on the editorial boards of several journals, including *Asian Journal of English Language Teaching, Journal of Second Language Writing, TESOL Quarterly*, and *WPA: Writing Program Administration*.

Liz Murphy is a lecturer in the English Department at Murcia University, Spain, where she has taught applied linguistics and didactic theory to undergraduates and is currently giving classes in academic literacy. She has co-written articles that have appeared in *Language Learning, Journal of Second Language Writing*, and *Learning and Instruction*. Her research centers on the use of the mother tongue in foreign language writing, although she is also interested in the role of the L1 in SLA in general as well as its uses in the classroom. Further interests involve bilingual education and teacher education.

Susan Parks is associate professor at Université Laval in Quebec City, Canada. Director of the undergraduate ESL teacher education program, she also teaches graduate courses in Applied Linguistics. Her research mainly focuses on exploring ESL literacy and enculturation processes in school and workplace contexts. Current research projects pertain to the use of information and communication technologies (ICTs) in ESL classes and preservice teacher education. Publications of her work are available in a variety of journals, including *Language Learning, Applied Linguistics, Journal of Second Language Writing, Canadian Modern Language Review, TESL Canada Journal, The Modern Language Journal*, and *Language Learning & Technology* (http://llt.msu.edu/vol7num1/parks/).

Julio Roca de Larios is associate professor at the University of Murcia, Spain, where he works in initial teaching education for primary EFL school teachers. His research interests include the analysis of written composition processes, classroom interaction processes, and the development of appropriate tools and strategies to foster reflective practice among preservice students.

Miyuki Sasaki was born in Japan and completed her undergraduate studies and an M.A. degree in English education at Hiroshima University. She also received an M.A. in TESO from Georgetown University, and a Ph.D. in Applied Linguistics from the University of California, Los Angeles. In her dissertation, she investigated the relationship among measures of L2 proficiency, foreign language aptitude, and two types of intelligence (verbal intelligence and reasoning) using structural equation modeling. She is currently a professor of Applied Linguistics at Nagoya Gakuin University. She is now very much interested in combining quantitative and qualitative approaches in one study so that the research targets can be analyzed from multiple perspectives. She hopes to conduct such a study in the field of L2 writing acquisition, cross-cultural pragmatics, and language testing.

Tony Silva is associate professor of ESL in the Department of English at Purdue University, where he directs the ESL Writing Program and teaches in the Graduate Program in ESL, which offers a Ph.D., M.A., and Certificate with a specialization in ESL. With Ilona Leki, he founded and edits the *Journal of Second Language Writing*; with Paul Kei Matsuda, he founded and hosts the Symposium on Second Language Writing and edited *Landmark Essays on ESL Writing* (Erlbaum, 2001) and *On Second Language Writing* (Erlbaum, 2001); with Colleen Brice and Melinda Reichelt, he edited the *Annotated Bibliography of Scholarship on Second Language*

Writing (Ablex, 1999). He currently serves on the Executive Committee of the Conference on College Composition and Communication and as a member of the Editorial Boards of *Assessing Writing*, *Journal of Assessing Writing*, *Journal of Basic Writing*, *TESL Canada Journal*, and *Writing Program Administration*.

Robert Weissberg directs an intensive English language program and teaches courses in TESOL and Applied Linguistics at New Mexico State University. He has also taught ESL/EFL, TESOL, and Applied Linguistics in Brazil, Mexico, Indonesia, and Afghanistan. He recently returned from a year teaching in Germany as a Fulbright Senior Scholar. His primary area of interest is in the developmental aspects of second language writing and the interconnections between speech and writing for adult second language learners. He has published extensively in these areas and is also the co-author of a textbook on technical writing for non-native speakers of English. He is currently at work on a project exploring the uses of oral language in the teaching of second language writing.

Author Index

H

I

J

K

L

R

S

T

U

V

W

Y

Z

Subject Index

C

D

M

N

O

R

S